The Ego and the Id

The Ego and the Id: 100 Years Later revisits Freud's classic 1923 essay, which developed key psychoanalytic concepts and presented a radical revision of his earlier theory.

International contributors explore the themes of this remarkable work from their own perspective, with novel and surprising results. There are mysteries uncovered, questions raised about the validity of Freud's perspective, problems in psychoanalytic technique based on those clinging to Freud's earlier model of the curative process in psychoanalysis, cybernetics as a way of evaluating Freud's model, and many other gems. With contributors highlighting the significance of the essay and offering critiques based upon new understanding gathered over the last century, *The Ego and the Id: 100 Years Later* offers a fresh, international perspective on this classic paper.

This book will be essential reading for psychoanalysts in practice and in training and of great interest to scholars of psychoanalytic studies.

Fred Busch, Ph.D., is Training and Supervising Analyst at the Boston Psychoanalytic Institute. He has published over eighty articles on psychoanalytic technique and has been invited to give papers and clinical workshops nationally and internationally. His last four books are *Creating a Psychoanalytic Mind* (2014); *The Analyst's Reveries: Explorations in Bion's Enigmatic Concept* (2019); *Dear Candidate: Analysts from Around the World Offer Personal Reflections on Psychoanalytic Training, Education, and the Profession* (2020); and *A Fresh Look at Psychoanalytic Technique* (2021). Forthcoming in 2023 is *Psychoanalysis at the Crossroads: An International Perspective*.

Natacha Delgado is a member of the Argentine Psychoanalytic Association and the International Psychoanalytic Association Publications Committee. She is a clinical psychoanalyst in private practice.

The International Psychoanalytical Association
Contemporary Freud Turning Points and Critical
Issues Series
Series Editor: Silvia Flechner

IPA Publications Committee
*Natacha Delgado, Nergis Güleç, Thomas Marcacci, Carlos Moguillansky, Rafael
Mondrzak, Angela M. Vuotto, Gabriela Legoretta (consultant)*

Titles in this series
On Freud's "A Child Is Being Beaten"
Edited by Ethel Spector Person

On Freud's "Analysis Terminable and Interminable"
Edited by Joseph Sandler

On Freud's "The Unconscious"
Edited by Salman Akhtar and Mary Kay O'Neil

On Freud's "Screen Memories"
Edited by Gail S. Reed and Howard B. Levine

On Freud's "Formulations on the Two Principles of Mental
Functioning"
Edited by Gabriela Legorreta and Lawrence J. Brown

On Freud's "The Question of Lay Analysis"
Edited by Paulo Cesar Sandler and Gley Pacheco Costa

On Freud's "The Uncanny"
Edited by Catalina Bronstein and Christian Seulin

On Freud's "Moses and Monotheism"
Edited by Lawrence J. Brown

For more information about this series, please visit: www.routledge.com/The-International-Psychoanalytical-Association-Contemporary-Freud-Turning/book-series/KARNIPACF

The Ego and the Id

100 Years Later

**Edited by Fred Busch
and Natacha Delgado**

Routledge
Taylor & Francis Group

LONDON AND NEW YORK

Designed cover image: Freud by Julia Kotulova, Charcoal & digital, 2019

First published 2024
by Routledge
4 Park Square, Milton Park, Abingdon, Oxon OX14 4RN

and by Routledge
605 Third Avenue, New York, NY 10158

Routledge is an imprint of the Taylor & Francis Group, an informa business

British Library Cataloguing-in-Publication Data
A catalogue record for this book is available from the British Library

ISBN: 978-1-032-37386-7 (hbk)
ISBN: 978-1-032-37385-0 (pbk)
ISBN: 978-1-003-33675-4 (ebk)

DOI: 10.4324/9781003336754

Typeset in Palatino
by Apex CoVantage, LLC

Contents

Contributors

Heribert Blass, Dr. med., is Training and Supervising Analyst for adults, children, and adolescents; member of the German Psychoanalytic Association (DPV); and President of the European Psychoanalytic Federation (EPF). He works in private practice in Düsseldorf, Germany. He has several publications on male identity and sexuality, the image of the father in human mental life and on supervision in psychoanalytic education, and the relation between internal and external reality, including the COVID-19 pandemic. His latest publication: Blass H. (2022). The Capacity to Think and Disorders of Thinking in Psychoanalytic Treatments and Institutions: from Mistakes and Failures to Boundary Violations. *The International Journal of Controversial Discussions*. May 2022, 100–120.

Claudia Lucía Borensztejn, M.D., is President of the Argentine Psychoanalytic Association (2017–2020). Former Director of the APA *Journal of Psychoanalysis*. Editor of the *Dictionary of Argentine Psychoanalysis*. Member of the publishing group and author of the APA Psychoanalysis Thesaurus for indexing documents from psychoanalytic libraries. Co-Chair for Latin America of the IPA International Congress, Boston, 2015. Member of the Latin American committee of the IPA Encyclopedic Dictionary. Member of the IJP Board for Latin America. IJP reviewer from 2014 to date. Latin American representative to the IPA Board (2021–2023).

Fred Busch, Ph.D., is Training and Supervising Analyst at the Boston Psychoanalytic Society and Institute and has been invited to teach at many institutes. He has published over eighty articles on psychoanalytic technique and six books. His work has been translated into many languages, and he has been invited to present over 170 papers and clinical workshops nationally and internationally. His last four books are *Creating a Psychoanalytic Mind* (2014); *The Analyst's Reveries: Explorations in Bion's Enigmatic Concept* (2019); *Dear Candidate: Analysts from Around the World Offer Personal Reflections on Psychoanalytic Training, Education, and the Profession* (2020); and *A Fresh Look at Psychoanalytic Technique* (2021).

Bernard Chervet, M.D., is Psychiatrist and Training Psychoanalyst of the Psychoanalytical Society of Paris (SPP). Former President SPP.

Representative on the IPA Board and on the IPA Executive Committee. Scientific Director of the Congress of French speaking Psychoanalysts (CPLF). Founder of SPP Editions. Author of numerous publications in French and international journals, which cover a wide range of clinical and theoretical psychoanalytic topics. Winner of the Bouvet Prize in 2017 for all his work. Keynote to the CPLF on the theme *The Après-coup*. Author of *Après-coup in Psychoanalysis: The Fulfilment of Desire and Thought* (to be published by Routledge). Contributor to the IPA encyclopedic dictionary.

Natacha Delgado is a member of the Argentine Psychoanalytic Association and the International Psychoanalytic Association Publications Committee. She is a clinical psychoanalyst in private practice.

H. Shmuel Erlich is Training and Supervising Analyst and past president of the Israel Psychoanalytic Society. He was Sigmund Freud Professor of Psychoanalysis (Emeritus) and Director of the Sigmund Freud Center at The Hebrew University of Jerusalem. He chaired the IPA Education Committee, served four terms as European Representative on the IPA Board, and is currently Chair of the IPA Institutional Issues Committee. He received the Sigourney Award for outstanding contributions to psychoanalysis in 2005. His publications span adolescent development and psychopathology, experiential dimensions of object relations, group and organizational processes, and two books: *The Couch in the Marketplace: Psychoanalysis and Social Reality* and *Fed with Tears, Poisoned with Milk: Germans and Israelis, The Past in the Present*. He is in private practice in Tel Aviv.

Gohar Homayounpour, Psy.D., is a psychoanalyst and award-winning author. She is a member of the International Psychoanalytic Association and the American Psychoanalytic Association. She is Training and Supervising Psychoanalyst of the Freudian Group of Tehran, of which she is also Founder and past President. She is a member of the scientific board at the Freud Museum in Vienna and of the IPA group Geographies of Psychoanalysis. Her first book, *Doing Psychoanalysis in Tehran* (2012, MIT), won the Gradiva Award and has been translated into many languages. Her latest book is titled *Persian Blues, Psychoanalysis and Mourning* (2022, Routledge).

Sudhir Kakar, Ph.D., has been Lecturer and Visiting Professor at Harvard; Visiting Professor at Chicago, McGill, Melbourne, Hawaii, and Vienna; and Fellow at the Institute for Advanced Study, Princeton, Berlin, and Cologne. His many honors include the Kardiner Award of Columbia University, Boyer Prize for Psychological Anthropology of the American Anthropological Association, and Germany's Goethe Medal and the Order of Merit. As "the psychoanalyst of civilizations", the French weekly *Le Nouvel Observateur* listed Kakar in 2005 as one of the world's twenty-five major thinkers. Kakar is the author/editor of eighteen books of nonfiction and six novels. Four volumes of his collected papers (Psychoanalysis, Culture and Society, Religion, Biography) will be published by Oxford University Press in the fall of 2023. His books have been translated into twenty languages around the world.

Eric R. Marcus, M.D., is Professor of Clinical Psychiatry at Columbia University College of Physicians and Surgeons and Training and Supervising Analyst at the Columbia University Center for Psychoanalytic Training and Research, where he was the director for ten years. He is Distinguished Life Fellow of the American Psychiatric Association. A proponent of modern ego psychology, he believes modern ego psychology is an umbrella meta-theory for psychoanalysis as a general psychology. His latest book is *Modern Ego Psychology and Human Sexual Experience: The Meaning of Treatment*. His previous book is *Psychosis and Near Psychosis: Ego Function, Symbol Structure, Treatment*, rev 3rd ed. Both by Routledge.

Amrita Narayanan, Psy.D., is Clinical Psychologist and Psychoanalyst in practice and Visiting Professor at the English Department of Ashoka University, New Delhi. She earned her doctorate in clinical psychology from Stanford University Psy.D. consortium in California. She trained as Psychoanalyst via the Indian Psychoanalytical Society (IPA, 2019). Amrita is Editor of *The Parrots of Desire: 3000 Years of Erotica in India* (Aleph Books, 2018) and Contributing Author in *Pha(bu)llus: A Cultural History of the Phallus* (Harper Collins, 2020) and to *Psychoanalysis in the Indian Terroir: Emerging Themes in Culture, Family, and Childhood* (Lexington Books, 2018). Her new book, *In a Rapture of Distress: Women's Sexuality in Modern India*, is forthcoming from Oxford University Press.

Ignácio A. Paim Filho, M.D., is Psychoanalyst and Plenary and Didactic Member of the Psychoanalysis Brazilian Society of Porto Alegre. His object of study is metapsychology and the Freudian method. Co-author of the books "Novos tempos, velhas recomendações: sobre a função analitica" (Paim Filho and Leite, 2012) and "Filicídio: uma introdução" (Paim Filho and Borges, 2017). Author of the books "Metapsicologia: um olhar a luz da pulsão de morte" (2014), "Inconfidências metapsicológicas: *Das Unheimliche*", (2019) and "Racismo por uma psicanálise implicada" (2021). His works have been published in collective books and in national and international journals.

Cecilio Paniagua, M.D., Universidad Complutense de Madrid. Fulbright Scholar. Psychiatrist at Thomas Jefferson University, Philadelphia. Doctoral thesis in Medicine at Universidad Autónoma de Madrid. Board Certified Member of the American Association of Psychiatry and Neurology.

Psychoanalyst at Institute Baltimore-Washington. Fellow of the American College of Psychoanalysis. Honorary Professor at Facultad de Medicina de la Universidad Autónoma de Madrid.

Cordelia Schmidt-Hellerau, Ph.D., is Training and Supervising Analyst of the Boston Psychoanalytic Society and Institute and the Swiss Psychoanalytic Society. She worked as a professor for clinical psychology at the University of Zürich, Switzerland, and published numerous papers on theoretical, clinical, and applied psychoanalysis. Her monograph *Life Drive & Death Drive, Libido & Lethe: A Formalized Consistent Model of Psychoanalytic Drive and Structure Theory* was published in German (1995), French (2000), English (2001), and Russian (2002). Her 2018 publication of *Driven to Survive* was a finalist of the American Board and Academy of Psychoanalysis book prize. She also published two novels, *Rousseaus Traum* (2019) and *Memory's Eyes: A New York Oedipus Novel* (2020). Since 2017, she is Chair of the IPA in Culture Committee. She works in private practice in Chestnut Hill, Massachusetts.

Mark Solms, Ph.D., is a member of the British Psychoanalytical Society and the American and South African Psychoanalytic Associations. He is Director of Neuropsychology at the Neuroscience Institute of the University of Cape Town. He is Honorary Fellow of the American College of Psychiatrists. He has received numerous honors and awards, including the Sigourney Prize. He has published 350 scientific papers and eight books, the latest being *The Hidden Spring* (Norton, 2021). He is the authorized editor and translator of the forthcoming *Revised Standard Edition of the Complete Psychological Works of Sigmund Freud* (24 volumes) and *Complete Neuroscientific Works of Sigmund Freud* (4 volumes).

Raúl Tebaldi, M.D., Medical School of La Plata. Residency in Psychiatry at Hospital José T. Borda. Specialist in Psychiatry. Psychoanalyst. Full Member and Training Analyst at the Argentine Psychoanalytic Association (APA). IPA full member and training analyst. Specialist in child and adolescent psychoanalysis. Former Coordinator of the Department of Children and Adolescents of the APA. Fellow of the Research Training Program at IPA, 1999. Former Chair of the IPA-APdeA (Asociación Psicoanalítica de Asunción) Liaison Committee. Secretary of the Institute of Psychoanalysis at APA. He has written numerous papers individually and in collaboration with others published in the *Revista de Psicoanálisis*, the *Journal of the Colombian Psychoanalytic Association*, and the *Journal of the Colombian Society of Psychoanalysis*. Author of the chapter "Metapsychology, limits, framing" in *Metapsychology: A Clinic with Foundation*. Compiler: Alejandra Vetzner Maruco. Ed. APA-Lugar (2014). Author of the chapter "Los límites del sueño" in *Perception and Dream*. Compiler: Fernando Martín Gómez. Editorial APA, 2019.

Series editor's foreword

The Publications Committee of the International Psychoanalytic Association is pleased to present a new book included in the International Psychoanalytic Series on Contemporary Freud, Turning Points, and Critical Issues: *The Ego and the Id: 100 Years Later*.

Fred Busch, Ph.D. (Boston, USA), and Natacha Delgado, Psychoanalyst and Translator (Buenos Aires, Argentina) – editors of this volume – belong to our Publications Committee and had selected very prominent psychoanalysts from our different regions to contribute with their ideas on the 100th anniversary of this breaking paper by Freud where he revised his basic theory. Our goal is to share with the psychoanalytic community new reflections and ideas that have arisen since Freud wrote his essay.

The Ego and the Id is a prominent essay by Sigmund Freud; it is an analytical study of the human psyche. His original title was *Das Ich und das Es* and was first published in April 1923. In his introduction, James Strachey states:

> The Ego and the Id are the last of Freud's major theoretical works. It offers a description of the mind and its workings that is at first sight new and even revolutionary, and indeed all psychoanalytic writings that date from after its publication But, despite all its fresh insights and fresh syntheses, we can trace, as so often with Freud's apparent innovations, the seeds of his new ideas in earlier, and sometimes in far earlier, writings.

Bear the unmistakable imprint of its effects – *at least regarding their terminology*. The key term phrase in Strachey's prediction is in *italics*. As Fred Busch has written, it is fascinating that this new model was never fully accepted by most psychoanalytic theories, with the French being an exception. This had important consequences for how different theories envisioned the best way to reach the unconscious.

We find the origin of the term "das Es" (Id or It) first used by Nietzsche and was taken up by Groddeck in a book he published named *Das Buch vom Es* just weeks before Freud's own book appeared in print.

Every creative mind has always taken a lot of seeds from others; perhaps the creative act is to take those seeds and make them ours in a new exercise of creation. One hundred years later, we see the validity of this text; let's ask ourselves why. Freud presents in this book a synthesis of the wholesale reorganization of a psychoanalytic theory, which was typical of his thinking from the 1920s on. Did we find another reorganization since then?

We can't set aside other concepts in psychoanalysis, such as, for example, narcissism and many others, but at the same time, we need to recognize the magnitude of this text. In *The Ego and the Id*, Freud concentrates on a strictly psychoanalytic point of view, reminding us that psychoanalysis is based on a fundamental premise: the distinction between what is conscious and what is unconscious.

Freud wrote this essay when he was 67 years old. In February 1923, he discovered a growth in his jaw, which he had removed just after *The Ego and the Id* was published. He had the feeling that his physicians might tell him to stop smoking, but instead of consulting a renowned specialist, he was treated by a physician not particularly competent as a surgeon. He underwent thirty-three operations for recurrent leukoplakia and received radiotherapy, this was very painful, and he was unable to work for six months.

But what struck me about this situation was that for several months, his physician and other friends said nothing to Freud about the cancerous nature of the tumor because they were afraid he might commit suicide. Maybe they never understood Freud's essential concepts about "knowing" what is not talked about or "thinking" what is not known. A clever mind like Freud's, who was also a physician and a great searcher, knows about his body signals. The way to pay attention to them is an individual matter. For Freud, his theory, writings, thoughts, and reflections were his priority.

I am writing this recommendation keeping in mind the terrible and painful time we are going through. It was not enough with the lockdown and isolation due to the COVID-19 pandemic also, the Russia and Ukraine war added a complex global instability. Freud also dealt with both situations, to have their boys as soldiers in the First World War and to survive the death of his beloved daughter, Sophie, from Spanish fever. We can't think about suicide ideation in Freud's mind. We need to think like Freud's mind. *We need to believe that a creative mind survives beyond life's avatars' limits.*

We will be able to continue delving into the work of the authors of this book on the influence that this text by Freud has left.

[1] Page numbers are those of *The Standard Edition of the Complete Psychological Works of Sigmund Freud*, vol. 19.

Dra. Silvia Flechner
Chair, *Publications Committee* IPA
Asociación Psicoanalítica del Uruguay

Introduction

In this monumental work, Freud rethinks the entire *metapsychological un-derpinnings of psychoanalysis*, based on clinical observation. He says in his preface:

> In these pages things are touched on which have not yet been the sub-ject of psycho-analytic consideration, and it has not been possible to avoid trenching upon some theories which have been put forward by non-analysts or by former analysts on their retreat from analysis. . . . If psycho-analysis has not hitherto shown its appreciation of certain things, this has never been because it overlooked their achievement or sought to deny their importance, but because it followed a particular path, which had not yet led so far. And finally, when it has reached them, things have a different look to it from what they have to others.
> (Freud, 1923, p. 21)

Here, we find the result of Freud's brilliance as a clinician-scientist, lead-ing to a new model of the mind that potentially had profound implications for psychoanalytic understanding and the psychoanalytic method.

The major themes are the following:

1 **Consciousness and What Is Unconscious** – Freud begins this work with a revolutionary reexamination of consciousness and what is un-conscious, along with the introduction of a new conceptualization of the ego as a *structure*.

> The decisive elements he points to are the difference between the *descriptive* and *dynamic* unconscious, and the ego as the source of repression. From a technical perspective he introduces the idea that the *analyst's main task consists in removing the resistances*. However, he came upon the puzzling fact that patients are unaware of these resistances, leading to the ground-breaking conclusion that a part of the ego itself are unconscious. He concludes that, "We recognize that the *Ucs*. does not coincide with the repressed; it is still true that

all that is repressed is *Ucs.*, but not all that is *Ucs.* is repressed. A part of the ego, too – and Heaven knows how important a part – may be *Ucs.*, undoubtedly is *Ucs*".

(p. 18)

The Ego and the Id – In this part of the essay, Freud emphasizes the importance of the preconscious, that parts of the ego are unconscious, the discovery of unconscious defenses, and the ego's role in serving the id.

He opens this section with a series of questions: "We can come to know even the *Ucs.* only by making it conscious. But stop, how is that possible? What does it mean when we say 'making something conscious'? How can that come about?" (p. 20). He then refines this by stating, "'How does a thing become conscious?' would thus be more advantageously stated: 'How does a thing become *preconscious*?' And the answer would be: 'Through becoming connected with the word-presentations corresponding to it'" (P. 20, italics added). This is an idea Freud (1915) already presented in his paper on "The Unconscious". He goes on to say that we bring the repressed to preconscious attention by supplying "preconscious intermediate links through the work of analysis" (p. 21). Although the idea that resistances are unconscious was first suggested by Freud in 1893, its importance in the analytic process was highlighted again in this 1923 essay. Freud mentions in passing that the ego is the actual seat of anxiety (p. 123) and elaborated this crucial point three years later in *Inhibitions, Symptoms and Anxiety. This set the stage for* a new guideline for psychoanalytic technique, where unconscious ego resistances need to be uncovered and worked through, leading to clarifications of preconscious links to the repressed.

Here, Freud also presents one his most famous analogies:

The functional importance of the ego is manifested in the fact that normally control over the approaches to motility devolves upon it. Thus, in its relation to the id it is like a man on horseback, who has to hold in check the superior strength of the horse; with this difference, that the rider tries to do so with his own strength while the ego uses borrowed forces. The analogy may be carried a little further. Often a rider, if he is not to be parted from his horse, is obliged to guide it where it wants to go;[1] so in the same way the ego is in the habit of transforming the id's will into action as if it were its own.

(P. 25)[2]

It is only in 1933 that Freud explores the role of the ego in more depth, with a decidedly clinical focus, and introduces the term "ego psychology". He is *prescient* in suggesting that this "ego psychology" will be difficult to understand in that there is something "in the material itself and of our being unaccustomed to deal with it. In any case, I will not be surprised if you show yourself even more reserved and cautious in your judgment than hitherto" (ibid., p. 58).[3]

The Ego and the Superego (Ego Ideal) – Although Freud noted *an unconscious sense of guilt* in patients as early as 1897 (p. 273), here, he introduces the concept of a *superego*. The idea stems from his clinical observation that there are patients where self-criticism and conscience dominate their mental functioning. He "reluctantly" describes an unconscious sense of guilt that he views as more prevalent than he at first realized and how he gradually came to see that in a great number of neuroses, an unconscious sense of guilt of this kind plays a decisive economic part and puts the most powerful obstacles in the way of recovery (pgs. 26–27). He notes that the "character of the ego is a precipitate of abandoned object-cathexes and that it contains the history of those object-choices" (p. 29). He also states that an erotic object choice can be transformed into an alteration of the ego helping to gain control of the id.

Freud then turns to the significance of the first identifications in early childhood and the ego ideal as the result of an identification with the father.[4] He describes what he calls the more *complete* Oedipus complex, which is both positive and negative, due to the inherent bisexuality in children. He concludes: "The broad general outcome of the sexual phase dominated by the Oedipus complex may, therefore, be taken to be the forming of a precipitate in the ego, consisting of these two identifications in some way united with each other. This modification of the ego retains its special position; *it confronts the other contents of the ego as an ego ideal or super-ego*" (p. 34). He then continues: "Its relation to the ego is not exhausted by the precept: 'You *ought to be* like this (like your father)'. It also comprises the prohibition: 'You *may not be* like this (like your father) – that is, you may not do all that he does, some things are his prerogative'" (p. 34).

The two classes of instincts

The two classes of instincts Freud proposes here are the sexual and death instinct, described first in *Beyond the Pleasure Principle* (Freud, 1920). While the sexual instincts were well known to analysts, the death instinct was controversial, even to this day. Freud states, "On the basis of theoretical considerations, supported by biology, we put forward the hypothesis of a death instinct, the task of which is to lead organic life back into the inanimate state" (p. 40). He goes on to say: "both the instincts would be conservative in the strictest sense of the word, since both would be endeavouring to re-establish a state of things that was disturbed by the emergence of life. The emergence of life would thus be the cause of the continuance of life and also at the same time of the striving towards death. and life itself would be a conflict and compromise between these two trends" (p. 40). The death instinct is seen expressing itself in destruction directed towards the external world. He concludes this section with the following thought: "Over and over again we find, when we are able to trace instinctual impulses back, that they reveal themselves as derivatives of Eros. If it were not for the considerations put forward in *Beyond the Pleasure Principle*, and ultimately for the sadistic constituents which have attached themselves to Eros, we should have difficulty in holding to our fundamental dualistic point of view. But since we cannot escape that view, we are driven to conclude that the death instincts are by their nature mute and that the clamour of life proceeds for the most part from Eros" (p. 46).[5]

The dependent relationships of the ego

In this section, Freud delves into the effect of the superego upon the ego and introduces the concept of the *negative therapeutic reaction*, which he describes in the following way:

> There are certain people who behave in a quite peculiar fashion during the work of analysis. When one speaks hopefully to them or expresses satisfaction with the progress of the treatment, they show signs of discontent and their condition invariably becomes worse. . . . One becomes convinced, not only that such people cannot endure any praise or appreciation, but that they react inversely to the progress of the treatment.
>
> (p. 49)

Freud elaborates that these patients suffer from a sense of guilt, finding satisfaction in illness. The patient feels no guilt, making it difficult to overcome except by slowly uncovering its unconscious roots and "gradually changing it to a *conscious sense of guilt*" (p. 50, italics added). He adds a fresh hypothesis to how the superego is formed in these individuals (i.e., a destructive component had entrenched itself in the superego and turned against the ego). What is now holding sway in the superego is, as it were, a pure culture of the death instinct due to an instinctual defusion where the exotic element "no longer has the power to bind the whole of the destructiveness that was combined with it, and this is released in the form of an inclination to aggression and destruction" (p. 53).

Finally, one momentous idea appears briefly (i.e., "The ego is the actual seat of anxiety" [p. 57]). This was elaborated on in Freud's (1926) paper, *Inhibitions, Symptoms and Anxiety*, differentiating it from his earlier idea of anxiety stemming from repressed libido.

While the unconscious sense of guilt has been accepted as an important part of understanding patients, the concept of a death drive has had mixed acceptance;[6] and it has been my view for some time that Freud's insights regarding the significance of analyzing unconscious resistances, the role of the preconscious in bringing what is unconscious to consciousness, and the introduction to ego psychology were rarely accepted as essential to psycho-analytic technique. There were exceptions. It took almost fifty years for a method of analyzing versus overcoming unconscious resistances was developed while appreciating the ego as the seat of anxiety (Gray, 1982, 1994; Busch, 1992, 1993, 1995; Paniagua, 1985, 2001). Green (1974) was one of the few who highlighted the importance of the preconscious in bringing what is unconscious to the fore in analysis. It is only recently that May (2002) pointed to how in the 1920s, analysts in Amsterdam, Berlin, and London emphasized the destructive instinct and diminished or excluded the sexual. In a series of papers and books, Schmidt-Hellerau (e.g., 2018) showed how the death drive can be the source of self and object preservation. However, it has not been so clear how some of the most important theorists, who positioned themselves as Freudians, turned away central aspects of this work (e.g., Klein, Bion, Winnicott).

Freud (1933) was, as it turns out, justifiably wary of how his introduction of ego psychology would be welcomed. "I must, however, let you know of my suspicion of this ego-psychology will affect you differently from the introduction into the psychic underworld which preceded it" (P. 58). He went on to say: "I now believe that it is somehow a question of the nature of the material itself and of our being unaccustomed to dealing with it. In any case, I shall not be surprised if you show yourselves even more reserved and cautious in your judgment than hitherto" (p. 58).

Chapter summaries

When we (the editors) invited an international group of psychoanalytic scholars to write about their thoughts on The *Ego and the Id*, 100 years after its publication, we had no idea what reactions we might receive. Indeed, what we received was surprising and eye-opening. We think the reader will find many new insights into this revered essay by Freud.

In Chapter 1, **Mark Solms** takes the bold position *that Freud made two errors* in *The Ego and the Id*. He believes that the problem, which led Freud to propose the structural theory, would be served better by assigning the function of consciousness to the id and by "distinguishing between the system *Ucs.* and the id". Solms believes that it was incorrect for Freud to claim that all "sense impressions are conscious from the start". He states that Freud made his claim on consciousness and perception from cerebral anatomy and gathers a large body of evidence from this field to show that Freud erred. He uses similar data to demonstrate what he describes as Freud's second error.

In another fascinating chapter (Chapter 2), **Cordelia Schmidt-Hellerau** describes her methodical reading of Freud's works and how she experienced reading *The Ego and the Id* as a rupture. She ends up understanding this puzzling feeling as a result of realizing that it was the first time Freud seriously grappled with how the psyche deals with what comes from the outside world. She describes how the mind starts out as an undifferentiated structure and is ready to be influenced by external forces leading to the building of the ego. Using cybernetics as a model theory to understand and evaluate Freud's theories, she describes his first view of the mind as being driven by *preservative and sexual drives* and fully elaborates this position, which she's described extensively in previous publications. She points out that Freud's drive theory is the most disputed part of his theory due to a concretistic misunderstanding. She notes that in *The Ego and the Id*, the new definition of drive became murkier.

In Chapter 3, **Gohar Homayounpour** asks a startling question (i.e., Why didn't Freud include the superego in his title, even though he spends considerable space writing about its role in his new model?) After a careful detailing of the role of the superego as Freud described in this metapsychological essay, Homayounpour presents an interesting speculation as to why Freud left out the superego in his title. She suggests that Freud taught us to be aware of *what isn't said* and, maybe in this way, drew our attention to the superego even more.

In Chapter 4, **Sudhir Kakar and Amrita Narayanan** make another new observation, when they point out that Freud didn't pay attention to the cultural dimensions of the ego. Based on the cultural myths of India, they point to how the father-son relationship is portrayed in many different ways than the rivalrous, murderous Oedipus complex described by Freud. For example, in Indian myth, the father may be seen more as a wished-for ally and protector. It is interesting that in clinical practice, this is also an important theme for men that complicates their rivalrous relationship with men. They also point out that culturally, the idealization of motherhood is reserved for mothers of sons, and it is hard to find examples of mother-daughter rivalry. They also describe a different view of bisexuality in Indian culture.

Heribert Blass, in Chapter 5, assumes that contemporary psychoanalysis would be inconceivable without the theoretical changes presented in this epochal work. He focuses primarily on four aspects in Freud's text: the concept of self, implicit in Freud's text, refers largely to a conflicted self; the special significance of the preconscious is still valid for our clinical practice today; the distinction between ideal ego and ego ideal can help us clinically, despite the fact that the superego is not mentioned in the title; and the intrapsychic and the interpsychic are always implicitly linked in Freud's work. Blass concludes that the interpretation of conflicts and the currently emphasized work on figurability are not mutually exclusive but build on each other.

Bernard Chervet (Chapter 6) takes us on a journey of Freud's theorization process by inviting the reader to really *listen* to the text – that is, to read Freud following his process of thought with its detours, its returns and regressions, and its productions and proposals that create new conceptions and new differences. In *"The advent of the superego: An après-coup of Beyond* *the Pleasure Principle"*, Chervet underlines the complexity in Freud's work by focusing not only on the process of theorization with regard to the mind of the author but also in the process that results in an epistemology of psychoanalytic theorization. Chervet's work in *The Ego and the Id* highlights Freud's dissatisfactions with his conceptions of the life drive and presents the dynamics of the process of après-coup in Freud's own elaboration of trauma and denial, thus showing how the advances of psychoanalysis may unfold.

In Chapter 7, **Cecilio Paniagua** describes a conundrum that's puzzled some analysts for over sixty years (i.e., that Freud's new view of an unconscious ego leading to resistances that are also unconscious, explained in *The Ego and the Id*, has done little to change analytic technique from its earlier model). Partly, this was due, he suggests, to Freud's own ambivalence towards the implications of his new model. He further argues that it is the magnetism of the id that leads us to make deep interpretations and thus bypassing the unconscious ego resistances, leading to intellectualized understanding.

In Chapter 8, **Fred Busch** continues Paniagua's theme about the importance of an unconscious ego in *The Ego and the Id*. He highlights that it is a curious thing that one of the major changes Freud made to his model of the mind, based upon a clinical fact which had immediate clinical consequences, was and continues to be ignored by the majority of the psychoanalytic world. Freud's clinical insight hasn't been proven wrong or dismissed for lack of clinical evidence: it is simply treated as if it never existed. In short, while other sections of *The Ego and the Id* gained general acceptance, the clinical implications of the new view of the ego were generally ignored.

Chapter 9 by **Eric R. Marcus** traces the development of the ego concept from 1923 up to the present and offers future directions. The ego as synthesizer and creator is described (i.e., its role in symbolic representation as the basic building block: to object relations, to relationships, to personality, to enactment, to psychic reality, to meaning, and to self and its story. The potential of modern ego psychology is a meta-theory of psychoanalysis as a general psychology. Metapsychologies describe different ego organizations of different affect validated organizations of symbolic representation. Metapsychologies are different aspects of a general psychology of the human mind.

Chapter 10 by H. Shmuel Erlich picks up on a theme that he believes did not receive the attention it deserves (i.e., the intertwined ideas of consciousness, the subject, and "the I"). He points out that Freud consistently used the term *Das Ich*, or *"the I"*, in different yet interrelated meanings, prominent at different periods, which he traces. The profound change brought about by *The Ego and the Id* is that "the I" (ego) is also largely unconscious, introducing the paradoxical notion of the subject, who is both conscious and unconscious and, in this sense, the master in his own house. With this formidable change, the therapeutic goal shifted profoundly from merely being aware to being responsible, introducing an ethical and social dimension into psychoanalysis.

In Chapter 11, **Ignácio A. Paim Filho** gives an account of how melancholia serves to explore not only the dependent relationship of the ego and the superego but mainly to reflect upon the vulnerability of mourning. Paim's detailed exposition reminds us about the vitality of the Freudian legacy, while his reflections on the narcissistic neurosis as a model for thinking about contemporary expressions of psychic suffering help us to understand the complex links held by an ego entangled in alienating identifications and prisoner of the superego's idealizations.

Claudia Lucía Borensztejn's (Chapter 12) contribution presents a review of different perspectives deriving from the reading of Freud's classic article. She sheds light over the impact of this within the post-Freudians, especially by showing how it became part of the Klein and Anna Freud controversies as well as in the developments of Isaacs, Heimann, Fairbairn, and Hinshelwood. She also focuses on the repercussions that this had on authors of the Argentinean Psychoanalytical School, such as Racker, Rascovsky, and more recently, Cosentino, with his comparative and translated edition into Spanish of the original manuscript of *The Ego and The Id*.

In Chapter 13, **Raúl Tebaldi** discusses *The Ego and the Id* from the perspective of the epistemology of complexity. He highlights that it serves as an example of Freud's model, anticipating modern epistemology. Tebaldi is interested in showing the co-existence of different psychic agencies and drives, the concept of "limit", and the interactions among them. The author underlines that in *The Ego and the Id*, there is an integration of different notions of psychic functioning from a stand-point that appeals to a humanist perspective, and he states that Freud confronted colleagues with other realities disturbing therapeutic success, such as negative therapeutic reactions, masochism, and so on. He suggests that post-Freudian authors have needed a common trunk to enable us to integrate different theories. For this purpose, Freud's methodological articulation in *The Ego and the Id* provides us with a fundamental model.

We hope you enjoy and are stimulated by reading Freud's work again, along with the discussions that bring to the fore new meaning and questions. It is truly a marvel that Freud, at age 67, was willing to rethink the underlying principles he discovered and produce this new metapsycholoical guideline. Most parts have remained at the center of psychoanalytic thinking for 100 years, some were modified, and some were ignored. We are very appreciative of our contributors who have enlightened us, surprised us, and added to the discussion about this historic work.

Fred Busch
Natacha Delgado

Notes

1 The importance of the preconscious remained unexplored for many years (Busch, 2006) until the work of Green (1974, 1975). However, it's centrality in the curative process is absent in most current theories, except for some French authors (Birksted-Breen, Flanders, Gibeault, (2010).
2 Freud's (1933) elaboration of what he then called "ego psychology" (p.58) is an important supplement to this section.
3 Hartmann (1956) noted that Freud, "sometimes used the term ego in more than one sense, and not always in the sense in which it was best defined (p. 432). Before the Ego and the Id the term ego became interchangeable with 'one's own person' or 'the self'."
4 It's my impression that Freud bypasses making a clear distinction between the ego ideal and super-ego. Of course, he is only referring to the situation of the male child.
5 May (2022) shows how from 1920 through 1925 analysts in Amsterdam, Berlin, and London championed aggression as the primary instinct, leading to the sexual instinct fading into the oblivion.
6 Schmidt-Hellerau (2018) proposes a new way of understanding the death drive.

References

Birksted-Breen, D., Flanders, S., Gibeault, a. (2010). *Reading French Psychoanalysis*. London: Routledge.

Busch, F. (1992). Recurring Thoughts on Unconscious Ego Resistances. *J Amer. Psychoanal. Assoc.*, 40: 1089–1115.

Busch, F. (1993). "In the Neighborhood": Aspects of a Good Interpretation and a "Developmental Lag" in Ego Psychology. *J Amer. Psychoanal. Assoc.*, 41: 151–177.

Busch, F. (1995). *The Ego at the Center of Psychoanalytic Technique*. New York: Jason Aronson Press.

Busch, F. (2006). A Shadow Concept. *International Journal of Psychoanalysis*, 87: 1471–1485.

Freud, S. (1915). The Unconscious. *S.E.*, 14: 159–215.

Freud, S. (1920). Beyond the Pleasure Principle. *S.E.*, 18: 1–64.

Freud, S. (1923). The Ego and the Id. *S.E.*, 19: 12–68.

Freud, S. (1926). Inhibitions, Symptoms and Anxiety. *S.E.*, 20: 75–176.

Freud, S. (1933). The dissection of the personality. *S.E.*, 22: 57–80.

Gray, P. (1982). "Developmental Lag" in the Evolution of Technique for Psychoanalysis of Neurotic Conflict. *J. Amer. Psychoanal. Assoc.*, 30: 621–655.

Gray, P. (1994). *The Ego and the Analysis of Defense*. New York: Jason Aronson Press.

Green, A. (1974). Surface Analysis, Deep Analysis (The Role of the Preconscious in Psychoanalytical Technique). *Int. Rev. Psychoanal.*, 1: 415–423.

Hartmann, H. (1956). The Development of the Ego Concept in Freud's Work. *Int. J. Psychoanal.*, 37: 425–438.

May, U. (2022). *Int. J. Psychoanal.*, 103: 328–349.

Paniagua, C. (1985). A Methodological Approach to Surface Material. *Int. Rev. Psychoanal.*, 12: 311–325.

Paniagua, C. (2001). The Attraction of Topographical Technique. *Int. J. Psychoanal.*, 82: 671–684.

Schmidt-Hellerau, C. (2018). *Driven to Survive*. New York: IP Books.

1 Freud's error

Mark Solms

I have argued elsewhere that Freud made two interrelated errors in *The Ego and the Id* (Solms, 2013, 2018, 2019, 2021). These errors were (1) incorporating the topographical system *Cs.* into his structural conception of the ego and (2) incorporating the topographical system *Ucs.* into his structural conception of the id. I believe that the problem that prompted Freud to propose a new "structural" conception of the mind would be resolved better by assigning the function of consciousness to the id, rather than the ego, and by distinguishing between the system *Ucs.* and the id. The invitation to contribute a chapter to the present book provides me with an opportunity to support these arguments with a detailed analysis of Freud's (1923) original text.

The problem that prompted Freud to revise his topographical model, and to replace it with the so-called structural one, is summarized succinctly in the following statement:

> We recognize that the *Ucs.* does not coincide with the repressed; it is still true that all that is repressed is *Ucs.*, but not all that is *Ucs.* is repressed. A part of the ego, too – and Heaven knows how important a part – may be *Ucs.*, undoubtedly is *Ucs.*
>
> (Freud, ibid., p. 18)

The part of the ego that Freud was referring to is the part that wields the mechanisms of defense. This part of the ego is not under voluntary control. It is unconscious and not only descriptively so; it is also dynamically unconscious.

Freud recognized on this basis that he was mistaken to have previously equated the ego with consciousness, or with the capacity for consciousness, since there is no special relationship between the ego and "the property of being conscious" (ibid.). This being so, one might think that he would have concluded that the property of being conscious belongs to some *other* mental system; but he didn't.

Why not? The answer is provided by the fact that the ego "starts out . . . from the system *Pcpt.*, which is its nucleus, and begins by embracing

DOI: 10.4324/9781003336754-1

the *Pcs.*, which is adjacent to the mnemic residues" (ibid., p. 23). This is axiomatic – the ego comes into being through the influence of external reality – so it must be "developed from its nucleus the *Pcpt.* system" (ibid., p. 24). Freud explains further that this means that the ego is ultimately derived from sensory stimuli "springing from the surface of the body" (ibid., p. 26 n. 1) and that it may, therefore, be described as "a mental projection of the surface of the body" (ibid.). He concludes: "If we wish to find an anatomical analogy for it we can best identify it with the 'cortical homunculus' of the anatomists, which stands on its head in the cortex" (ibid., p. 26).

So far, so good. But now we come upon Freud's first error. Six years before he wrote this work, Freud (1917) decided that the system *Pcpt.* should be combined with the system *Cs*. Accordingly, he coined the hybrid term "system *Pcpt.-Cs*".

The assumption upon which Freud's (1917) identification of consciousness with perception was based is restated in *The Ego and the Id*:

> Consciousness is the *surface* of the mental apparatus; that is, we have ascribed it as a function to a system which is spatially the first one reached from the external world – and spatially not only in the functional sense but, on this occasion, also in the sense of anatomical dissection. Our investigations too must take this perceiving surface as a starting-point. All perceptions which are received from without (sense-perceptions) . . . are *Cs*. from the start.
>
> (ibid., p. 19)

This is factually incorrect. *It is not true that all sense perceptions are conscious from the start.* I am surprised that Freud claimed this, since subliminal perception is easily recognized in everyday life (and as we shall see later, his claim is contradicted also by what he says about the defense mechanisms). Be that as it may, by the end of the 20th century, the existence (and ubiquity) of unconscious perception had been thoroughly proven by a variety of experimental methods. The accumulated evidence for this is summarized in a well-known review by Kihlstrom (1996), the title of which says it all: "Perception without awareness of what is perceived, learning without awareness of what is learned".

Put simply, we are conscious of what we perceive only if we *attend* to it. It would have been more correct, therefore, for Freud to link perception with the function of attention, rather than with consciousness, and to have assigned this function – attention – to the ego (which, in fact, he always did; e.g., Freud, 1900, 1911). The ego's attentional function has everything to do with its *defensive* function; the unconscious nature of which provided the impetus for *The Ego and the Id*.

Now the question becomes: If consciousness does not flow in through the senses, where does it spring from? The empirical evidence that answers this question first came to light ten years after Freud's death. Moruzzi and

Magoun (1949) discovered that if the cortex is separated from a part of the brainstem known as the reticular activating system, it is rendered unconscious. Many subsequent observations of a similar kind have firmly established that *all* consciousness is contingent upon arousal of the cortex by the reticular activating system. In other words, *cortical consciousness is a secondary, derivative form of consciousness*. The extent to which cortical consciousness depends upon brainstem arousal is amply demonstrated by Fischer et al.'s (2016) identification of a "coma-specific" region in the reticular activating system: all that is required to fall into a coma is to suffer a 2 mm^3 lesion in the parabrachial complex.

These findings demonstrate that, far from arising from the surface of the mental apparatus, consciousness arises from its inmost interior. Freud (1923, p. 19 n. 1) states explicitly that his alternative assumption (quoted earlier) was derived not only from his (1917) metapsychological study but also from ideas he set out in *Beyond the Pleasure Principle*. There, Freud (1920, p. 24) wrote:

> What consciousness yields consists essentially of perceptions of excitations coming from the external world and of feelings of pleasure and unpleasure which can only arise from within the mental apparatus; it is therefore possible to assign to the system *Pcpt.-Cs.* a position in space. It must lie on the borderline between inside and outside; it must be turned towards the external world and must envelop the other psychical systems. It will be seen that there is nothing daringly new in these assumptions; we have merely adopted the views on localization held by cerebral anatomy, which locates the 'seat' of consciousness in the cerebral cortex – the outermost, enveloping layer of the central organ. Cerebral anatomy has no need to consider why, speaking anatomically, consciousness should be lodged on the surface of the brain instead of being safely housed somewhere in its inmost interior.

The irony is that consciousness is, in fact, housed in the brain's inmost interior. I have quoted this passage not only to reveal the irony but also to address a concern that may have arisen in some readers' minds: Why am I using neuroanatomical findings to resolve metapsychological questions? The quoted passage makes clear that Freud adopted his assumption of an intrinsic relationship between consciousness and perception *from cerebral anatomy* (as do several other remarks by him, some of them also quoted here). This being so, it is entirely legitimate to correct his assumption on the basis of subsequent developments in that discipline.

There is something else in the passage just quoted that requires our attention. Freud says that consciousness consists not only in perceptions coming from the outside world but also in "feelings of pleasure and unpleasure which can only arise from *within* the mental apparatus" (emphasis added).

It is odd, therefore, for him to say in the same breath that the system *Pcpt.-Cs.* "must be turned towards the *external* world" (emphasis added); but that is what he says.

That is because Freud adopted another assumption from cerebral anatomy, namely, that feelings of pleasure and unpleasure, too, are registered in consciousness only when they reach the superficial cortex. Here is his most explicit (and last) statement to that effect:

> The process of something becoming conscious is above all linked with the perceptions which our sense organs receive from the external world. From the topographical point of view, therefore, it is a phenomenon which takes place in the outermost cortex of the ego. It is true that we also receive information from the inside of the body – the feelings [*Gefühle*], which actually exercise a more peremptory influence on our mental life than external perceptions . . . Since, however, these sensations ([*Empfindungen*][1] as we call them in contrast to conscious perceptions) also emanate from the terminal organs and since *we regard all these as prolongations or offshoots of the cortical layer*, we are still able to maintain the assertion made above. The only distinction would be that, as regards the terminal organs of sensation and feeling, the body itself would take the place of the external world.
>
> (Freud, 1940, pp. 161–162, emphasis added)

The assumption that feelings are registered via interoceptive terminal organs, which are "prolongations or offshoots" of the cortex, is highly questionable. The most dramatic evidence against it is the fact that children who are born without cortex (a condition called hydranencephaly) are not only conscious – since their brainstems are preserved – but they are also *emotionally* responsive. Figure 1.1 shows a brain scan of one such child, and Figure 1.2 shows the pleasurable response when her baby brother is placed in her lap. Several other lines of evidence point to the same conclusion, namely, that *affect is generated not in the cortex but in the brainstem.* For example: electrical stimulation of deep reticular nuclei – but not of the cortex – generates intense affective states (e.g., Blomstedt et al., 2008); functional brain imaging of people gripped by strong emotion reveals that the correlated brain activity is located not in the cortex but in the brainstem and its ascending arousal pathways (Damasio et al., 2000); pharmacological manipulation of the neurotransmitter systems sourced in the reticular activating system provides the mainstay of modern psychiatric drug therapy (e.g., serotonin, dopamine, noradrenaline; Solms, 2021);[2] and so on.

All this demonstrates that the reticular activating system does not merely "switch on the lights" in some purely quantitative sense (as was originally thought by Moruzzi & Magoun, 1949); it actually generates pleasurable and unpleasurable *qualities.* Since we know already that all consciousness is contingent upon brainstem arousal, this evidence suggests that *the*

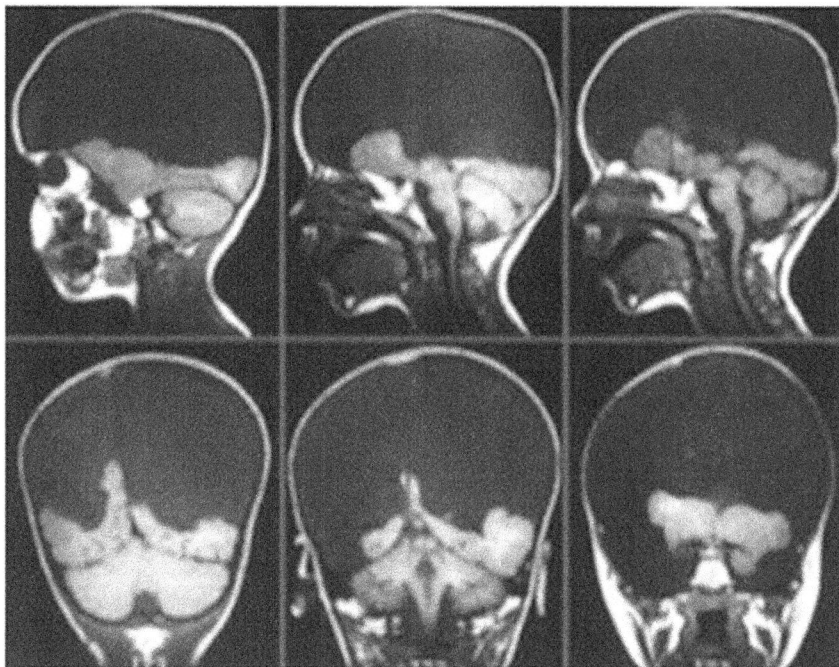

Figure 1.1 MRI of the brain of a hydranencephalic child, showing absence of cortex.

Figure 1.2 Hydranencephalic child showing a normal emotional response.

fundamental form of consciousness is affect (for reviews, see Panksepp, 1998; Merker, 2007; Damasio, 2010; Solms, 2021).

Against this background, it is of the utmost interest that the authors just cited argue that pleasurable and unpleasurable feeling is, to quote Freud (1915a, pp. 121–122), "a measure of the demand made upon the mind for work in consequence of its connection with the body". In other words, feeling is the conscious manifestation of oscillations in *drive* demand:

> The id, cut off from the external world, has a world of perception of its own. It detects with extraordinary acuteness certain changes in its interior, especially oscillations in the tension of its drive[3] needs, and these changes become conscious as feelings in the pleasure–unpleasure series. It is hard to say, to be sure, by what means and with the help of what sensory terminal organs these perceptions come about. But it is an established fact that self-perceptions – coenaesthetic feelings and feelings of pleasure–unpleasure – govern the passage of events in the id with despotic force. The id obeys the inexorable pleasure principle.
>
> (Freud, 1940, p. 198)

Now, if consciousness is not sourced in the cortex (which Freud equated with perception and the ego) but rather in the reticular activating system, and if the latter system is the source of what Freud called drive energy, then we have to conclude that *the id (and not the ego) is the wellspring of consciousness.*

Freud himself addressed this possibility:

> Whereas the relation of *external* perceptions to the ego is quite perspicuous,[4] that of *internal* perceptions to the ego requires special investigation. It gives rise once more to a doubt whether we are really right in referring the whole of consciousness to the single superficial system *Pcpt.-Cs.* Internal perceptions yield sensations of processes arising in the most diverse and also certainly the deepest strata of the mental apparatus. Very little is known about these sensations and feelings; those belonging to the pleasure-unpleasure series may still be regarded as the best examples of them. They are more primordial, more elementary, than perceptions arising externally and they can come about even when consciousness is clouded. I have elsewhere [Freud, 1920] expressed my views about their greater economic significance and the metapsychological reasons for this. These sensations are multilocular, like external perceptions; they may come from many different places simultaneously and may thus have different or even opposite qualities.
>
> (Freud, 1923, pp. 21–22)

So, the relation of feelings to the ego gave rise to understandable doubt in Freud's mind as to whether he was right to link all consciousness with the superficial system *Pcpt.* How did he resolve this doubt? He continued:

> Sensations of a pleasurable nature have not anything inherently impelling about them, whereas unpleasurable ones have it in the highest

degree. The latter impel towards change, towards discharge, and that is why we interpret unpleasure as implying a heightening and pleasure a lowering of energic cathexis. Let us call what becomes conscious as pleasure and unpleasure a quantitative and qualitative 'something' in the course of mental events; the question then is whether this 'something' can become conscious in the place where it is, or whether it must first be transmitted to the system *Pcpt.*

(ibid.)

This is precisely the right question. How did Freud answer it? He said: "Clinical experience decides for the latter" (ibid.); i.e., that the "something" (drive demand) is felt consciously only after it is transmitted to the system *Pcpt.* Freud explains: "It [the 'something'] can exert driving force without the ego noticing the compulsion" (ibid.). So the "something" behaves exactly like external perception: it becomes conscious only if the ego pays *attention* to it. But Freud claimed earlier that perception is always conscious. This is inconsistent. If perception and the "something", both, can sometimes influence the ego without it noticing it, then a failure of attention on the part of the ego cannot be used as grounds for concluding that the "something" (but not perception) is unconscious "in the place where it is".

This brings us to the heart of the matter: back to the problem that prompted Freud to revise his topographical model in the first place. It brings us to the problem of *defense* and the fact that the ego wields its defenses unconsciously.

This problem leads us to another contradiction in Freud's account. He said that perception is inherently conscious, but he included among the ego's mechanisms of defense scotomization (and others, including disavowal)[5] – a not "noticing" of external perceptual events. One way to resolve these inconsistencies and contradictions is to conclude what I suggested Freud should have concluded: if there is no special relationship between the ego and consciousness, then perhaps the ego is unconscious, and it *derives* its consciousness from some other mental system. This conclusion would be more consistent with the neuroscientific facts we have just reviewed. The cortex, with its perceptual function (and its attentional and defensive functions, all of which Freud assigned to the ego), is intrinsically unconscious, and it derives its consciousness from the reticular activating system, with its drive function (which can only be assigned to the id). Since drive and affective consciousness then become one and the same thing,[6] we are obliged to conclude that Freud's "something" *is* consciously felt "in the place where it is".

This yields the following simple formulation: *the unconscious ego, with its defensive functions, strives to gain control of affective consciousness.* This goal of the ego can be achieved in various ways. At one theoretical extreme, the ego can convert affective consciousness into cognitive consciousness entirely. This coincides with the fictitious case of Mr. Spock, where the (affective) drive – or "demand made upon the mind for work" – exerted by the id upon the ego yields perfectly efficient (cognitive) work. At the opposite extreme, the ego can fail entirely to achieve this goal. In which case, it will be overwhelmed by affect and cognitively incapacitated. At yet another extreme, the ego can exclude affective consciousness from its (cognitive) realm entirely. This results in the id generating negative affects of which the ego has no *knowledge* – a common-enough situation, as every psychoanalyst will attest.[7]

My proposed formulation is consistent with what Freud said about feelings becoming conscious directly. Unconscious ideas, by contrast, become conscious only indirectly – that is, only when they are attached to *Pcs.* word-presentations. "With *feelings*, which are themselves transmitted directly, this does not occur. In other words, the distinction between *Cs.* and *Pcs.* has no meaning where feelings are concerned; the *Pcs.* here drops out" (ibid., p. 23). This means that what stands between drive demand and the so-called system *Pcpt.-Cs.* is the *Ucs.* ego only – that is, the mechanisms of defense.

All the common-and-garden varieties of defense can be located between the theoretical extremes I have just described. I will focus on one of them shortly – namely, sublimation – but before I can do that, I must discuss a further contradiction in Freud's structural theory.

This contradiction is contained in two sentences I have quoted already:

> It is an established fact that self-perceptions – coenaesthetic feelings and feelings of pleasure–unpleasure – govern the passage of events *in* the id with despotic force. The id obeys the inexorable pleasure principle.
>
> (Freud, 1940, p. 198, emphasis added)

In *The Ego and the Id*, Freud likewise speaks of "the pleasure principle which reigns unrestrictedly *in* the id" (p. 25, emphasis added). How can the pleasure principle reign *in* the id if it is unconscious? What is the point of pleasure and unpleasure if you don't feel them? Surely, the pleasure principle regulates affective *consciousness*. That is why Freud says that the id is "guided by the pleasure principle – by the *perception* of unpleasure" (ibid. p. 47, emphasis added). If he meant that feelings become conscious only when they reach the cortex (the system *Pcpt.*, the nucleus of the ego), then the pleasure principle would have to exert a *top-down* influence over the id. This makes no sense. The reality principle exerts a top-down influence; the pleasure principle exerts a *bottom-up* influence – from the id upon the ego.

It is remarkable that this logical contradiction in the structural model had not been noticed before; it became apparent only when the empirical errors summarized earlier in this chapter were first revealed (Solms, 2013).

Against this background, it is interesting to note that Freud made many other statements in *The Ego and the Id*, which likewise imply that drive demand must be felt directly. Here are some representative examples. When he first introduced the notion of a "something", on p. 22, he wrote: "Let us call what becomes conscious as pleasure and unpleasure a quantitative *and qualitative* 'something' in the course of mental events" (emphasis added). How can something unconscious be qualitative? From the beginning to the end of Freud's writings (i.e., from 1950 [1895] to 1940), he used the term "quality" to denote the most essential characteristic of consciousness (as philosophers still do; cf. "qualia").[8] On the same page, Freud says that this "something" is equivalent to "unconscious feelings". He is obliged to add immediately that this phrase is actually "condensed and not entirely correct". That is because, once again, from the beginning to the end of his writings, Freud had always insisted that feelings *must* be conscious. Here is just one example:

> It is surely of the essence of an emotion that we should be aware of it, i.e., that it should become known to consciousness. Thus the possibility of the attribute of unconsciousness would be *completely excluded* as far as emotions, feelings and affects are concerned.
>
> (Freud, 1915b, p. 177, emphasis added)

The notion of "unconscious feelings" must, therefore, be completely excluded. The notion only becomes coherent if it is expanded to mean "cognitively unconscious but affectively conscious". That is, the phrase "unconscious feelings" properly denotes the situation I described earlier, where the ego *defensively* repels id demands (i.e., affect). Just one year later, Freud (1924b) conceded that "we [should] give up the term 'unconscious sense of guilt', which is in any case psychologically incorrect, and speak instead of a 'need for punishment'" (p. 166). The latter need is *felt*, of course; what is unconscious is *knowledge* of where it comes from.

In a similar vein, Freud tells us in *The Ego and the Id* that "object-cathexes proceed from the id, which *feels* erotic trends as needs" (p. 29, emphasis added). What makes erotic trends erotic is the fact that they feel so. This is only consistent with Freud's earlier comment to the effect that drive demand (i.e., the "something") possesses both quantitative and qualitative characteristics. The fact that erotic trends proceed from the id must also be read in conjunction with the following statement:

> For the ego, perception plays the part which in the id falls to drive. The ego represents what may be called reason and common sense, in contrast to the id, which contains the passions. . . . Thus in its relations to the id it is like a man on horse-back, who holds in check the superior strength of the horse; with this difference, that the rider tries to do so with his own strength while the ego uses *borrowed* forces.
>
> (ibid., p. 25, emphasis added)

Later – again referring to the erotic object choices of the id – Freud says that the ego gains control over them "at the cost, it is true, of acquiescing to a large extent in the id's *experiences*" (ibid., p. 30).

This brings us, finally, to the matter of sublimation. Freud writes: "The problem of the *quality* of drive impulses and of its persistence throughout their various vicissitudes is still very obscure and has hardly been attacked up to the present" (ibid., p. 44, emphasis added). One of these vicissitudes, he continues, is a desexualization of the libidinal drive, which then becomes a "displaceable and *neutral* energy" (ibid., emphasis added). This can only mean that, in becoming neutral, it has *lost* its erotic quality. He continues:

> If this displaceable energy is desexualized libido, it may also be described as *sublimated* energy; for it would still retain the main purpose of Eros. . . . If thought-processes in the wider sense are to be included among these displacements, then the activity of thinking is also supplied from the sublimation of erotic driving forces [*Triebkraft*].[9]
>
> (p. 45)

This is a model example of the process I formulated earlier concerning how the unconscious ego, via its defensive function, gains control over affective consciousness. This is how the drive *demand* for work exerted by the id yields efficient *work* by the ego. *Sublimation, I submit, is the means by which the primary affective form of consciousness is converted by the ego into the secondary cognitive form.*

There is much more to say about how drive demand is transformed into conscious perception (see Solms, 2021). Likewise, considering how much Freud said on the subject of hallucination in *The Ego and the Id*, it is unfortunate that I do not have space here to describe how perception is understood in modern neuroscience as "controlled hallucination" (Hohwy, 2013; Clark, 2015). Perception entails outward projection onto external reality of "predictions" (what Freud called "wishes"), which are secondarily constrained by incoming "prediction errors" (what Freud called "reality testing").

Be that as it may, I must use the remaining space to make some condensed remarks on the relationship between the id and the *Ucs.*

I do not want my assertion that the id is conscious – that it is the primary source of consciousness, the wellspring of sentient being – to be read as a denial of the existence (and importance) of the *Ucs.* My claim is only that *they are not the same thing.*

The id is a drive system, but the *Ucs.* is fundamentally a *memory* system (as one glance at the diagrams in Chapter 7 of *The Interpretation of Dreams* suffices to demonstrate). The former system *cathects* the latter system. So they can't be the same thing. Freud (1894) puts it like this at the very beginning of his metapsychology: "Quotas of affect spread over the memory-traces of ideas somewhat as an electric charge is spread over the surface of a body" (p. 60). Strachey called this distinction (between quotas of affect and memory traces of ideas) Freud's "most fundamental" hypothesis.

What is distinctive about the *Ucs.* is not that it is a reservoir of affect – what Freud later called drive energy, or libido (in *The Ego and the Id*, he identified the id as this "reservoir"). Rather, what distinguishes the *Ucs.* and *Pcs.* memory systems is the fact that the drive energies, which cathect them, behave differently in the two systems: *Ucs.* cathexes are "freely mobile" whereas *Pcs.* cathexes are "bound". This, in turn, underwrites the distinction between the primary and secondary processes. To repeat: the energy producing these two modes of cathexis does not spring from the memory systems themselves; rather, it comes from the demands *made upon them* in consequence of the mind's connection with the body.

What I am proposing here is simply that drive demands arise from outside the *Ucs.* and the *Pcs.* both – that they come from the id. Drive makes demands upon the ego to perform such work as is required to satisfy the needs of the organism, which it can only do by drawing upon *previous* "experiences of satisfaction" (which gradually supplement and augment what Freud called "inherited" memories, which are properly described as "instincts", as opposed to "drives"). In short, the ego's memory systems derive from *learning from experience*.

But as the title of Kihlstrom's review (cited earlier) showed, learning can occur both with and without "awareness of what is learned". Freud's system *Ucs.* coincides, therefore, with what cognitive scientists nowadays call the "nondeclarative" memory system, and the *Pcs.* coincides with what is now called the "declarative" memory system. The nondeclarative system (which, like Freud's primary process, functions automatically, stereotypically, and rapidly) is mainly subcortical,[10] and the declarative system (which, like the secondary process, functions voluntarily, flexibly, and "holds things in mind") is *cortical*. The most important thing to note is that neither of these systems is located in the brainstem (and related) structures that are the anatomical substrate of the drives.

Readers who want to know more about these memory systems, and what contemporary neuroscience teaches us about them, may fruitfully consult Solms (2018). There, I argue, just as Freud did in *The Ego and the Id*, the following:

> the [nondeclarative] *Ucs.* does not coincide with the repressed; it is still true that all that is repressed is *Ucs.*, but not all that is *Ucs.* is repressed. A part of the ego, too – and Heaven knows how important a part – . . . undoubtedly is *Ucs.*
>
> (p. 18)

Psychoanalysts interested in advancing our metapsychology have much to gain by acquainting themselves with what has been learned since Freud (1923) about the distinction between the repressed and the unrepressed *Ucs.*

Notes

1 The German word *Empfindungen* is barely distinguishable from the English "feelings". Readers should bear this in mind whenever Strachey's word "sensations" appears in my quotations from Freud.
2 Cf. Freud (1940, p. 182): "The future may teach us to exercise a direct influence, by means of particular chemical substances, on the amounts of [drive] energy and their distribution in the mental apparatus. It may be that there are still undreamt-of possibilities of therapy".
3 Strachey's translation of Freud's term *Trieb* as "instinct" is misleading. I have accordingly changed it to "drive" in all the Freud quotations used here.
4 As we have just learned, it is really not.
5 Cf. Freud (1924a, p. 151): "the delusion is found applied like a patch over the place where originally a rent had appeared in the ego's relation to the external world".
6 Bodily needs (the needs to hydrate, to sleep, to urinate, to breathe, etc.) illustrate this. They are present all the time, but they become *drives* (they make demands upon *the mind* for work) only when we feel them.
7 Here, we recognize the oxymoronic "unconscious feelings".
8 Cf. Freud (1950 [1895], p. 308): "Consciousness gives us what are called *qualities* – sensations which are *different* in a great multiplicity of ways".
9 Translated by Strachey as "motive forces".
10 It is located mainly in the basal ganglia, amygdala, and cerebellum.

References

Blomstedt, P., Hariz, M., Lees, A. et al. (2008). Acute severe depression induced by intraoperative stimulation of the substantia nigra: A case report. *Parkinsonism and Related Disorders*, 14: 253–256.

Clark, A. (2015). *Surfing Uncertainty: Prediction, Action, and the Embodied Mind*. New York: Oxford University Press.

Damasio, A. (2010). *Self Comes to Mind*. New York: Pantheon.

Damasio, A., Grabowski, T., Bechara, A. et al. (2000). Subcortical and cortical brain activity during the feeling of self-generated emotions. *Nature Neuroscience*, 3: 1049–1056.

Fischer, D., Boes, A., Demertzi, A. et al. (2016). A human brain network derived from coma-causing brainstem lesions. *Neurology*, 87: 2427–2434.

Freud, S. (1894). The neuro-psychoses of defence. In *Standard Edition of the Complete Psychological Works of Sigmund Freud*, 3. London: Hogarth, pp. 45–61.

———. (1900). The interpretation of dreams. In *Standard Edition of the Complete Psychological Works of Sigmund Freud*, 4 & 5. London: Hogarth.

———. (1911). Formulations on the two principles of mental functioning. In *Standard Edition of the Complete Psychological Works of Sigmund Freud*, 12. London: Hogarth, pp. 215–226.

———. (1915a). Instincts and their vicissitudes. In *Standard Edition of the Complete Psychological Works of Sigmund Freud*, 14. London: Hogarth, pp. 117–140.

———. (1915b). The unconscious. In *Standard Edition of the Complete Psychological Works of Sigmund Freud*, 14. London: Hogarth, pp. 166–204.

———. (1917). A metapsychological supplement to the theory of dreams. In *Standard Edition of the Complete Psychological Works of Sigmund Freud*, 14. London: Hogarth, pp. 219–234.

————. (1920). Beyond the pleasure principle. In *Standard Edition of the Complete Psychological Works of Sigmund Freud*, 18. London: Hogarth, pp. 7–64.

————. (1923). The ego and the id. In *Standard Edition of the Complete Psychological Works of Sigmund Freud*, 19. London: Hogarth, pp. 12–59.

————. (1924a). Neurosis and psychosis. In *Standard Edition of the Complete Psychological Works of Sigmund Freud*, 19. London: Hogarth, pp. 149–153.

————. (1924b). The economic problem of masochism. In *Standard Edition of the Complete Psychological Works of Sigmund Freud*, 19. London: Hogarth, pp. 157–170.

————. (1940 [1939]). An outline of psycho-analysis. In *Standard Edition of the Complete Psychological Works of Sigmund Freud*, 23. London: Hogarth, pp. 144–207.

————. (1950 [1895]) Project for a scientific psychology. In *Standard Edition of the Complete Psychological Works of Sigmund Freud*, 1. London: Hogarth, pp. 283–397.

Hohwy, J. (2013). *The Predictive Mind*. New York: Oxford University Press.

Kihlstrom, J. (1996). Perception without awareness of what is perceived, learning without awareness of what is learned. In M. Velmans (ed.), *The Science of Consciousness: Psychological, Neuropsychological and Clinical Reviews*. London: Routledge, pp. 23–46.

Merker, B. (2007). Consciousness without cerebral cortex: A challenge for neuroscience and medicine. *Behavioral and Brain Sciences*, 30: 63–68.

Moruzzi, G. & Magoun, H. (1949). Brain stem reticular formation and activation of the EEG. *Electroencephalography and Clinical Neurophysiology*, 1: 455–473.

Panksepp, J. (1998). *Affective Neuroscience: The Foundations of Human and Animal Emotions*. New York: Oxford University Press.

Solms, M. (2013). The conscious id. *Neuropsychoanalysis*, 14: 5–85.

————. (2018). The neurobiological underpinnings of psychoanalytic theory and therapy. *Frontiers in Behavioral Neuroscience*, 12: 294. DOI: 10.3389/fnbeh.2018.00294

————. (2019). The hard problem of consciousness and the Free Energy Principle. *Frontiers in Psychology*, 10: 2714. https://doi.org/10.3389/fpsyg.2018.02714

————. (2021). *The Hidden Spring: A Journey to the Source of Consciousness*. London: Profile Books.

2   The meeting of minds

Cordelia Schmidt-Hellerau

I'll never be done with Freud. Reading his work, I always find something new to think about, something in need of clarification, elaboration, or revision. About thirty years ago, I embarked on a deep exploration of Freud's metapsychology from its beginning in his 1895 *Project for a Scientific Psychology* to his last reflections posthumously published (Schmidt-Hellerau, 2001). I understood that Freud's big theoretical moves occurred in three boosts, namely, 1895–1900, 1913–1915, and 1920–1923. Each burst of conceptual creativity reorganized previous assumptions and introduced new elements into Freud's "psychic apparatus" – leaving behind a trail of challenging questions while opening new insights into the intricate ways of psychic processes. Chronologically working my way through the growing body of Freud's model of the mind, when I arrived at his 1923 essay, *The Ego and the Id*, I was surprised to feel something akin to a rupture. Even though many aspects of this essay seemed to expand on familiar themes – the distinction between the *Ucs.* and the *Cs.*, the elaboration of the complete Oedipus complex, the formation of the ego ideal/superego, as well as a summary of his new drive theory (which had been my particular focus of interest) – I felt there was something puzzling, something different in this paper, something I first couldn't quite put my finger on.

I think this rupture or shift has to do with the fact that in this essay, Freud, for the first time, seriously grapples with the question how the psyche deals with and responds to what comes to it from the outside world. Of course, before 1923, the mind Freud was studying didn't exist in isolation. It was the infant's, the child's, the adolescent's, and the adult's mind as it aims for, experiences, fantasizes, and transfers to the nursing object, the oral, the anal, the genital, and the oedipal objects, the feared parental authority, the hysterically embraced, obsessionally avoided, melancholically mourned objects and so on. It was *the look from inside out* initiated by the subject's needs and desires that helped Freud build his developmental theory, the mind according to the subject's drives and representations. What he had left out so far was the question on how the mind receives and deals with the object's drives. What if the subject finds itself as the aim of another's wishes?

DOI: 10.4324/9781003336754-2

These questions aren't fully fleshed out in *The Ego and the Id*. Only after Freud's death they were taken up and articulated (e.g., in the discussions about the analyst's countertransference, in Laplanche's "enigmatic messages", in the debate about a "one-person" versus "two-person" psychology, or in the relational turn). And yet in 1923, this seems to be one of the essential questions that Freud tried to grapple with in his extensive efforts to distinguish between the perception of internal and external stimuli, object-cathexis and identification, and the fusion and defusion of the drives.

The outside-impact

The puzzle of the outside-impact had been on Freud's mind for a while. At the beginning of his 1923 essay, he refers back to 1920: "The present discussions are a further development of some trains of thought, which I opened up in *Beyond the Pleasure Principle*, and to which, as I remarked there, my attitude was one of a kind of benevolent curiosity" (Freud, 1923, p. 12). What he now picks up is his "far-fetched speculation" (Freud, 1920, p. 24): to "picture a living organism in its most simplified possible form as an undifferentiated vesicle" (ibid., p. 26), which is "suspended in the middle of an external world charged with the most powerful energies" (ibid. p. 27). While in Freud's previous considerations this "little fragment of living substance" (ibid.) was mainly concerned with its own inner life, namely, the drives and defenses as well as their organization, now two new tasks are put into focus: the *reception of* and the *protection against* outside stimuli.

Departing from the idea that the mind has to deal with internal drive pressures as well as "the ceaseless impact of external stimuli" (ibid., p. 26), in 1923, Freud places the ego right at the border between both. This may be a bit concretistic because a structure/system assigned with the task to receive and process such excitations could be placed anywhere in the mind; however, this particular location helped picture the clash of internal and external forces and conceptualize how such a "coming together" of energies might form and inform the structures of the mental apparatus. Curious to see where this idea would lead him and referring to Groddeck, Freud suggests:

> We shall now look upon an individual as a psychical id, unknown and unconscious, upon whose surface rests the ego, developed from its nucleus the *Pcpt*. System. . . . The ego is not sharply separated from the id; its lower portion merges into it.
>
> (Freud, 1923, p. 24)

It is easy to see that the ego is that part of the id which has been modified by the direct influence of the external world through the medium

of the *Pcpt.-Cs.*; in a sense it is an extension of the surface-differentia-
tion (. . .). For the ego, perception plays the part which in the id falls
to the drive.[1]

(Freud, 1923, p. 25)

Hypothetically, the mind starts out as this undifferentiated bit of living substance, an id, which by its nature (like in embryology) has the capacity,
expectation, and readiness to be modified by the external world, thereby
building the ego. The external world primarily consists of the infant's objects. They foster and shape the unfolding mind and its ego. While the ego
increasingly adapts to the principles of reality, it also remains rooted in the
id (ibid., p. 24), which eventually will contain next to the repressed a vast
array of perceptions that never reached a state of conscious awareness. The
importance of the infant's objects for the formation of psychic structure
is common sense and agreed upon, whether by contemporary Freudians,
object relations theorists, the Bionian paradigm of beta-to-alpha transformation, or modern infant observation. Still, how can it be conceptualized
within Freud's metapsychology?

Structure formation

As I have shown extensively elsewhere (Schmidt-Hellerau, 2001), Freud's
model of the working mind can be researched and clarified by using cybernetics, a control theory that is successfully applied (amongst other fields)
to describe the regulation of complex biological as well as psychological
systems. Cybernetics works with sensors and rulers (here, our mental
structures) that respond and adjust to input and output variables (here, our
drives and their energies) to maintain the homeostasis of the system (here,
the pleasure [constancy] principle of the mind). In the spirit of cybernetics,
we can say that Freud's metapsychology rests upon only two notions, drive
and structure. The drives energize the mental system; the structures organize, balance, and direct these energies.[2]

In its 1915 definition, the drive is defined as the mental representation of
the body's demands (Freud, 1915, p. 121f.). Freud suggested to think of the
infant's mind as being stirred by preservative and sexual drives, hunger and
love (in the widest, including metaphorical sense). The mother receives the
infant's quest (hunger) and responds by offering the breast, a nurturing as
well as sensorially pleasing (erotic) present. But the nursing object herself is
also driven, namely, to feed and play with her baby, and the baby responds
with suckling and smiling. We can say: in the act of nursing, the infant's and
the mother's needs and desires are mutually satisfied.[3] Mother and baby
are both subjects with their own needs and each other's objects, aims of the
other's drives. It's this meeting of minds that characterizes their interaction.

Ideally, the nursing object functions as a mature structure (auxiliary ego)
that more or less correctly perceives the infant's needs and desires. "For

the ego, perception plays the part, which in the id falls to the drive" (ibid.). In this sense, *perception functions as or equals drive excitation*. Since mental structures (sensors/rulers) can only read or react to varying quantities of drive energy (variables), infant and object are mutually receptive for each other's drive messages, conscious or unconscious ones and be they overt or enigmatic.

This is the new challenge in Freud's 1923 conception of mental processes: How does this little bit of living substance, the newborn mind/id, receive and react to what comes from the object, namely, the object's drives? If the subject's and object's actions are motivated, energized, and registered in the mind as drive excitations (the variables), how exactly do they impact the mind, namely, form and inform structure?

Needs and desires can be regulated by providing satisfaction ("Here you go", mother says) or by being limited and repressed ("Stop it", mother says).[4] *Satisfaction* is a *concordant* move; the infant's hunger (self-preservation) excites the mother's urge to nurse (object-preservation). *Limitation* is *complementary*: the subject's (over-)excitement is calmed down by the object, or the subject's lack of excitement leads the object to stimulate arousal. Thus, the mother contributes to the regulation of the infant's drive activities by either satisfying them with the same drive's response (concordant) or moderating them with the antagonistic drive (complementary) – usually a combination of both drives. How does this impact the formation of mental structures? Freud sketches his ideas as so often with regard to the sexual drives:

> At the very beginning, in the individual's primitive oral phase, object-cathexis and identification are no doubt indistinguishable from each other. (. . .) The ego, which to begin with is still feeble, becomes aware of the object-cathexes, and either acquiesces in them or tries to fend them off by the process of repression.
>
> When it happens that a person has to give up a sexual object, there quite often ensues an alteration of his ego which can only be described as a setting up of the object inside the ego. (. . .) It may be that this identification is the sole condition under which the id can give up its objects. At any rate the process, especially in the early phases of development, is a very frequent one, and it makes it possible to suppose that the character of the ego is a precipitate of abandoned object cathexes and that it contains the history of those object-choices.
>
> (ibid., p. 29)

Here, Freud describes how he envisions structure formation. In the beginning, the infant's quest and the mother's nursing response form what we could call a self-object-structure, which represents the drive-satisfaction experience. It is only through the developmental process of structural differentiation that the object is "given up" (as part of the self-object-unit) and "set up" as a separate entity within the mind. This is possible when the self can take over ("identify" with) the object's function of regulating the level of excitation. A "transformation of object-libido into narcissistic libido" (ibid., p. 30) takes place. "It may be that this identification is the sole condition under which the id can give up its objects" (ibid., p. 29). Now we have two distinct types of structures, self representations and object-representations "inside the ego".

It may be worth emphasizing here that the notion of "object-cathexis" always refers to the activation of an object representation within the mind, not directly to a real object out there.[5] The real object in the external world only exists insofar as it is perceived, represented, and energized within the mind of a person. That's why positive as well as negative hallucinations are so compelling. The adherence to the reality principle, the ego's task, requires to continuously register and integrate new information about the object that arrives through the perception of the outside world and adjust the drive responses accordingly.

Differentiation and integration are foundational to all structure formations and their hierarchical organization. In the same sense as from a certain degree of complexity on the hypothetical original self-object-representation will be split into two distinct representations, self and object, the id and the ego gradually – but never completely – separate from each other by erecting what Freud called the barrier of repression. And finally, the ego and the superego (ego ideal) will separate out, organized around distinct functions. In his 1923 essay, Freud describes these functions most detailed for the superego in his elaboration of the Oedipus complex as the subject's wish for, use of, as well as struggle with and against the object. It is a formative, structure-building struggle in which the will (drives) of the subject meets, clashes, and eventually reconciles with the will (drives) of the object. All mental structures, whether on a micro-level (such as single representations) or on a macro-level (such as the ego, the id, and the superego), are shaped that way. They register significant deviations from tolerable tension levels established as their homeostatic value and initiate the arousal of drive energies, which activate existing, associated, or newly forming structures in quick succession with varying compositions of drive energies. This is what we call mental processes: the continuous anticipation of and matching of the subject's and object's drives and its elicited responses.

Reflections on metapsychology

Drive theory is probably the most disputed part of Freud's metapsychology. Over the years, I have extensively responded to the various lines of criticism (Schmidt-Hellerau, 1997, 2001, 2005), and I will not again take up these arguments here. The opponents suggested to get rid either of drive theory altogether or of the one or other part of it (most decisively the death drive, as for example, also recently, Solms, 2021) or the energy concept or the economic/quantitative point of view of metapsychology. Looking back to these suggestions, I think for the most part the denial of drive theory is due to a concretistic misunderstanding or a narrow reading of the essential function of the concepts of drive and drive energy in Freud's model of the mind.

We know that Freud's drive concept picks up Darwin's finding that self-preservation and procreation are the two fundamental success categories in the evolution of the species. What do these categories include? For instance: self-preservation means eating, drinking, and sleeping but also chasing for food, making sure to be safe, bonding with protective others, and so on; and procreation requires searching for, choosing, and courting the desirable object but also competing by becoming stronger, more beautiful, more successful, and more enjoyable, all in order to be attractive and mate. Most of man's activities – like creativity, recreation, research, relating to others, progressive or conservative activism – serve either primarily one or more often both objectives to varying degrees. As we can see, the ultimate goals of the two primal drives encompass a wide variety of cognitive, emotional, and behavioral attitudes, all of which aim at self-preservation and/or procreation – and this nota bene not only on a momentary or daily basis but also as trajectories reaching across a lifespan. In this process, a multitude of processes is coordinated, involving the mind, the brain, and the body, and in each new effort, different environmental circumstances have to be considered and will require different responses, *just in order to reach these goals*.

Relating to Darwin, as early as in his 1895 *Project*, Freud considered self-preservation and sexuality as man's main motivations, and that's why he placed them as the two primal drives in his psychic apparatus. Even though keenly interested in the mind-body-connection, he was fully aware that it would not be possible to specify detailed physiological processes for or assign particular brain structures to either of them. His restraint is not simply a reflection of the early and underdeveloped state of neuroscience at Freud's time. More importantly, given the complexity and diversity of physiological processes activated in the short- as well as long-term goals of self- and object preservation as well as self- and object love, it makes no sense to even try. Metapsychological concepts are merely theoretical constructs, which *organize our clinical experience* of psychic processes. There is no such thing as an ego, a superego, or an id as a fact or reality or a region in the brain. All we can suggest is, for example, to think of mental processes as organized by three macro-structures – called the ego, superego (ego ideal), and id – to which we assign specific functions explaining these processes or to stipulate two antagonistic drives, which express man's basic motivations and account for the psychodynamics in the mental processes we observe. That's why with regard to the drives, a statement like "there is no death drive" would be an error in thinking. The question can only be the following: Does it make sense, and is it clinically useful to introduce the concept of "death drive" into our theory of the mind, and what does it help to better see and understand?

Solms (2021), following Panksepp, distinguishes between bodily and "emotional drives" and focuses on the latter:

> The "emotional" drives are distinguished from the "bodily" ones mainly by virtue of the fact that they do not arise from bodily needs so much as from what might be called *object-relational* ones. That is, they arise from biological needs in relation to other mental *agents*.
>
> (Solms, 2021, p. 1062; *italics* in the original)

The emotional drives, Solms proposes, are a LUST drive, a SEEKING drive, a RAGE drive, a FEAR drive, a PANIC/GRIEF drive, a CARE drive, and a PLAY drive, arguing that these drives "can be reliably elicited by electrical or (specific) chemical stimulation at exactly the same brain sites, in all mammals, from mice to men" (ibid., p. 1064). Stimulating these brain sites and eliciting these emotions may very well move the mammal. But such move is not what the function of two primal drives in psychoanalysis is about. In keeping with Freud's 1915 definition that the drive represents the body's demand on the mind – namely, that self-preservation and procreation shall be reached – the two primal drives capture man's basic motivations in the widest, most encompassing sense. Psychoanalysis postulates that they are the trajectories of all human endeavor. These two primal drives are what motivates us and keeps us going over a lifespan, whether we are momentarily hungry or not or whether we want to concretely procreate or not. And in addition, Freud positioned them as antagonists in his theory, which allowed him to think of them as balancing forces in all human strivings, enabling the structures to maintain the dynamic stability (homeostasis) of the mind.

Life and death drives

This conceptual clarity got lost in Freud's second drive theory of 1920. While the antagonistic position of the drives was maintained in the notions of *life* and *death*, the new general definition of the drive got murky:

> it seems, then, that a drive is an urge inherent in organic life to restore an earlier state of things which the living entity has been obliged to abandon under the pressure of external disturbing forces; that is, it is a kind of organic elasticity, or, to put it another way, the expression of the inertia inherent in organic life.
>
> (Freud, 1920, p. 36)

As I have previously elaborated on,[6] here, the drives are defined as *intelligent beings*, knowing what they want and remembering where to return to. Maybe confusion is an essential part of creativity, and it remains to later generations to do the work of clarification. Working on Freud's theory development, I noticed that most of the logical breaks and conceptual inconsistencies occurred when Freud mixed up the function of drive and structure. The previous definition of his new drive concepts is an example of such a confusion. Thus, it seems expedient to stay with the original conceptions: the drives (variables) do nothing else other than driving, thereby activating the associated structures with drive energy; and the structures (sensors and rulers), formed by experience (memory traces), regulate and steer these energies to ensure the satisfaction of these drives.

Freud's first drive theory was represented by the pair "hunger and love". His second drive theory embraced the opposite feelings of "love and hate", assigning aggression to the death drive. This decision led Freud to compare the aims of the life and death drives with the physiological processes of *anabolism* and *catabolism* (ibid., p. 41), concluding that the purpose of Eros be *uniting* and *binding* (as if in loving), whereas the death drive's aim be *unbinding* and *destruction* (as if in hating). Freud was not quite sure about this, but he tried to feel his way ahead:

> This hypothesis throws no light whatever upon the manner in which the two classes of drives are fused, blended, and alloyed with each other; but that this takes place regularly and very extensively is an assumption indispensable to our conception.
>
> (ibid., p. 41)

Here again, Freud confused the functions of drive and structure. Cybernetic consistency requires that "binding" and "unbinding" is not the drives but the structure's function. At the structure, both antagonistic drives come together – and it's the structure that "mixes", "binds", "fuses", "blends", or "alloys" them as it were – whereby (through computation) a subsequent drive response will be created and released. Therefore, we better keep up the drives' separate antagonistic values (rather than thinking of their energies as mixed or "neutral").

And yet, as imperfect as it was, Freud's idea of life and death drives captured something new worth thinking about. His struggle with transitioning his first into his second drive theory is understandable: the sexual drive fit well into the broader concept of a life drive, but the self-preservative drive seemed to contradict a death drive[7] – unless we now integrate the formative impact of the object. As shown earlier and over the years (Schmidt-Hellerau, 2006, 2018), it's the object that responds to and interferes with the subject's drives, thereby satisfying, limiting, and structuring them. Thus, it's the object's nurturing care that prevents the death drive from racing towards death and ensures the infant's survival, thereby establishing the structures of self-preservation. And it's the object's loving care that focusses the joy of life on the immediacy of the available erotic object initiating the sexual drive. Green made the structuring function of the object very clear:

> Even if drives are considered as basic, first entities, that is to say, primary, we nevertheless must assume that the object reveals the drives. It does not create them – and no doubt it can be said that it is at least partly created by them – but it is the condition for their coming into existence.
>
> (Green, 1999, p. 84f.)

This is how Freud's important papers of 1920 and 1923 belong together: His new theory of the primal drives had expanded their reach from the momentary stirrings of and preoccupations with hunger and sexuality to the overarching goals and tasks of mastering life and death. But as general as these human tendencies are, they are mutually structured by the interaction with the object. The individual mind is inherently the product of a meeting of minds.

Concluding remarks

The Ego and the Id is one of Freud's richest and theoretically most challenging essays. In its merely 50 pages (of the *Standard Edition*), so many ideas about the formation and function of the mind are addressed – and more still insinuated – that hardly any one paper could thoroughly speak to all of them. It is my sense that one of the questions he wanted to answer by introducing the structural theory is how to conceptualize the object's impact on the subject, namely, how the interaction between the subject's and the object's needs and wants (drives) leads to structure formation in all three parts of the mind. For reasons of space limitation, I did not address another central theme in this essay, namely, how to understand the conscious and unconscious parts of mental processes. But this is how it is, reading Freud: there always remains more to think about.

One hundred years after it was first published, Freud's essay, *The Ego and the Id*, can still inspire us. At the same time, its language may sound old-fashioned, in particular in its anthropomorphic gestures (e.g., when Freud speaks of the ego as "a poor creature", which tries to mediate between the menacing dangers and demands of the id, the superego, and reality – all of which are informed by the object's wishes and urges towards subject – thereby behaving sometimes submissive like a slave, at other times, opportunistic like a lying politician and so on) (ibid., p. 56). Is this acceptable as the language of our theory? Some may turn up their noses at such formulations. However, this is how Freud made his theory serviceable to our clinical work. This is exactly how our patients' inner struggles sound like and how the clinical material can be relayed back to the concepts and processes developed in Freud's model of the mind. The tools of cybernetics serve at clarifying the logical coherence and consistency of metapsychology. The language of metapsychology points to the workings of the individual mind in all its human peculiarities and complexities and in interaction with the minds of others.

Notes

1 The Standard Edition translates "Trieb" with "instinct"; for reasons elaborated elsewhere (Schmidt-Hellerau, 2005), I use the notion of "drive" throughout.
2 In his recent "Revision of Drive Theory", Solms (2021) confuses the functions of structures (sensors/rulers) and drives (variables) stating: "The fundamental mechanism of drive is homeostasis" (ibid., p. 1048). However, it seems self-evident that homeostatic regulation is done by a ruler, a structure which has stored (learned [memory trace]) what can count as homeostasis and can initiate the necessary measures (steer the flow and distribution of drive energy). Also, I disagree with Solms' statement: "Had Freud been familiar with the concept of homeostasis, (. . .) he would have formulated his drive theory differently" (ibid.). What Cannon in the 1930s called "homeostasis" had its forerunners in Fechner's 1873 reflections on the stability, which Freud used already in 1895 as "Principle of Inertia" and then "Principle of Constancy" and for most of his work as "Pleasure Principle" and finally as "Nirvana Principle"; even though different by names, they all describe the work of the psychic apparatus to maintain dynamic stability (Homeostasis).
3 For a detailed description of these interactions leading to structure formation, see Schmidt-Hellerau, 2018, pp. 410–413.
4 Freud's notion of drive discharge is only a way to describe the expression of drive activity.
5 Also, the notion of "transference" refers only to an inner process, whereby the representations of a (usually infantile) object and a current (real) object are confused and invested according to the former's anticipated or wished for responses.
6 For a detailed discussion of Freud's second drive theory and its shortcomings, see Schmidt-Hellerau, 1997, 2001, pp. 171–208.
7 Short of a convincing solution, Freud decided to have the self-preservative drive join with the sexual drive under the umbrella concept of his life drive and appointed aggression as the representative of the death drive.

References

Freud, S. (1915). Instincts and their vicissitudes. *SE*, 14.
———. (1920). Beyond the pleasure principle. *SE*, 18.
———. (1923). The ego and the id. *SE*, 19.
———. (1950). A project for a scientific psychology. *SE*, 1.
Green, A. (1999). *The Work of the Negative*. London and New York: Free Association Books.
Schmidt-Hellerau, C. (1997). Libido and Lethe: Fundamentals of a formalized conception of metapsychology. *Int. J. Psycho-Anal.*, 78: 683–697.
———. (2001). *Life Drive & Death Drive, Libido & Lethe: A Formalized Consistent Model of Psychoanalytic Drive and Structure Theory*. New York: Other Press.
———. (2005). We are driven. *Psychoanalytic Quarterly*, 74: 989–1028.

————. (2006). Surviving in absence: On the preservative and death drives and their clinical utility. *Psychoanalytic Quarterly*, 75: 1057–1095.

————. (2018). *Driven to Survive*. Selected Papers on Psychoanalysis. New York: International Psychoanalytic Books.

Solms, M. (2021). Revision of drive theory. *Journal of the American Psychoanalytic Association*, 69(6): 1033–1091.

3 *The Ego and the Id* and . . . the *superego*

Gohar Homayounpour

As we begin the centennial celebrations of Sigmund Freud's significant and monumental 1923 book, *The Ego and the Id*, starting with this collection of essays edited by Dr. Fred Busch, I cannot help but be reminded of my surprise upon my first reading of this text many years ago. I have always been surprised and curious about why Freud chose not to include the superego in the title of this book. This absence has intrigued me over the years. While it is clear in this book that he formally introduces this radical idea of a superego and while this comprises a significant part of the text, why is the superego omitted from *The Ego and the Id*'s title? Even though he says: "among the dependent relationships in which the ego stands, that to the superego is perhaps the most interesting" (Freud, 1923, p. 57).

Precursors to the concept of the superego arise in Freud's much earlier writings, from the function of the ego ideal in his paper *On Narcissism* (Freud, 1914) to the origin of the conscience in *Totem and Taboo* (1912–1913) and the idea of the separation of the ego from the ego ideal in *Group Psychology and the Analysis of the Ego* (Freud, 1921). But it is in *The Ego and the Id* that he formally introduces the concept of the superego while omitting it from the title of the book.

As psychoanalysts, we know that often, what is not said is far more significant than what is said and that omissions and absences are never to be overlooked.

Let us look at Freud's conceptualization in *The Ego and the Id* on the formation of the superego, where he explains the origin of the ego ideal. But first, let's highlight that although it sometimes appears that Freud uses the term ego ideal and ideal ego almost interchangeably, there is a clear distinction for him between the two terms. In short: the ideal ego is the memorial site of the narcissism and omnipotence of our infancy, the nostalgic idealization of that lost paradise. The ego ideal is a much more dynamic formation and closely related to the superego (also used almost interchangeably at times by Freud) comprised of identifications with our earliest and most important object choices. The ideal ego is a concrete state of being, while in the ego ideal, there are possibilities of movement; hence, for Lacan, the ideal ego is imaginary and the ego ideal symbolic (Lacan, 1966, p. 414).

DOI: 10.4324/9781003336754-3

In *The Ego and the Id*, Freud goes on to explain that the origin of the ego ideal is formed from the individual's first and most significant identifications. Primary among these is the individual's identification with the father of his prehistory so that the object choices belonging to the first sexual period and relating to the parents seem normally to find their outcome in an identification of this kind, thereby reinforcing the primary one.

Freud continuous to elaborate two factors that greatly complicate matters: the triangular characters of the Oedipus situation and the constitutional bisexuality of each individual. Whatever the formulation of these oedipal constellations, with their active and passive counterparts, the road towards the dissolution of the Oedipus complex, albeit never fully realized, emerges inescapably from the giving up of the object-cathexis towards the oedipal object and the replacement of those very cathexes by ambivalent identifications. Out of these identifications, the superego is formed. Hence, the superego is the inheritor of the Oedipus complex.

Freud goes on to explain that the superego is not just the residue of these early object choices by the id but is also comprised of vehement reaction formations against those choices. It is not just a command to be like this or that; it is also a strong prohibition: to not be like this or that. In both cases, the superego is a command. And this double command comes from the ego ideal's task of repressing the Oedipus complex, and it is to this significant and revolutionary event that the superego owes its existence.

It is through the resolution of the Oedipus complex that we develop a superego and enter the neurotic structure, with the ability to sublimate in which the original sexual aim is exchanged for another one, which is no longer sexual but which will always psychically be related to the first aim. For the resolution of the Oedipus complex becomes the example par excellence of sublimation, a blueprint for possibilities of sublimations to come. In *The Ego and the Id*, Freud beautifully elaborates on sublimation, saying that if this displaceable energy is desexualized libido, it may also be described as sublimated energy, for it would still be in the service of Eros's main task, that of uniting and binding, clarifying that since thought processes are among these displacements, then the activity of thinking is also supplied from the sublimation of erotic motive forces.

He goes on to emphasize the role of the ego in the process of sublimation, as he has repetitively reminded us that the ego is largely formed out of identifications that replace the abandoned object-cathexis of the id and that it is the FIRST of these identifications that behaves as a special agency in the ego and stands apart from it in the name of a superego.

> The transformation [of erotic libido] into ego-libido of course involves an abandonment of sexual aims, a desexualization. In any case this throws light upon an important function of the ego in its relation to Eros. By thus getting hold of the libido from the object- cathexes, setting itself up as sole love-object, and de-sexualizing or sublimating

the libido of the id, the ego is working in opposition to the purposes of Eros and placing itself at the service of the opposing instinctual impulses. It has to acquiesce in some of the other object-cathexes of the id; it has, so to speak, to participate in them.

(Freud, 1923, p. 46)

The formation of the superego has the clearest link to the individual's own unconscious archaic heritage, and yet its development is a necessary step in the becoming of the subject, for the possibility of the development of a mind and for the possibility of sublimation. The recognition of the symbolic law of the father, our passport to the reality principle, to language, and to our entrance into the symbolic is not possible without the elaboration of the Oedipus complex and the development of the superego.

Hence, the superego has a clear protective function for the psychic apparatus, but this is not the end of the story either. It is indeed merely where the narrative of the subject begins, for this protection comes at a colossal price, and this is where things start to get perverted, albeit within a neurotic structure.

In what I consider to be a significant passage on page 36 of *The Ego and the Id*, Freud insists that since the ego ideal is the heir to the Oedipus complex, it is, therefore, the expression of the most powerful impulses and libidinal vicissitudes of the id.

By setting up this ego ideal, the ego has mastered the Oedipus complex and at the same time placed itself in subjection to the id. Whereas the ego is essentially the representative of the external world, of reality, the super-ego stands in contrast to it as the representative of the internal world, of the id. Conflicts between the ego and the ideal will, as we are now prepared to find, ultimately reflect the contrast between what is real and what is psychical, between the external world and the internal world.

(Freud, 1923, p. 36)

So for Freud, the superego is the closest to the id, for in the process of attempting to master the Oedipus complex, it subjugates itself to the id. And hence, the superego is, for Freud, clearly not related to the external but to the internal and not to reality. As such, the "unconscious sense of guilt" stemming from a need for punishment has nothing to do with an actual crime in the outside world. And hence, as Freud further elaborates in this article, this increase in the *unconscious* sense of guilt can turn people into criminals, so the guilt is often not the result but the motive of the crime. The guilt, in such cases, finally attaches itself to something real on the outside, satisfying this need for punishment that comes from cruel intentions alone. For in the unconscious, mere intentions can send you to the dungeon. For in the unconscious, wishing to kill your father is one and the same as having killed him: the distinction between a wish and an act is not clear in the land of the unconscious. The same kind of unrealistic judgment makes up the nucleus of the superego, a perversion of the law, so to speak. In all these situations, the superego shows its independence from the conscious part of the ego and its dependence on the unconscious id. Freud goes on to tell us that the superego always knew more than the ego about the unconscious id.

For Freud, the superego owes its special position in the ego, or in its relation to the ego, to a two-sided factor. On the one hand, it was the first identification that initially took place when the ego was still fragile, and on the other, because the superego is the heir to the Oedipus complex, it has introduced the most fundamental objects into the ego. Here, he compares the superego's relation to the later alterations of ego to the relation of the influence of infantile sexuality to later sexual life.

Although it is accessible to all later influences, it nevertheless preserves throughout life the character given to it by its derivation from the father-complex – namely, the capacity to stand apart from the ego and to master it. It is a memorial of the former weakness and dependence of the ego, and the mature ego remains subject to its domination. As the child was once under a compulsion to obey its parents, so the ego submits to the categorical imperative of its superego.

But the derivation of the superego from the first object-cathexes of the id, from the Oedipus complex, signifies even more for it. This derivation, as we have already seen (Freud, 1923, p. 36ff.), brings it into relation with the phylogenetic acquisitions of the id and makes it a reincarnation of former ego-structures, which have left their precipitates behind in the id. Thus, the superego is always close to the id and can act as its representative vis-à-vis the ego. It reaches deep down into the id and, for that reason, is farther from consciousness than the ego itself is (Freud, 1923, pp. 48–49).

Freud is clearly saying that the superego is closest to the id and is unconscious.

We are not so far, then, from what Jacques Lacan is trying to elaborate when he says: "The Superego is thus the expression of the will to enjoy [volonté de jouissance], which is not the subject's own will but the will of the Other, who assumes the form of Sade's 'supreme Being in Evil'" (Lacan, 1966, p. 773). Or when, in his seminar 1, Lacan says the superego has a relationship to the law and is at the same time a senseless law, where he says the superego is one and, at the same time, the law and its destruction (1988, p. 102).

In a sense, the superego is not exactly the voice of an ethical authority but simply that of an authority, and I believe this is an important and, at times, misunderstood notion. The superego for Freud is an unrelenting command, one that we can never satisfy: the harder you try, the guiltier you become, in a deeply Kafkaesque sense. The superego is an insatiable master operating within the sadomasochistic realm: the more you feed it, the hungrier it becomes. The superego takes the subject's own drives and turns them against themselves. So in a way, we can say that the superego becomes a perverse agent within the ego.

And yet it is a necessary step in becoming social/thinking, desiring beings, and so Freud wrote a great deal on the topic in *Civilization and its Discontents* (Freud, 1930). We need our superego to become civilized, and yet it becomes a law within a law. It wants to domesticate one's drives so that one can become social, but it will turn that very thing against you in the form of a superego, split, and against the ego, with the same aggressiveness, sadism and . . . .

So this is how the story gets perverted:

For if the superego is the agent of the command of *thou shalt or shalt not*, even if according to Lacan the utmost command of the superego for the subject is to enjoy, it is an enjoyment that is far from desire. It is enjoyment which gets dangerously close to beyond the pleasure principle, to an excess, to transgressions and the pleasure of prohibitions, within the territory of the forbidden.

For Adam Phillips (2016), we are being instructed what to desire by the forbidders (the agents of our superego), and that is truly a shame because most of our pleasures, like the pleasures of our childhood, are unforbidden. Is it not that the celebration of unforbidden pleasures is our visa out of the territory of the puritanism of guilt and the superego? The moment the forbidders instruct us not to do something, a wish is created to do that exact forbidden deed – a tantalizing wish, according to Phillips. Hence, in our search for forbidden pleasures, we are confirming that we are the slaves of the forbidders. He essentially says that rules and the temptation to break them confuse our sense of pleasure with notions of self-control. So, basically, when we are in the claws of taboos and forbidden pleasures, we are being obedient to the forbidders.

Thus, when it comes to forbidden pleasures, we are in the terrain of crime and punishment, in the plot of guilt for our forbidden wishes, and ultimately, in the land of the sadomasochist, where pleasures always have the aroma of pain, and pleasure is eroticized death, sexualized pain.

We do not want to know what we know, and the more troubling our desire, the more repressed it is, the more unconscious we are of it. We think we are doing what we want, but it is out of the fear of desire because nothing is more fearful than desire, to get what we want, to do what we want. Phillips goes on to say: "Our perversions could be no problem except that often they are an attack on something else that we really want" (Phillips, cited in Homayounpour, 2022, p. 82).

The superego casts us as a certain kind of character and tells us in its essentialist way who we are. The superego knows us best. It is repetitive, it is redundant, and it confuses our sense of the law and the superego's law within a law. And its power stems from the fact that we are *a priori* guilty beings. The superego knows our sins. It is the memorial site of our sinful wishes. It is, after all, the expression of the most powerful impulses of the most important vicissitudes of the id.

In a sense, the famous clinical dictum of doing superego work is really to get to know the wishes of one's id, its darkest, most hidden, unacceptable, and strange longings – all that makes the subject *a priori* guilty, all that drives the subject to criminality in a vain attempt to reduce some of his unconscious guilt with an actual received punishment in the outside world. Although this could temporarily reduce the guilt, it can never last, and the subject needs her fix over and over again. The superego bombards us with impossible, unrealistic demands and mocks our inevitable failed attempts, and the more we try to obey, the guiltier we become.

Hence, the superego gives way to a violence in the subject. A violence colored by ambivalence towards others. A regressive, narcissistic violence from object libido to ego libido. A violence that felt too dangerous to perform in the external world and, hence, has been directed back against ourselves, raging towards our egos. A violence that stokes us mercilessly, becoming an all-knowing master that we fear and must obey in order not to get to know ourselves and the sexuality and violence a part of us recognizes within ourselves, so this not wanting to know comes at the cost of the slavery to the superego. It's a kind of blackmail: it says, "If you don't obey me, if you do not feed my existence, I will divulge your secrets. I will expose you". Or as Adam Philips tells us:

> Freud is showing us how conscience obscures self-knowledge, intimating indeed that this may be its primary function: when we judge the self it can't be known; guilt hides it in the guise of exposing it. This allows us to think that it is complicitous not to stand up to the internal tyranny of what is only one part – a small but loud part – of the self. So frightened are we by the super-ego that we identify with it: we speak on its behalf to avoid antagonizing it (complicity is delegated bullying).
>
> (2015)

Yet we know that the superego is a necessary part of developing a mind and that we don't have a shot at becoming subjects without it, so we are in a pickle; the psychoanalytic pun is intentional here. But as neurotic subjects, WE ARE IN A PICKLE. Yet a better metaphor has been offered to us by Freud himself.

Somehow, it all feels like the Battle of Châlons, described by Freud in *The Ego and the Id* (1923, p. 39), a battle in which the infamous Attila was finally defeated by the Romans and Visigoths, which Wilhelm von Kaulbach made the subject of one of his mural paintings. In this mural, the dead warriors are depicted as continuing their fight in the sky above the battlefield. This, to me, is a beautiful metaphor for the superego, the memorial site of the decathexis of our most crucial and ambivalent early object choices and identifications. The site of the process of desexualization, the giving up of the sexual aim towards these objects, and a sort of regression to the introjection of objects and what remains of them, their commands to do or not to do, what to be, what not to be, what to enjoy, and how to enjoy it but constant is the essentialist command.

The superego claims to force the ego to act morally but not realistically, and this lack of connection to the external world is part and parcel of how the story of the superego, which started as a necessity in the history of our becoming, gets perverted: the superego is excessive, unrealistic, cruel, and insatiable in the realm of narcissism, aggression, the death drive, and beyond the pleasure principle. The superego is intertwined with narcissism. With the death drive, it is regressive in the sense of taking object libido back to ego libido, where in melancholia, it becomes blatantly clear and dangerous for our psychic apparatus.

Freud taught us throughout his writings to be aware of what is not said, of what at times cannot be said, and of what is at the edge of language. Perhaps, and this is just one small interpretation, he omitted the superego from the title of *The Ego and the Id* to draw our attention to it even more, to this radical, fundamental idea he had introduced in his last metapsychological contribution. To remind us that when we believe we have beaten Attila, the dead soldiers will continue to fight in the sky, just as the battle with the superego, if we are subjects within the neurotic structure, will continue in one way or another; we just have to endure our unreasonable, at times futile, quest in an attempt to hear what is not said, what cannot be said.

References

Freud, S. (1914). On narcissism: An introduction. In J. Strachey et al. (Trans.), *The Standard Edition of the Complete Psychological Works of Sigmund Freud*, 14. London: Hogarth Press.

———. (1921). Group psychology and the analysis of the ego. In J. Strachey et al. (Trans.), *The Standard Edition of the Complete Psychological Works of Sigmund Freud*, 18. London: Hogarth Press, pp. 65–144.

———. (1923). The Ego and the Id. In J. Strachey et al. (Trans.), *The Standard Edition of the Complete Psychological Works of Sigmund Freud*, 19. London: Hogarth Press.

———. (1930). Civilization and its discontents. In J. Strachey et al. (Trans.), *The Standard Edition of the Complete Psychological Works of Sigmund Freud*, 21. London: Hogarth Press.

Homayounpour, G. (2022). *Persian Blues, Psychoanalysis and Mourning*. Abingdon, UK: Routledge.

Lacan, J. (1966). *Écrits*. Paris: Seuil.

———. (1988). *The Seminar, Book I: Freud's Papers on Technique, 1953–1954*. Trans. John Forrester. New York: Norton.

Phillips, A. (2015). Against self-criticism. *London Review of Books*, 37(5): 13–16.

———. (2016). *Unforbidden Pleasures: Rethinking Authority, Power, and Vitality*. London: Hamish Hamilton.

4 The capacious Freud

Sudhir Kakar and Amrita Narayanan

Reading one of Freud's more influential essays, *The Ego and the Id*, almost a hundred years after its first publication is a cautionary reminder that human beings never seamlessly fit into even the most convincing of paradigms. That there is always something that remains and is missing from our explanatory models. What is left out from Freud's wide-ranging essay could not be discerned as long as psychoanalysis considered itself as a universal enterprise, where "one size fits all" rather than as a global one that reflects cultural nuances. Freud's world (as also Jung's) was still that of a colonial Europe, which regarded itself as the center of the world, culturally, intellectually, and politically. It was a world untouched by the globalization and decolonization of our times, and it is unfair to expect that Freud should be an exception who transcends the rule of rootedness of thought in culture and history.

In his elaboration of the formation of the ego, the ego ideal, and the superego, Freud does not attend to the cultural dimension of the ego, the fact that the essence of the ego is cultural, the reality of the reality principle, which the ego endeavors to substitute, for the pleasure principle of the id is essentially cultural.

We have little difference with Freud when he remarks that "speaking broadly, perceptions may be said to have the same significance for the ego as instincts have for the id" (p. 25). As long as we could add that research into cognitive processes since the 1960s (Segall et al., 1966) shows that perception, a nucleus of the ego, is strongly influenced by cultural differences (Nisbett & Miyamoto, 2005). Commenting on cultural variations in perception in the Müller-Lyer illusion, where lines of equal length give impressions of different length, an illusion created by the orientation of the arrow caps placed at their ends, Alfred Margulies (2018) observes:

> our cultural environment in its everyday structures, practices and aesthetics shapes the way our brains process visual information. . . . And, if this circular complex of experience and structure is true for neurobiological non-conscious visual processing, it seems almost

DOI: 10.4324/9781003336754-4

certain it would be true for psychoanalytically relevant unconscious processes and the impact of culture.

(p. 182)

Reading *The Ego and the Id* in 2022 in India, it is crucial, then, that we speak of cultural imagination when discussing the role of culture in ego formation. For clinical psychoanalysis, generally limited to a small sample from three or four large Indian metropolises, cannot adequately take into account the heterogeneity of a country of over a billion people with its regional, linguistic, religious, and caste divisions. While clinical work can tell us how an individual's cultural imagination, their civilizational heritage, has been modified by the specific cultures of his family, caste, class, or ethnic group, they can, at best, generate hypotheses about cultural particularities. The further testing of these hypotheses is done (and remains true to psychoanalytic intention and enterprise) by testing them in the crucible of the culture's imagination – its myths, folklore, proverbs, art, fiction, cinema, and so on – before psychoanalytic propositions about a culture can be advanced.

Disseminated through myths and legends, proverbs and metaphors, iconic artworks, the stories its members tell each other, enacted in rituals, conveyed through tales told to children, given a modern veneer in films, our cultural imagination is equally glimpsed in the admonitions of parents and in the future vistas they hold out to their children or even in the way children are touched and fed and carried about. Indeed, a society's way of reasoning and making inferences, that is, its organization of knowledge, is starkly influenced by its cultural imagination.

To focus a cultural lens on some of the issues Freud discusses around the development of the ego requires a particular reading of *The Ego and the Id*, one that exploits Freud's literary style to open up pathways in the elaboration of cultural difference. Describing Freud's literary style, the literary critic Michael Maar writes: "he always lucid as he begins to consider an issue, evidently deliberating, apparently scrupulous, although in the next paragraph(s) he rakes in with a tiger's leap all that had just before been possible though by no means assured" (Maar, 2020, p. 29). Our reading of *The Ego and the Id* pays greater attention to Freud considering and deliberating, the hidden Freud, than following Freud on the path he finally chooses to take.

The two places in which we interrupt Freud are in his consideration of the Oedipus complex and of bisexuality. In each case, we will interrupt where Freud deliberates and insert within the deliberation Hindu narratives from the Indian geography that widen the cultural ambit of Freud's deliberations.

First, the Oedipus complex. Freud hints that there is room for more complexity in his consideration of the little boy's relationship with the father when he writes, "For one gets an impression that the simple Oedipus complex is by no means its commonest form, but rather represents a simplification or schematization which, to be sure, is often enough justified for practical purposes".

As an example of a culturally congruent simplification, the Freudian Oedipus is rife with "rivalry with the father" and the son's unconscious wishes of parricide, but parricide is almost completely absent in both myths and folklore of India. Instead, the Indian father is at the periphery of the mother-son dyad, hovering in the background, a barely palpable presence yet nonetheless vital to masculinity development to mute the overwhelming presence of an engulfing or sexually threatening mother, who looms larger than life in the Indian imagination.

The story of Devi and Mahisasura, a myth involving the powerful, sexual mother, is visually represented in dance performances and carved on innumerable temple walls in Hindu India. In the myth, a demon, Mahisasura, who had conquered all the three worlds, fell in love with the goddess Devi, Shiva's wife. He sent a message to make his desire known to her. Devi replied that she would accept as her husband only someone who defeated her in battle. Mahisasura entered the battlefield with a vast demon army and a huge quantity of fighting equipment. Devi came alone, mounted on her lion. She rode without armor or clothes, entering the combat naked. Dismounting, Devi started dancing and cutting off the heads of millions and millions of demons with her sword to the rhythm of her movement. Mahisasura, facing death, tried to run away by becoming an elephant. Devi cut off his trunk. The elephant became a buffalo, and against its thick hide, Devi's sword and spear were of no avail. Angered, Devi jumped on the buffalo's back and rode it to exhaustion. When the buffalo demon's power of resistance had collapsed, Devi plunged her spear into its ear, and Mahisasura fell dead.

The omnipotence and sexual energy of the goddess, dancing and riding naked, is stark in its immediacy, as she exhausts even the most powerful male to abject submission and, ultimately, death. As the myth continues, the Devi's frenzied dancing does not come to an end, even after the killing of the buffalo demon. The gods become alarmed at the ongoing naked dancing and ask Shiva for help. Shiva lies down on his back, and when the naked goddess steps on her husband (Shiva), she hangs out her tongue in shame and stops.

Pictured as Shiva, who enters the scene supine, yet a container for the great mother goddess's energy and power, the father in the Hindu-Indian imagination may be unassuming and remote but is still powerful. He is more likely to be experienced as a wished-for ally and a protector than a rival to his son in myths and folklore. Where rivalry does occur, in popular Indian myths and, most of the case, histories, is not so much that of Oedipus, where the power of the myth derives from the son's guilt over a fantasized and eventually unconscious parricide. The Indian context stresses more the father's envy of what belongs to the son – especially the mother – and thus the son's persecution anxiety as a primary motivation in the father-son relationship.

The boys' persecution anxiety comes clearly through in the popular origin myth of the god Ganesha, the remover of obstacles and the god of all beginnings, who is perhaps the most adored of the Hindu gods. Iconically represented as a pot-bellied toddler with an elephant head and one missing tusk, he is represented proportionately as a small child when portrayed in the family group with his mother, Parvati, and father, Shiva. His image, whether carved in stone or drawn up in a colored print, is everywhere: in temples, homes, shops, roadside shrines, calendars.

In the myth, Ganesha was created solely by his mother, Parvati, from her bodily substances. Parvati's husband, Shiva, was away for a long time, busy doing penance on the mountain, so Parvati, using her own power, conceived her son, Ganesha. Consequently, the father and the son never met each other. One day, when Parvati was taking a bath, she instructed the little boy, Ganesha, to stand guard outside the door and let no one in. While the boy was standing guard, his "father", Lord Shiva, returned from his penance and asked the boy to step aside so he could visit his wife. Ganesha, following his mother's strict instructions, refused. Enraged, Lord Shiva cut off his head. Hearing the commotion, Parvati came outside. Seeing her son lying dead, Parvati was furious and inconsolable. Shiva promised to restore the boy to life and ordered a servant to go out and bring back the first head he found so Shiva could replace the boy's head. The servant brought the first head he found – that of an elephant. That is how Ganesha came to have a little boy's body and an elephant's head.

Elsewhere (Kakar, 2005), the *Ganesha* complex has been called the hegemonic developmental narrative of the male self in Hindu India. The major cadences of the Ganesha complex are also characteristic perhaps of the major Iranian myth of father-son relations – that of Rustam and Sohrab.[1]

As another example of the diversity presented by Oedipus in India, some Indian myths and legends depict the rivalry between father with a spotlight on the *father*'s attempt to defy generational barriers rather than the son's wishes for sexual union with the mother. In the father-son relationship presented by Santanu and Bhishma, the father falls in love with a fisher girl. When he goes to the girl's father to ask her hand, the fisherman agrees to the match on the condition that the son born to his daughter inherit the kingdom. Santanu cannot give his consent to this condition because he already has a son. He returns to his palace where he sinks into a depression born of an old man's unfulfilled passion for a young girl. Bhishma, on coming to know the reason for his father's grief, goes to the fisherman. Bhishma promises both the renunciation of the kingdom and of his own sexual life – which could result in a progeny, which threatened the rights of the sons born to the fisher girl.

In another similar myth, King Yayati, cursed by a sage to suffer a sudden old age, asks his five sons, one after another, to give him their youth for a thousand years so that he may continue his life of sensual pleasure. The elder sons refuse and are cursed by the father. Puru, the youngest son, agrees. "Take my youth from me and enjoy the pleasures you are seeking", he says. "Covered with old your old age and wearing your aged body, I shall live as you say and give you my youth". Puru is blessed by the father and later inherits the kingdom.

Both these myths spotlight a son's self-castration that sacrifices to the father the son's right to sexual activity and generational ascendancy. The son does so in order to deflect the father's envy and his primal fear of annihilation at the father's hands while keeping the bond of love between father and son intact. These myths, as also the one on Ganesha's beheading, invert the psychoanalytically postulated causality between the fantasies of parricide and filicide. They are charged with the fear of filicide rather than the oedipal guilt of parricide and emphasize the son's persecution anxiety as primary motivation in Hindu-Indian cultural imagination.[2] With exceptions in psychoanalysis (e.g., Ross, 1982; Levy, 2011) and in literature – James Joyce, for example – where the father's envy[3] is accurately highlighted, the Western cannon has greatly underestimated the father's envy and rivalry with the son (as of the mother with the daughter).

In the clinic, the male longing for the oedipal alliance – the inverse of a rivalrous father – and the terror of female sexuality is reflected in the following case history (Kakar, 1997, p. 94). A patient with a long history of depression accompanied by spells of impotence: Soon after getting married, he dreams that a gang of dacoits, led by a female bandit, attacks his house. As the woman chases him around the house, they pass his father, who is lying on the bed with a gun, but the gun does not work. The girl bandit mocks him for not being able to defend himself (p. 94).

In the individual and cultural unconscious, the father-son stories are saturated with the little boy's need for an oedipal alliance: the father's firm support, solidarity, and emotional availability at a stage of life where the wishes and fears related to being smed by the mother and femaleness are at their peak.

The wish for a protective father is mirrored, with a difference, in the father-daughter dyad. "Positive" Oedipus myths that narrate the father's desire for his daughter are easily found in ancient Indian texts. Prajapati – elsewhere identified as Brahma, the Creator[4] – is described in the Śatapatha Brāhmaṇa as casting his eyes upon his own daughter and saying, "May I pair with her?" (Ramanujan, 1999a, p. 388). When he consummates his desire, Prajapati is punished by the other gods: his body is pierced through. Numerous versions of this myth reflected in ancient myths as well as folk tales narrate the untrustworthy nature of the father's desire and the need for forces outside the family to step in to protect the daughter from the father's lust. The mother is never the protective force – that role is reserved for other men – but it is worth wondering that as much as the son requires an oedipal alliance to protect him from overwhelming femaleness, the daughter, too, requires an oedipal alliance with the mother to protect from the overwhelming nature of her father's desire.

To continue our refraction of Oedipus complex from the vantage point of culture, it remains to look at the dyad of girls and their mothers. Here, another sentence from *The Ego and the Id* glimmers with possibility for refraction: "If we come back once more to our scale of values, we shall have to say that not only what is lowest but also what is highest in the ego can be unconscious" (p. 26). If, as numerous theorists have argued (Kakar, 1989; Ramanujan, 1999a; Obeyesekere, 1981), motherhood is the highest conscious cultural value, then maternal envy – a mother who is rivalrous instead of loving – must be the lowest and, therefore, the least spoken of. The fact that the cultural celebration of mothers is reserved for the mothers of sons (Kakar, 1978) makes a search for mother-daughter rivalries even more difficult because there is an overall absence of mother-daughter dyads in myth and popular narratives (Johri & Sachdev, 2009). The unconscious presence of the envious mother of daughters, the counterpart to the Devi who kills men, is always costumed as a mother-in-law, as A.K. Ramanujan (1999a) reminds us in his essay *The Indian Oedipus*. Narratives of barren queen mothers who fight with their young daughters-in-law are plentiful in folk tales all over India, and these altercations are, Ramanujan asserts, "blatantly for sexual success with the king" (Ramanujan, 1999a, p. 391). In a rare example of a clear mother-daughter rivalry, one Kannada folk tale speaks of a mother so rivalrous of her daughter's beauty that she puts a clay-mask over the young girl's face (Ramanujan, 1999b, p. 361). In the clinic, the daughter's fantasy of maternal envy and retribution is always partially in disguise: it shows up as women's sexual self-suppression (Narayanan, 2013, 2018, 2022) and as extended, even excessive, periods of mourning for mothers' erotic losses that must be lived out before a girl's erotic life can begin (Oberoi, 2019).

These examples taken together are by no means exhaustive of the diversity of Oedipus-style myths. Indeed, they are limited in their diversity, for they only touch upon Hindu India. But we hope this beginning might serve to illuminate the importance of reading Freud's "the simple Oedipus complex is by no means its commonest form" through the refractive prism of the cultural imaginations of non-Western civilization like that of India. Viewed in this prism, Freud's observation reveals no one universal, "commonest" narrative of parent and child. Each of the various cultural narratives, highlighting one or other aspect of the parent-child relationship, is but a partial developmental truth.

Freud comments in *The Ego and the Id* on bisexuality, to which he attributes considerable importance, particularly in its effect upon the Oedipus complex. The innate bisexuality of children, he explains, complicates the initial simplicity connoted by Oedipus. Here, he makes an extraordinary statement:

> It is this complicating element introduced by bisexuality that makes it so difficult to obtain a clear view of the facts in connection with the earliest object-choices and identifications, and still more difficult to describe them intelligibly. It may even be that the ambivalence displayed in the relations to the parents should be attributed entirely to bisexuality and that it is not, as I have represented above, developed out of identification in consequence of rivalry.
>
> (p. 30)

To us, this seemed significant: Freud admitting to even the slightest doubt in one of the bedrocks of psychoanalytic canon – the fateful developmental consequences of rivalry with a parent. However, in the subsequent paragraphs, in the characteristic literary style that we mentioned at the beginning of our essay, Freud begins to retreat from the capaciousness of this statement, and the commonly known form of the oedipal complex comes to the fore.

As early as 1929, Girindrasekhar Bose, the founder-president of the Indian Psychoanalytic Society, had written to Freud that "the desire to be female is more easily unearthed in Indian male patients than in European" (Sinha, 1966). Freud was politely dismissive of this challenge from Calcutta to the psychoanalytic claim of universality of its theories and models, and the discussion did not go further.

Indeed, the easier access into awareness of the wish to be female is not only to be found in male patients but is also ubiquitous in Indian cultural imagination.

Thus, for instance, when Mahatma Gandhi (1940) publicly proclaims that he has mentally become a woman or, quite unaware of Karen Horney and other deviants from the orthodox analytic position of the time, talks of man's envy of the woman's procreative capacities, saying, "There is as much reason for a man to wish that he was born a woman as for woman to do otherwise" (p. 13), he is sure of a sympathetic and receptive audience brought up on Hindu-Indian myths of bisexuality. One of these myths is of Mahadeva – "Great God", Shiva, iconically represented as half man and half woman that is often encountered in street and popular dance performances. Much more ubiquitous throughout the land is another iconic representation of Shiva, the lingam. Sculpted in stone and worshipped in countless homes, roadsides, and temples, the phallus in the lingam is always represented as arising out of the yoni, the symbol of female creative energy. The lingam then symbolizes the unity of the male and female and the cosmic energy generated by this union. In its ritual worship in temples and homes, cups of cold milk are poured on the lingam to cool the heat of the energy rising from the union, the vitality of bisexuality.

Unconsciously absorbed since childhood, it is our cultural variations of bisexuality that determine for the individual what it means to be, look, think, or behave like a man or a woman. As another example, think of a Greek or Roman sculpture with their hard, muscled men's bodies and chests without any fat at all, familiar to most Europeans from childhood visits to museums or reproduced in countless visual mediums, and compare it with the sculpted representations of Hindu gods in the temples or the Buddha, where the bodies are softer, suppler, and, in their hint of breasts, nearer to the female form. Between a minimum of sexual differentiation needed to function heterosexually with a modicum of pleasure and a maximum, which cuts off any sense of empathy and emotional contact with the other sex that is experienced as a different species altogether, there is a whole range of positions, all of which should be recognized by psychoanalysis as part of being human rather than closely identifying with any particular position on the continuum as the only one that is "healthy and mature" (Kakar, 1989).

Whether bisexuality is an openly acknowledged part of the cultural imagination or whether is relatively repressed will thus play a significant role not only in a male child's identifications but also in case of a girl child as Freud acknowledges:

> Analysis very often shows that a little girl, after she has had to relinquish her father as a love-object, will bring her masculinity into prominence and identify herself with her father (that is, with the object which has been lost), instead of with her mother. This will clearly depend on whether the masculinity in her disposition – whatever that may consist in – is strong enough.
>
> (p. 31)

Clinical experience in India suggests that the girls' identification with the father might be elusive. For example, the psychoanalyst Honey Oberoi (2019) argues that a preoccupation with mothers – what Kakar (1989) has elsewhere called maternal enthrallment – is as much the lot of girls as of boys. If we accept the Oberoi's clinical testimony, then the "masculinity in a girl's disposition" that Freud refers to often appears not strong enough. Oberoi argues that the psychoanalytic focus on the bad-mother, and maternal ambivalence, while necessary, represses mother-love – including the homosexual dimension of mother-love. She writes:

> At the conscious (and at times, not so conscious level) a girl believes that she will search for a partner who is like (or different from) her father. However, deeper than this layer of identification is a woman's desire (often not fully in her realm of conscious awareness) to relive with her lover, husband or partner, the longings which were fulfilled, interrupted or which remained frustrated with her mother. Also, to be

noted is the fact that in intimate relations, many women possess their husbands and partners, in forms which are reminiscent of the wishes, desires, anxieties and insecurities they felt in childhood vis-à-vis their mothers.

Before we close our chapter, we would like to turn our attention to the section entitled *The Dependent Relationships of the Superego*. Here, in a cultural refraction of Freud's choice to focus on a male child's identification with the father, a range of superego positions become available. Freud writes about the formation of the superego:

> Although it is accessible to all later influences, it nevertheless preserves throughout life the character given to it by its derivation from the father-complex – namely, the capacity to stand apart from the ego and to master it. It is a memorial of the former weakness and dependence of the ego, and the mature ego remains subject to its domination. As the child was once under a compulsion to obey its parents, so the ego submits to the categorical imperative of its super-ego.
>
> (p. 3)

Freud's vocabulary is categorical here: the ego is weak and dependent like a child. The superego is derived from the father-complex and is associated with the capacity to stand apart and to master (the child-ego). In an earlier section on the subject of the superego, Freud emphasizes the father: "The super-ego retains the character of the father, while the more powerful the Oedipus complex was and the more rapidly it succumbed to repression (under the influence of authority, religious teaching, schooling and reading)". But still earlier, embedded in a footnote, Freud gives us a cautious caveat to his confident focus on the father identification:

> Perhaps it would be safer to say "with the parents"; for before a child has arrived at definite knowledge of the difference between the sexes, the lack of a penis, it does not distinguish in value between its father and its mother.
>
> (p. 28)

Subsequent to this caveat, Freud's focus on the father-son relationship has the consequence of overemphasizing the role of the father and his signifier, the penis. It glosses over the fact that the child's valuation of its mother must surely be higher than its father, given the preoccupation of women with child-rearing and children's organic preoccupation with breasts rather than penises. If the ego is a skin-ego, dependent upon the physical body to find its mental representation, then does the early life of skin – shaped after all by culture – impact how ego gets constructed in a cultural context? We might wonder whether ego formation is different in India, where urban-area breastfeeding, UNICEF (2018) tells us, continued for over a year for children of both genders, at a rate of 79%, compared to the United States, where extended breastfeeding rates are around 6.2%? From breastfeeding, the Indian child proceeds not to spoon-feeding but to hand-feeding, less frequently to strollers than to being carried on the mother's side or back in skin contact, and extended co-sleeping with parents or elder relatives. In this social atmosphere of early life, togetherness with the parents – especially the mother – is valued over independence and conveyed by visible skin contact.

If we look at gender and culture through a stereoscopic lens, more possibilities open up. For Indians, the ambit of the oedipal triangle opens up to another shape, a quadrangle representing the home, perhaps, that houses a larger family impact, whose skin contact with the child shapes her or his early life of desire and its attendant guilt. It may be worth considering whether these touch dynamics of Indian childhood – virtually absent in adulthood – later replaced by customs and traditions can then be read as a diversity of object-cathexes that far exceed the oedipal triangle. Implicit in Freud's discussion of the ego and superego is his self-admitted over-simplification: as he discusses the oedipal triangle in the formation of the superego, he focuses on the boy's need to define himself as masculine via identification with his father and a disinvestment from his mother. In the linearity of this "developmental" task, a fixed position gets created for the woman-mother in order for the boy-son to individuate – male subjectivity depends on an objective female standing still.

The idea of a female standing still as a substrate for male development is, of course, at best, an illusion, complicated by cultural child-rearing practices, where there might be not one but skin-caretakers, and further complicated by a culturally valued bisexuality in which the male longing to be female prevents undue clarity on who is father and who is mother in the formation of the superego, even as it opens up the possibilities for the values of other objects – uncles, grandparents, and older cousins – to become part of the child's superego formation process, the objects that need to be replaced with identifications.

When we watch for when Freud seems to catch himself in each of these three situations – the Oedipus complex, bisexuality, and the formation of the superego – cultural complexity and a range rather than a single position open up. Freud's pauses, the way in which he hesitates in places of murkiness before he sallies forth with confidence onto clearer pathways, are part of what allows contemporary readers to keep his work relevant. They allow us to exercise our imagination to add what Freud might have suggested had he had a glimpse into our time and geography. Capacious Freud, whose unique writerly voice seemingly commands its audience to follow a line of thought, always also leaves rooms for other lines of thought.

Notes

1 In this legend, one of the Persian culture's "master narratives", it is the son and not the father who is killed in the father-son conflict. The father Rustam does not recognize his son Sohrab on the battlefield. That the Iranian Oedipus, too, has as its Oedipal outcome, filicide rather than parricide, it is still central to the organization of a boy's object relations.
2 The boys persecution anxiety comes clearly through in the popular origin myth of the god, Ganesha, in which Ganesha, conceived independently by his mother, is beheaded by his father Shiva during their first meeting.
3 "He [the son] is a new male: his growth is his father's decline, his youth his father's envy, his friend his father's enemy". James Joyce, Ulysses.
4 The Hindu trinity consists of Brahma, the Creator; Vishnu, the Preserver; and Shiva, the Destroyer.

References

Gandhi, M. K. (1940). The role and status of woman. *Harijan*, 24(2).

Johri, R. & Sachdev, D. (2009). Yashoda, Kaushalya, Kunti, Sunayana: Remembering the forgotten mother of daughters in the Hindu family. Paper presented at the *M(o)ther Trouble: An International Conference on Feminism, Psychoanalysis and the Maternal*, May 31, 2009, Birbeck College, University of London.

Kakar, S. (1978). *The Inner World: A Psychoanalytic Study of Childhood and Society in India*, 4th edition. Delhi: Oxford India Perennials.

———. (1989). The maternal-feminine in Indian psychoanalysis. *International Review of Psychoanalysis*, 16(3): 1989.

———. (1997). Maternal enthrallment: Two case histories. In *Culture and Psyche: Selected Essays*, 2nd edition. New Delhi: Oxford India Paperbacks.

———. (2005). Hindu myth and psychological concepts: The Ganesha complex. In W. Tseng, S. C. Chang & M. Nishizono (eds.), *Asian Culture and Psychotherapy*. Honolulu: University of Hawaii Press, pp. 76–84.

Levy, I. (2011). The Laius complex: From myth to psychoanalysis. *International Forum of Psychoanalysis*, 20: 222–228.

Maar, M. (2020). *Die Schlange im Wolfspelz, Das Geheimnis großer Literatur*. Reinbek: Rowohlt Verlag (our translation).

Margulies, A. (2018). Imagining the real: An essay on Sudhir Kakar's "Culture and Psyche: A Personal Journey". In M. Kumar, A. Mishra & A. Dhar (eds.), *Psychoanalysis in the Indian Terroir: Emerging Themes in Culture, Family and Childhood*. Lanham, MD: Lexington Books.

Narayanan, A. (2013). Ambivalent subjects: Psychoanalysis, women's sexuality in India and the writings of Sudhir Kakar. *Psychodynamic Practice*, 20(3): 213–227.

———. (2018). When the enthralled mother dreams: A clinical and cultural composition. In M. Kumar, A. Mishra & A. Dhar (eds.), *Psychoanalysis in the Indian Terroir: Emerging Themes in Culture, Family and Childhood*. Lanham, MD: Lexington Books.

———. (2022, In Press). *In A Rapture of Distress: Women's Sexuality and Modern India*. New Delhi: Oxford University Press.

Nisbett, R. E. & Miyamoto, Y. (2005). The influence of culture: Holistic versus analytic perception. *Trends in Cognitive Sciences*, 9(10): 467–473.

Oberoi, H. (2019). Singing to the tune of feminine desire: Crucial strands from the melody of mother-daughter relationship. Presentation at the *Second COWAP Conference (International Psychoanalytic Conference)*, November 22–23, 2019, Kolkata.

Obeyesekere, G. (1981). *Medusas Hair*. Chicago: University of Chicago Press.

Ramanujan, A. K. (1999a). The Indian Oedipus. In V. Dharwadker (ed.), *The Collected Essays of A.K. Ramanujan*. New Delhi: Oxford University Press, pp. 377–397.

———. (1999b). Some folk tales from India. In V. Dharwadker (ed.), *The Collected Essays of A.K. Ramanujan*. New Delhi: Oxford University Press, pp. 358–368.

Ross, J. (1982). Oedipus revisited: Laius and the "Laius complex". *The Psychoanalytic Study of the Child*, 37: 169–200.

Segall, M. H., Campbell, D. T. & Herskovits, M. J. (1966). *The Influence of Culture on Visual Perception*. Indianapolis: Bobbs, Merrill.

Sinha, T. C. (1966). Psychoanalysis in India. In *Lumbini Park Silver Jubilee Souvenir*. Calcutta: Lumbini Park.

UNICEF. (2018). *Infant and Young Child Feeding Data*. UNICEF Data. Accessed online at https://data.unicef.org/resources/dataset/infant-young-child-feeding/

5 Some thoughts of Freud's epochal work

100 Years Later

Heribert Blass

To reread such an epochal work as *The Ego and the Id* from 1923 100 years later and against the background of the manifold further development of psychoanalytic theory and practice inevitably raises the question of the appropriate perspective. In any case, it is a historical view, but as in psychoanalysis in general, the view into the past is at the same time shaped by the present. Conversely, traces of the past are always found in the present. Thus, when we let this historical text affect us 100 years after its first publication, we know simultaneously that we are encountering a central turning point in Freud's thinking. Our appreciation stands in marked contrast to Freud's own initial skepticism, for after reading the proofs, he had described his text to Ferenczi as "downright unclear, artificially put together, and terrible in its diction" (Freud, 1923b). As posteriors, however, we know the significance of this work for progress in Freud's thinking, even if the title remained strangely incomplete: although only the ego and the id are mentioned, with the introduction of the superego, at least three psychic instances now became significant in the text for understanding human psychic life. We also know that in addition to the distinction of the descriptive and dynamic unconscious, the juxtaposition of *sexual drives* or *Eros* versus *death drive* made earlier (Freud, 1920) became further significant. And we know that Freud saw the ego "first and foremost as a bodily ego", which "is not merely a surface entity but is itself the projection of a surface" (1923a, p. 26). Interestingly, for the translation first published in London in 1927, Freud added a footnote in which he characterized the ego more specifically as "as a mental projection of the surface of the body. . . representing the superficies of the mental apparatus". A German version of this footnote has not been preserved (cp. ibid. footnote p 26). However, this emphasis on the connection between body and mind in the English edition makes it clear that psychoanalytic theorizing did not stop in 1923 and that Freud himself repeatedly subjected his own views to critical revision. Insofar it is consistent that we, as Freud's descendants, look at this text today with an expanded knowledge of human mental development. On the other hand, without this work, authors after Freud and all psychoanalysts practicing today would not have been able to develop concepts beyond him. Freud's

DOI: 10.4324/9781003336754-5

concepts have been explicitly or implicitly incorporated into the work of subsequent psychoanalytic authors.

In the following, I would like to deal with those aspects of *The Ego and the Id* which seem to me particularly significant for our present psychoanalytic theory and practice. Naturally, this is a very subjective selection.

I will address the following questions:

- How can the transition from Freud's first topic with the *systems conscious, preconscious, and unconscious* to the second topic of *id-ego-superego*, which can be traced in *The Ego and the Id*, be related to our contemporary concept of the self? In other words, which form of the self shines through in *The Ego and the Id*?
- To what extent is Freud's attitude of not considering the first and second topics alternatively, but formulating them in the text as a kind of complementary series, still relevant for us clinically? I am thinking especially of the role of the *preconscious*, which Freud emphasizes at the beginning of his treatise.
- How can the distinction between the two drives – *sexual drive*, or *Eros*, versus *death drive*, described again in Chapter 4 – be used for a conceptual differentiation within the newly introduced instance of the superego? In *The Ego and the Id*, Freud equates the superego with the ego ideal, determining it predominantly as the heir of the Oedipus complex. In *On Narcissism: An Introduction* (1914), he had still used synonymously the terms *ideal ego (Idealich)* and *ego ideal (Ichideal)*. Freud does not justify the later renunciation of the naming of an ideal ego, but it might be worthwhile to distinguish the concept of the ideal ego from the ego ideal.
- What does it mean for our conceptualizations today that Freud repeatedly switches in his text between the description of intrapsychic processes and the effects of interpersonal relationships? How does the representation of object relations in the individual psyche lead to the formation of psychic structure through *interpsychic* interactions?

On the shape of the self

Which shape of the self shines through in Freud's text? Freud did not use the term self, but implicitly, the concept of self is included when he speaks of the "individual" or the "person". As we understand it today, the self encompasses the experience of the whole person and includes feeling and thinking, emotion and cognition in equal measure. It can be understood as a kind of mental body for the three instances of id, ego, and superego, which in their various manifestations in turn have an effect on the shape of the self. Of course, it emerges only gradually during childhood-adolescent development, and it undergoes further transformations in adult life. The earliest forms of the infant self and self-experience can be grasped only sensorimotorly, and the states of being associated with them are initially prelinguistic. At the same time, the infant is in a vital, extreme dependency relationship with its environment, which is usually its parents. The developing self is thus in an *autistic-contiguous position* (Ogden, 1989), and at this stage, it is not yet possible to speak of a mentally organized self. Rather, a sensory-dominated, pre-symbolic mode of generating experience prevails. Freud, with his focus on the importance of *word-presentations*, did not describe this pre-symbolic phase in such detail, but he nevertheless made it the basis of the first self in the form of an unconscious early id: "We shall now look upon an individual as a psychical id, unknown and unconscious" (ibid. p. 24). Our attempts to describe this early form from the perspective of experience cannot do without the first-person singular. In our language, we can only try to put ourselves in a feeling, perceiving, and acting "I plus verb", as is done in the statements "I feel", "I am", "I hear", or "I see". The attempt to formulate the unstructured of an early bodily experience from the first-person perspective must also fail. The syntax of a simple sentence, such as "I feel something" is likely to be more complex than the early sensation on one's own body, of which the infant does not yet know that it is one's own. The "I plus verb" cannot yet be identical with the "ego" of structural theory. Moreover, we know today that the earliest "I am" coincides with a "you are" or "you belong to us" (cf. Personnier, 2022, p. 80), which is conveyed through the physical-mental contact with parents and their culture. For parents, it usually evokes smirks when their child refers to him/herself as "you" at the beginning of language development. As adults, we can only imagine how this second person singular "you" feels before language acquisition begins as first-person singular "I". The notion of a "Skin-Ego" (Anzieu, 2016), which evolves from the fantasy of "one skin for two", comes closer to feeling these bodily emotions in connection with the early dyad. Through this common area of the skin arises the fantasy of "one thought for two", which I would like to grasp tentatively with the intertwining of the second- and first-person singular in "you are". The philosopher Ernst Bloch (1963) described the beginning of human existence as follows: "I am. But I don't have myself. That is why we are only becoming" (p. 11, Transl. HB.).[1] This formulation of Bloch, which quasi musically captures the existential tension between the early being-there and only gradual becoming of the subject, can, in my opinion, also be applied to Freud's developmental series of id « bodily ego « ego but with the crucial addition of the interpersonal and interpsychic dimension.

Today, we know that these early, body-bound, and interpersonal processes are stored in procedural memory and are not as accessible to perception as the linguistically formulated memories in declarative memory (cf. Kandel, 2005). Freud also already knew this with his distinction of the systems *Ucs.* and *Pcpt.-Cs.* According to him, "sensations and feelings, too, only become conscious through reaching the system *Pcpt.*" (1923a, p. 22), and only through the interposition of word-presentations "internal thought-processes are made into perceptions" (ibid., p. 23). Having arrived at the word-presentations, it is worth returning to Bloch once again: "I am" is not yet a "becoming". As mentioned earlier, the perception of being as "I am" undergoes a refraction through the sensing of a gap: "I do not have myself". To come to oneself and to be able to feel oneself as one's own object in "I have myself", the child must first have become the recognized object of another. In an adultomorphic language, this sequence could perhaps be formulated like this: child feels "I am!" – "Who am I?" Mother/father feel and convey: "You are my/our everything!" But the existential identification with this "you are our everything" can only lead to a growing structural ego if the parents simultaneously convey the deviating message: "You are indeed our everything, but you are also an other and may be". Thus, the object-oriented sense of self will mature in the child from "you are" to the more subjective "I am". Only gradually the "body for two" transforms into a body of one's own, which in the favorable case becomes the home of the self with its own ego, but in the unfavorable case remains alien. In these early interpersonal processes, the parents' ability to affirm their child's true affects and self plays a central role. Equally important is the child's ability to incorporate the parents' emotional messages. We know these affective exchanges between self and object today from the perspectives of a wide variety of conceptualizations, whether as holding, transitional space and use of an object (Winnicott, 1971), container/contained (Bion, 1962), mirroring (Kohut, 1971), alterity (Laplanche, 1997), inner object relations (Sandler et al., 1998), or mentalization and epistemic trust (Fonagy & Allison, 2014), to name a few. All confirm that it takes a long interpersonal and intrapsychic journey to get from "I am" to "I have myself". Freud's concept of the body-ego emerging from the unknown id laid the foundation for a deeper knowledge of these early processes, even if he initially did so in terms of a one-person psychology. Implicitly, however, this interpersonal and interpsychic dimension is already present in his conception of the relationship between ego and id; thus, he speaks of the fact that "in the individual's primitive oral phase, object-cathexis and identification are no doubt indistinguishable from each other", and the initially "still feeble" ego emerges to mediate the "object-cathexes [which] proceed from the id" with the "real external world". The ego can either follow the id "which feels erotic trends as needs" or try "to fend them off by the process of repression" (ibid. p. 29). It is shown that the processes within the individual psyche are not possible without an interaction with the interpersonal external world.

In our contemporary psychoanalytic theory and practice, this connection is more explicitly formulated. The "unknown" of the child's "psychical id" is, as has been said, connected with the unconscious images and affective messages of the parents and their culture. The child's gradually developing ego remains strongly influenced by these messages, along with the onset of his/her own unconscious fantasies. In an analogous way, the personal influence of the psychoanalyst on the shape of the psychoanalytic process assumed increased importance – besides the role of countertransference (Heimann, 1950), the concept of the "analytic third" (Ogden, 1994), and the inevitable co-creation in the analytic field may be mentioned as key words (cf. Baranger & Baranger, 2008; Ferro, 1999). This interpersonal/interpsychic dimension works against a reductionist objectifying view within the psychoanalytic process. However, Freud's approach of obtaining a picture of the individual human psyche is not thereby obsolete. Today, we are in the advantageous position of being able to grasp intrapsychic and interpsychic processes, not separately but in interplay with each other.

Particularly in his preoccupation with the emergence of the "superego", Freud also conformed to this view. By dealing with the fate of the further identifications of the infantile ego with persons of its environment, he finally arrived at the conception of the superego. Its emergence from pre- and post-oedipal idealizations with subsequent identifications further clarified the interdependence of infantile fantasy and real object experiences. I will return to the differences between pre- and post-oedipal identifications later. First, however, it seems important to me to note the *existential dependence of* both the infantile self and an ego growing beyond the early bodily ego. It was Winnicott who made the first absolute, then relative dependance of the child and later "interdependence" of the adult his central theme (cf. Abram 2022, p. 35), but already Freud spoke of "the lengthy duration in man of his childhood helplessness and dependence" (1923a, p. 35), and he saw the ego as a "poor creature owing service to three masters and consequently menaced by three dangers: from the external world, from the libido of the id, and from the severity of the super-ego" (ibid. p. 56). His comparison of the id to a "man on horseback, who has to hold in check the superior strength of the horse [the id, HB]", often only by "transforming the id's will into action as if it were its own" (ibid., 25) on the one hand, and as an "actual seat of anxiety", even from the hatred and persecution on the part of the superego on the other, made the ego seem almost without a chance in its effectiveness, especially since the realms of the passions (id) and morality (superego) had secretly allied with each other. But we can ask: Is the ego really that weak? Or better: When does it remain weak? Freud saw its real strength in an attitude of wise modesty as a "frontier-creature" or "politician" by which it could consolidate its position vis-à-vis id and superego. If we consider the gradual emergence of the ego from the body and the increasingly mentally represented relationships associated with it, we can discover another strength: people unconsciously "tell" the story of their early object experiences in new, later relationships and interpersonal situations – whether as *embodied memories* via the body or whether by means of unconscious shaping of specific situations with other people. This form of *repetition compulsion* serves not least to find new solutions to old conflicts both interpersonally and intrapsychically. For these coping attempts, Argelander (2013) has attributed to the ego a *scenic function* by which unconscious, infantile configurations can be communicated within a relationship in connection with psychically relevant situations. Referring to Freud's definition: "Psycho-analysis is an instrument to enable the ego to achieve a progressive conquest of the id" (ibid. p. 56), the shape of affectively toned "scenes" between patient and analyst can now be used to gain insight into similar forms of earlier conflicts and subsequent symptom formations of the analysand. From an intrapsychic perspective, it can be seen as a strength of the ego to bring its conflicts with libidinal passions or moral severity into the relationship with the analyst as a potentially new object. In my opinion, this is not contradicted by the fact that Lorenzer (2016) located the corresponding scenic structure in the id and not in the ego. He saw psychoanalysis as "hermeneutics of the body" (cited after Bohleber, 2016, p. 1394), by means of which a shared language between patient and analyst should transform a bodily communication into more mental representation. From my point of view, both authors describe different levels of organization of the development of the mind, but both share the goal of scenically reviving within analytic relationship recurrent conflicts that are not yet regulable for the ego within the self. The analyst's benevolent attitude, directed towards an understanding of the conflicting patterns reestablished in the relationship, can serve as a template for the patient's ego: as a template to leave room for the passions and morality but to set limits where destructive versus libidinous developments threaten to take over. Fundamentally, the ego will tend to remain weak within the self when its bodily and linguistic narratives go unheard. In the psychoanalytic process, however, where analyst and patient "ride out" together, mastering difficult situations along the way, the patient's ego can become an emotionally competent rider.

Nevertheless, Freud's anthropomorphic description of the "poor" ego within the self, always struggling for its place, recognized man as a mentally conflicted being. The self is a conflicted self. Freud's central legacy is to conceptualize psychoanalysis as conflict psychology, as clearly expressed in *The Ego and the Id*. The opposites and conflicts occur in various areas of psychic life, whether as movement between unconscious, preconscious, and conscious experience or as wrestling between the different instances inside the self, or whether as the constant polarity between Eros and Thanatos.

A new self today?

What do we think today of this conception of man as a mentally conflicted being, or of a human self in which different areas of motivation are in conflict with each other and the instance of a feeling-acting ego struggles to find a personal fit between passion and morality?

In contrast to Freud's time, psychoanalytic research and literature of the last decades has increasingly shifted its focus to the study of non-neurotic states. In them, psychic representation is weakly developed or absent altogether (cf. Bohleber, 2014). Very often, especially in borderline states, narcissistic disorders, traumatization, or pronounced somatization, the aim is no longer to uncover processes of repression within an established mental structure. Rather, it is a matter of first establishing a psychic structure in the self by means of the psychoanalytic process. Freud's conflictual self seems to have become the self of "psychic holes". Alongside the conflict model, a deficit model of psychic life has emerged, which, according to many authors, requires a changed approach on the part of the psychoanalyst: not direct interpretations of inner-psychic conflicts but the work on the framework of analysis (Green, 1975), or the mediation of the analyst's waking dream thoughts in connection with his alpha function (Bion, 1962), or the promotion of sensually palpable and representable images within the framework of "the work of figurability" (Botella & Botella, 2005) are central. Instead of formulated, "saturated" interpretations, "unsaturated" interpretations (Ferro, 2004; Civitarese, 2015) should enable the analysand to feel himself and to represent or to create her/his mind (cp. Levine, 2012).

Has Freud's mental conflict model become obsolete with these approaches? At least the uncovering interpretation derived from it has come under suspicion of being antiquated (cf. e.g., Scarfone, 2016). In its place in many case presentations today, the work of figurability is seen as transformative, without pursuing intrapsychic conflicts in more detail. Busch (2022) makes a similar observation in an essay on the relationship between conflict theory and trauma theory. According to him, "many analysts singularly emphasize trauma interpretations in clinical work (based on interferences in development or countertransference enactments), without at some point addressing its intrapsychic meanings" (ibid. P. 112). He rightly points out, however, that any trauma – I would add: even if it seems psychically unrepresented at first – stimulates feelings and fantasies that become "part of a dangerous intrapsychic field". In agreement with Busch, I am convinced that it is not sufficient to stop at the analysand's current moment of feeling. Of course, sensing the current mental state, including the feeling of the body, represents the indispensable first step. And indeed, only an ability to perceive one's own (and others') feelings leads to a lively self. However, to be able to "have oneself", a deeper understanding of the intrapsychic consequences of trauma or other "psychic holes" seems necessary. These consequences include conflicts within the individual psyche. Work on the importance of figurability and emotional presence in the psychoanalytic process has greatly expanded our range of understanding and interpretation of differentially organized forms of the self. Hallucinatory activity of the analyst as an "animistic double" (Botella & Botella, 2005) to locate memory without existing memory images is one of them. One hundred years after the appearance of *The Ego and the Id*, we have the advantage of being able to draw on a wider variability of suitable forms of interpretation in psychoanalysis (cf. Tuckett et al., 2008). However, if we take as the basic model of these pre-neurotic forms of the mind the unsuccessful or incomplete constitution of an integrated self on the basis of inappropriate affect perceptions and attunements or gross impingements in the earliest subject-object relations, we thus again arrive at a conflictual area: in the unfavorable case, the initial perception of a "you are" remains unchanged in the evolving self because of the absence of the object's acknowledging and differentiating response "you are other than I am". In this way, the "you" remains in the "you are" and cannot mature into a structural ego in the sense of "I am, and I have myself". According to Winnicott, in healthy development, there is a "healthy split" between false self and true self that results in a core self, which protects a necessary isolation from the external reality because "each individual is an isolate, permanently non-communicating, permanently unknown, in fact unfound" ([1963] 1965, p. 187). Abram (2022) has shown that for Winnicott, this "isolated incommunicado self" serves as a "resting place" and as a place to "be" and "feel real", based on the experience of unintegration when the mother is in a state of primary maternal preoccupation. She calls the experience of unintegration "a precursor to the capacity to enjoy" (p. 15). The contrary is a psychotic core self, and this result of repeated traumatic violations of the "incommunicado self" does not allow an inner place to rest. Instead, it "becomes a place of retreat from persecutions" (Abram, ibid. p 15). I would like to emphasize that we thus already find conflicts on an interpersonal and intrapsychic level during the earliest development, even if they are less clearly structured and represented. In the analytical process, we must not ignore these already early antagonisms alongside the work of the figurability. And what can feel like an inner hole – a sense of inner strangeness – can form the nucleus for a surviving self. As a school child, Mr. A had developed diffuse body pain after the early death of his father and regularly received painkillers in the form of anal suppositories from his mother. Only during his analysis was he able to discover how sad he had been about his father's death, without his depressed mother being able to recognize and accept his sadness. For many years, he had felt like a "pain child" on an exclusively physical level. "But I always knew", he said, "that something central was never right". In one session, the image of a hunched figure with severely swollen eyes suddenly emerged in me so that I could say, "Yes, it hurts so much when sad tears can't flow". The discovery of being sad enabled him to gradually distinguish mental pain from physical pain. Sometime later, however, he reproachfully asked why I hadn't put him in touch with his sadness earlier. The anger originally directed at his mother was now represented and actualized within the transference relationship with me, as was his sadness, which had been nameless for years.

The meaning of the preconscious

The example of Mr. A shows that the expansion of the scope of psychoanalytic therapy to less represented or even unrepresented states of the mind confirms the importance of the *preconscious* emphasized by Freud. The analyst's *oneiric work*, or the work of figurability, contributes to creating access to previously informulable sensations. In this respect, they deepen the possibility of connecting to word-presentations (ibid. p. 20), even if the associated affects are not "repressed" in the structural sense but must first be figured. In both cases, the analytic work consists in establishing "preconscious intermediate links" between the unconscious and the conscious, which bring together "the thinking in pictures" and "the thinking in words" (ibid. p. 21) in such a way that within the self, an ego with living connections can mature into both a pre-oedipal, vital id and a post-oedipal, guiding superego. Green (1974) also emphasized the importance of the preconscious as a transitional space between the unconscious and the conscious and between the id and the ego. Similar to his recommendation not to interpret a repressed affect directly but "to link the repressed affect to the preconscious presentation" (p. 417), Bolognini (2022) speaks of the "practicability of the Preconscious". He offers the beautiful comparison of the preconscious with underground routes and tunnels between distant castles in medieval times. These had enabled a secret mutual exchange of intermediaries with their messages, and likewise, the preconscious with its more or less secret passages "allow the customs of the defensive Ego and the Superego to be bypassed without duties, controls or disputes" (p. 11/12). These secret passages can serve not only for facilitating intrapsychic communication but also for easier exchange between persons, as it takes place in contact within the analytic couple. Against the background of this comparison, both the work on the figurability of unrepresented states and the understanding of interpersonal scenes that express configured conflicts serve to expand the realm of the preconscious. The two ways of working are not antagonistic, but they represent different ways of accessing the preconscious, from which sometimes the tracing of vital affects and sometimes the working through of intrapsychic and interpersonal conflicts can become possible. In the case of Mr. A, it was helpful to establish a connection between bland sensations of pain, feeling his grief, and ego-enhancing confrontation with me in the transference via different pathways to the preconscious. Each element contributed to his gradually growing ego, with which he could use the power of his id.

Superego, ego ideal, and ego

Although Freud did not mention the superego in the title of his work, its definition as a psychic structure is one of the major advances in his thought. Thus, he wrote: "Among the dependent relationships in which the ego stands that to the superego is perhaps the most interesting" (ibid p. 57). It embodies an ideal of the ego and thus conveys a moral orientation for the ego-righteous action of the person. This moral orientation can develop in two opposite directions: paraphrased, it can be said that there can be a loving, libidinous quality but also a cruel severity of the superego, which resembles the archaic violence of the id in its exaggerated moral sense of guilt. For an understanding of our present time, whose culture is characterized by a far-reaching secularization up to the abandonment of ideals on the one hand and radical political idealizations on the other hand – for example, in nationalistic populism or in terrorist ideal formations – a closer look at the term "ideal" can be helpful. In connection with the *two classes of instincts* and thus the juxtaposition of Eros and Thanatos, it seems to me justified to distinguish a *life-affirming ideal formation* from a *regressive and potentially destructive* ideal formation. An ideal formation turned towards Eros serves the unfolding of life and represents a drive for emotional and cognitive growth associated with pleasure. An ideal formation oriented towards Thanatos tends to idolization with rigidity, potentially hostile to life.

As Freud's derivations for the emergence of an ideal ego or ego ideal clearly show, ideals always arise in connection with object relations, even if they are perceived as personal value attitudes or moral ideas in the individual psyche, where they can be shaped by one's own imagination. This becomes even more evident the more we examine a different understanding of the structural concepts, ego ideal, ideal ego, and superego alongside the ego and the id.

A short digression: the terms ideal and idol have an etymological root in the ancient Greek "idéa". The diverse development in the history of the term deserves attention because the infinitive of the verb "idéin" means "to see, to behold", while the noun derived from it, "eidós", or "idéa", denotes what is seen (i.e., the figure and the impression it evokes). Connected with this is a movement from the inside to the outside and from the outside to the inside: what I see has a shape, and in return, this shape has an aesthetic-emotional effect on me, for example, if I find it beautiful or ugly. Plato turned the association of "idéa" with the externally visible into the opposite: for him, "idéa" became *mental* seeing. As psychoanalysts, we know the tension between inside and outside, and it belongs to the core of our profession to deal with inner images in relation to outer perception. In this sense, Canestri (2001) also emphasized "the necessity of a constant oscillation between seeing and thinking, form and imagination, image and abstraction" (p. 158).

The development of the superego can equally be understood in terms of an oscillation between object experience and imaginative elaboration. In addition to the drive-theoretical orientation, Freud repeatedly dealt with the interplay between subject and object in *The Ego and the Id* as well as he did in his earlier work *On Narcissism: An Introduction* (1914). In both works, he develops his understanding of the ideal ego, ego ideal, and superego alongside the ego and the id. Initially, he does not explicitly distinguish between the ideal ego and the ego ideal; rather, in *On Narcissism*, he first uses the term *ideal ego*, but in the rest of the text, he mostly speaks of the *ego ideal*. In the later work of 1923, he does not use the term ideal ego anymore. He speaks only of the ego ideal and the superego. In both texts, however, we find two different forms of the emergence of the "ideal I", and these different derivations seem significant for a definitional distinction. The decisive difference lies in the absence or recognition of limitation. Thus, Freud describes in 1914, following his conception of primary narcissism a connection between the individual's "ideal ego" and the self-love of the "infantile ego", which "finds itself possessed of every perfection that is of value" (p. 94).

Only a few lines further on, he introduces a limitation of the narcissistic perfection, which comes from interpersonal and intrapsychic sources: from "the admonitions" and critical influence of parents and others as well as from one's own critical judgment. The "new form of the *ego ideal*" is now to recover this perfection *(italics HB)* (ibid p. 96).

This juxtaposition of different forms of identification is also found in *The Ego and the Id*. Freud describes the pre-ambivalent origin of the ego ideal as the "individual's first and most important identification, his identification with the father in his own personal prehistory" (ibid p. 31) – in a footnote, Freud adds that it is better to say "with the parents".

After describing the oedipal phase, however, Freud calls the ego ideal, synonymous with the superego, the "heir of the Oedipus complex" (p. 36). It conveys the two-faced admonition and prohibition to the ego: "You should be like (the father)" but also, "You may not be like this (like your father)-that is, you may not do all that he does; some things are his prerogative" (p. 34). I like to follow Cavell (1996, p. 225), who has pointed to the preservation of the child's separate state in the admonition to be "like" the father and not to be the father himself.

Of Freud's successors, I would briefly mention Klein, Winnicott, and Lacan. In contrast to Freud, Klein (1984) assumed the early existence of a persecuting superego at the level of the paranoid-schizoid organization. However, as the child reaches the depressive position, it develops a capacity to feel sadness and gratitude towards the object. This appreciation of another person becomes, for Winnicott, a stage of object love, which is marked by "the subject's perception of the object as an external phenomenon, not as a projective entity, in fact recognition of it as an entity in its own right" (1971, p. 89).

The other subject is also decisive for Lacan (1966) because his concept of the ideal self (Moi idéal) includes admiration for an idealized other, while it is only the ability to accept judgments about the ideal self from this other that leads to the formation of the ego ideal (idéal du Moi). The ideal ego belongs to the imaginary realm, whereas the ego ideal belongs to the symbolic.

Why do I relate these concepts, in a very abbreviated form, here? I think that regarding the dichotomy of life-affirming ideals and potentially destructive ideals, there is a clarification: we find early ideals, which, by means of projective-identificatory processes, can be connected with omnipotent self-admiration or idealization of the object but also with rage and persecution. And we find ideals as result of the oedipal phase, which gain their strength through the recognition of limitation and difference. The ideal ego embodies the earlier form, the ego ideal the latter. Both forms belong to individual persons, also to groups. In our clinical psychoanalytic work, we often encounter relationships in which the subject and object representations carry the absolute claim of an ideal ego. Our working through in the analytic relationship, however, strives for subject-object representations in the sense of a post-oedipal ego ideal. It is connected with recognizing the value of other persons and other ideas without having to give up one's own self-esteem or one's own ideas. Vital, post-oedipal ideal formations know an acceptance of difference and the possibility of productive doubt, of oneself, of objects, and of one's own convictions. They form a basis for interpersonal debates with a direction towards the future. In this respect, they have a generative effect. In contrast, pre-oedipal idolizations, which persist beyond the first and psychologically necessary illusion of omnipotence, tend to perpetuate fusionary dedifferentiated object relations. As a defense against early fears, they contain a corresponding potential for violence. This distinction seems to me important not only clinically and in terms of cultural theory but it also acquires significance for current debates among psychoanalysts. The ongoing exchange about diverse psychoanalytic concepts and the necessary discussion about the preservation or possible loss of psychoanalytic ideals in times of accelerating change, virtuality and artificial intelligence can only be conducted in the sense of a benign superego and an ego ideal of scientific investigation and respectful, mutual exchange.

Closing remark

It was in this spirit of scientific inquiry and research that Freud unfolded his thoughts on the emergence of individual mental structure in the form of id, early body-ego, ego, and superego. Even if we today grasp the corresponding object relations more explicitly than Freud himself did, his emphasis on understanding the individual psyche was never detached from interpersonal and interpsychic references. Even 100 years after the publication of *The Ego and the Id*, its reading remains a stimulating source for examining contemporary issues, albeit in an expanded form. The goal of a psychoanalytic process is still to give an individual a greater sense of self and more of his or her own room for agency in the relationship with the analyst. The experiencing and acting subject will be able to become all the stronger the more in the psychoanalytic process one's own body is experienced as a source of vital power and one's own ideal formations retain a post-oedipal, life-affirming quality. The hope is that this grown ego, both within itself and in contact with others, can harness the powers of Eros and contain the inevitable human destructiveness. Freud has shown us a narrow but realistic dimension of hope within a threatened world, and this legacy is a cornerstone for the further future of psychoanalysis.

Note

1 German original text: "Ich bin. Aber ich habe mich nicht. Darum werden wir erst."

References

Abram, J. (2022). *The Surviving Object: Psychoanalytic Clinical Essays on Psychic Survival-of-the Object*. London and New York: Routledge.

Anzieu, D. (2016). *The Skin-Ego*. London: Karnac Books.

Argelander, H. (1970/2013). The scenic function of the ego and its role in symptom and character formation. *International Journal of Psychoanalysis*, 94: 337–354.

Baranger, M. & Baranger, W. (2008). The analytic situation as a dynamic field. *International Journal of Psychoanalysis*, 89: 795–826.

Bion, W. R. (1962). *Learning from Experience*. London: Heinemann.

Bloch, E. (1963). *Tübinger Einleitung in die Philosophie*, 1. Frankfurt am Main: Suhrkamp Verlag.

Bohleber, W. (2014). Auf der Suche nach Repräsentanz – Analytisches Arbeiten an der Schnittstelle von Ungedachtem und symbolisch Repräsentiertem. *Psyche – Psychoanal*, 68: 777–786.

———. (2016). Introduction to Alfred Lorenzer's paper "Language, Life Praxis and Scenic Understanding in Psychoanalytic Therapy". *International Journal of Psychoanalysis*, 97: 1393–1398.

Bolognini, S. (2022). *Vital Flows between the Self and Non-Self: The Interpsychic*. London and New York: Routledge.

Botella, C. and Botella, S. (2005). *The Work of Psychic Figurability: Mental States without Representation*. London and New York: Routledge.

Busch, F. (2022). *A Fresh Look at Psychoanalytic Technique*. Selected Papers on Psychoanalysis. London and New York: Routledge.

Canestri, J. (2001). Changing scientific ideals and idols in the history of psychoanalysis. *EPF Bulletin*, 55: 159–164.

Cavell, M. (1993/1996). *The Psycho-Analytic Mind: From Freud to Philosophy*. Cambridge, MA and London: Harvard University Press.

Civitarese, G. (2015). Transformations in hallucinosis and the receptivity of the analyst. *International Journal of Psychoanalysis*, 96: 1091–1116.

Ferro, A. (1999). *The Bi-Personal Field: Experiences in Child Analysis*. London and New York: Routledge.

———. (2004). Interpretation: Signals from the analytic field and emotional transformations. *International Forum of Psychoanalysis*, 13: 31–38.

Fonagy, P. and Allison, E. (2014). The role of mentalizing and epistemic trust in the therapeutic relationship. *Psychotherapy*. DOI: 10.1037/a0036505

Freud, S. (1914). On narcissism: An introduction. *S.E.*, 14: 67–102.

———. (1920). Beyond the pleasure principle. *S.E.*, 18: 1–64.

———. (1923a). The Ego and yhe Id. *S.E.*, 19: 1–66.

———. (1923b). Letter from Sigmund Freud to Sándor Ferenczi, April 17, 1923. *The Correspondence of Sigmund Freud and Sándor Ferenczi*, 3(1920–1933) 27: 102.

Green, A. (1974). Surface analysis, deep analysis (the role of the preconscious in psychoanalytical technique). *International Review of Psychoanalysis*, 1: 415–423.

———. (1975). The analyst, symbolization and absence in the analytic setting (on changes in analytic practice and analytic experience): In memory of D. W. Winnicott. *International Journal of Psychoanalysis*, 56: 1–22.

Heimann, P. (1950) On counter-transference. *International Journal of Psychoanalysis,* 31: 81–84.

Kandel, E. R. (2005). *Psychiatry, Psychoanalysis und the New Biology of Mind.* Washington, DC and London, UK: American Psychiatric Publishing, Inc.

Klein, M. (1984). *Envy and Gratitude and Other Works, 1946–1963.* London: The Hogarth Press.

Kohut, H. (1971). *The Analysis of the Self.* London: Hogarth Press.

Lacan, J. (1966/2007). *Écrits.* Trans. Bruce Fink. New York and London: W. W. Norton & Company.

Laplanche, J. (1997). The theory of seduction and the problem of the other. *International Journal of Psychoanalysis,* 78: 653–666.

Levine, H. B. (2012). The colourless canvas: Representation, therapeutic action and the creation of mind. *International Journal of Psychoanalysis,* 93: 607–629.

Lorenzer, A. (2016). Language, life praxis and scenic understanding in psychoanalytic therapy. *Int. J. Psycho. Anal.,* 97(5): 1399–1414.

Ogden, T. H. (1989). *The Primitive Edge of Experience.* Northvale, NJ and London: Jason Aronson and Karnac Books.

———. (1994). The analytic third: Working with intersubjective clinical facts. *International Journal of Psychoanalysis,* 75: 3–19.

Personnier, G. (2022). Ich? – Was meinst Du? Eine essayistische Reise über Identität. *Kinderanalyse,* 30: 75–98. DOI: 10.21706/ka-30-1-75

Sandler, J., Sandler, A. M. and Kernberg, O. F. (1998). *Internal Objects Revisited.* London: Routledge.

Scarfone, D. (2016). Deutung jenseits der Bedeutung. *ZpTP,* 31: 54–58.

Tuckett, D., Basile, R., BirkstedBreen, D., Böhm, T., Denis, P., Ferro, A., Hinz, H., Jemstedt, A., Mariotti, P. & Schubert, J. (2008). *Psychoanalysis Comparable and Incomparable: The Evolution of a Method to Describe and Compare Psychoanalytic Approaches.* London and New York: Routledge.

Winnicott, D. W. (1963). Communicating and not communicating leading to a study of certain opposites. In D. W. Winnicott (1965/2018). *The Maturational Process and the Facilitating Environment: Studies in the Theory of Emotional Development.* London and New York: Routledge, pp. 179–192.

———. (1971). *Playing and Reality.* London: Tavistock.

6 The advent of the superego

An après-coup of *Beyond the Pleasure Principle*

Bernard Chervet[1]

Reading *The Ego and the Id* (1923a) allows us to follow the process of Freud's theorization as it is highlighted in an exemplary way by the introduction in 1920 of his new conception of the nature of the drives defined by their tendency to regress to an earlier state of things, even to the inorganic and inanimate state. This process of complexification was driven by what had remained unelaborated since his internalization of the traumatic quality of the drive in *Beyond the Pleasure Principle* (1920).

In the very first lines of *The Ego and the Id*, Freud points out that this text takes up again the process of theorization opened up in 1920. The etiology of the traumatic dimension was first linked to an early awakening of an unconscious desire by a seducer (the *neurotica*), then to a conflict of sexualization of the ego drives and was finally understood as being the consequence of the elementary quality of every drive. He, therefore, proposed to reconceptualize the previously described psychic dualities (wish/defense, sexual drive/ego drive, sexual libido/narcissistic libido) as manifestations of a more fundamental drive duality – that between the life drive and the death drive, both characterized by this regressive tendency to extinction. This internalization resulted in a revision of the conception of mental functioning not only the topography but also its dynamics and economy.

In *Beyond the Pleasure Principle*, Freud calls this internalization of the traumatic regressive tendency defining every drive his third step in the theory of the drives, following the first two, namely, infantile sexuality and narcissism. He specifies that it is a regressive tendency to return to a previous state of things and even to the inorganic state. This new definition applies easily to the death drive, but it leaves Freud more circumspect with regard to the life drive. He thus ends his text with unresolved questions regarding the return to an earlier state of things, even to the inorganic state of the life drive and/or Eros.

This was obviously not a failure of intellectual resolution but a necessity of the mind to carry out momentary regressive work in order to be able to resume the process of theorizing itself after recovering from the traumatic effect. The two texts are thus linked by a two-stage process. This regressive work of the mind, whose prototype is that of the dream but also the session,

DOI: 10.4324/9781003336754-6

allows for the integration of the novelties and differences that require this two-stage process because they are associated with the traumatic dimension. Since *Beyond the Pleasure Principle*, the new theoretical object to be integrated was the traumatic dimension itself.

This integration requires a period of latency during which regressive work on thought processes is carried out; this process may require several nights of dreams and several articles of regressive writing with the aim of attenuating the traumatic quality by means of hallucinatory wish-fulfilments. This is the work of latency, of this interval period that is part of the two-stage process of the operation of après-coup. This process turns out to be involved in the process of theorization of any novelty because of the link that exists between it and the traumatic quality. This necessity is obviously intensified when the reality to be integrated is the traumatic dimension itself.

The *non liquet* (i.e., "it is not clear") present in the last chapter of *Beyond the Pleasure Principle* particularly concerns the life drive. The question of its regressive tendency, of its return to an earlier state of things, remained unresolved despite the appeal to the poets (Plato and primal hermaphroditism). Freud recognized that he had to finish his text limping and that this was not a sin. He thus suspended his reflection and postponed the resolution of this question.

In 1923, he wanted to resume this theoretical development. To do this, he followed a precise method. He recalled what psychoanalysis had made it possible to elaborate until then concerning the role of the ego in making unconscious contents conscious by means of sensory perceptions, ideas, endogenous perceptions (such as affects, emotions, and feelings), and all the sensations and experiences emanating from thought processes. But, in fact, he introduced new differences, which, in order to be taken into account, required a new approach to the composition of the mind. His method, therefore, consisted in starting from the knowledge acquired and in introducing new differences that called for a revision of the whole. The appeal to a new agency, the superego/ego ideal, was the consequence of these new differences. Freud could then return to the drive duality introduced in 1920 and redefine the ego in terms of its plural dependent relations and the task that falls to it of managing heterogeneities, both external and internal, with an aim of allowing them access to consciousness. But once again, in concluding *The Ego and the Id*, he had the feeling that he had not completely treated the question of Eros:

> It would be possible to picture the id as under the domination of the mute but powerful death instincts, which desire to be at peace and (prompted by the pleasure principle) to put Eros, the mischief-maker, to rest; but perhaps that might be to undervalue the part played by Eros.
>
> (1923a, p. 59)

This last sentence announced another stage in the theorization, which can be found in the *32nd Lecture* – "Anxiety and Instinctual Life", where Freud returns to extinctive drive regression, the tendency to "do away with life once more life and to re-establish the inorganic state" (1933, p. 107).

I will follow Freud's two-stage approach as well as the consequences of his attempts to theorize the life drive (and Eros) in terms of the elementary traumatic quality of all drives, their extinctive regressivity.

This approach will allow me to show how, through his attempts, Freud offers us an exemplary depiction of his thought processes, an enactment of the latter in the theorization of metapsychology; hence, a reflection on the process of theorization and an invitation to build an epistemology of psychoanalytic theorization.

It was with such an epistemological remark that Freud began *The Ego and the Id*:

> If psychoanalysis has not hitherto shown its appreciation of certain things, this has never been because it overlooked their achievement or sought to deny their importance, but because it followed a particular path, which had not yet led so far.
>
> (1923a, p. 12)

Reading Freud and psychanalytic epistemology

The two sides of theorization

Reading Freud as a psychoanalyst requires us to really listen to the text; it certainly calls for an exegesis of the contents produced by the theorization but also requires us to listen to the function of this process of theorization with regard to the mind of its author. In fact, theorization has two faces: one is to propose and advance the intelligibility of the observed phenomena, while the other is to respond to the theoretician's mental needs, to treat the traumatic quality he experiences. This is the function of infantile sexual theories. In order to diminish the traumatic effect, the psyche produces theories, affects, pictorial scenarios, and experiences. Before manifesting itself through such registrations, it must first effect an anti-traumatic restraint that is the foundation of primary masochism, a masochism of functioning. The whole development of the mind, of thought and desire, is based on this primary masochism. Just after *The Ego and the Id*, in 1924, Freud (1924) tackled this question of the masochism underlying his theorization of the extinctive tendency begun in 1920 and continued in 1923. The introduction of a new agency, the superego/ego ideal, was directly linked to this need to carry out a work of restraint and registration.

Reading Freud is not just a question of chronology; it is also necessary to follow the process of thought with its detours, its returns and regressions, its productions and proposals, and its advances on the basis of new differences that create new conceptions and new differences. This process is haunted by what has been glimpsed and not elaborated – that is, by what is marked by the traumatic quality and needs to be elaborated subsequently.

This reading, therefore, takes place on two levels. It is possible to follow the theorization itself, with its contents, contradictions, stumbling blocks, variations, hesitations, rejections, abandonments, regressions, and dynamic in two stages. We can find numerous examples of this two-stage dynamic in Freud's work – for example, in his two short texts on Signorelli of 1898 and 1900 but also in the elaboration of fetishism and in the elaboration of a dream from *The Interpretation of Dreams* taken up again in *The Future of an Illusion* (1927) and so on. Freud's entire work can be approached in this way, as a series of two stages and interval periods between them, and each new text is an après-coup that attempts to elaborate a part of what in the previous contributions had remained dominated by the traumatic regressive attraction.

The second level of reading Freud is more specifically psychoanalytic. As psychoanalysts, we know that every psychic production is the result of a process that has a value for the mind of its author and that every work portrays an associative process that seeks to fulfil hallucinatorily an unconscious wish under the guise of the work of theorization. Renunciation is not achieved without its obverse, the search for satisfaction, seeking to impose itself. This double meaning of theorization is in line with Freud's text on the double meaning of primitive words. We know to what extent the work of desexualization and sublimation can be used by the mind's attempts to maintain compensatory hallucinatory satisfactions. Desexualization is always accompanied by this other attempt.

Listening to an associative process, even when it is a path of theorization, obliges the analyst to give equal value to all the texts to the whole work. Any rigorous study is, therefore, coupled with an evenly suspended attentive reading that accords equal value to the whole work. It has as its ideal the rule of not discarding anything, of not eliminating anything but of taking the work as a whole, of not choosing this or that fragment or vertex.

Contextualization

As a corollary, another obligation arises – that of recontextualizing an article within the work as a whole, an infinite task that involves going back over the entire work each time not only its previous determinants and its later extensions but also its overdeterminations linked to private aspects of the author, which we are necessarily lacking, hence, the appetite for biographies and correspondence. This impossibility of completeness places limits on recontextualization, hence, the incompleteness of any reading.

With regard to *The Ego and the Id*, I have already emphasized the fact that Freud immediately links this essay to *Beyond the Pleasure Principle*. He also states that he is no longer making borrowings from what turns out to have been a diversion and a metaphor, cellular biology. In *The Ego and the Id*, he gives it up in favor of metapsychology. This detour was necessary for the elaboration of what he had only intuited at the time, the presence of tendencies within the mind leading it to its extinction, or even to death. We know to what extent *Beyond the Pleasure Principle* has been criticized for this reason, for having drawn on the biological science of the time, which has since evolved. In the name of this evolution, the detractors of Freud and psychoanalysis deny that his elaboration has any value. The same criticism can be made of *Totem and Taboo* (1912–1913) in the name of new anthropo-logical discoveries, as well as those of linguistics, physics, and so on. In fact, these detours belong to the very process of the theorization of metapsy-chology, and the fact that the knowledge acquired is of a temporary nature does not undermine the metapsychological advances that these detours have allowed. The same criticism has been made using the mistranslation between vulture and kite, an error that is supposed to nullify Freud's in-terpretation of the shape of the Virgin's dress in Leonardo's painting *The Virgin and Child with Saint Anne*, a shape in which Freud recognized a child-hood memory of Leonardo. In fact, the translation error liberated and high-lighted the process of theorization itself.

Transposition

This method of detour belongs to the epistemology of Freud's theorizing process. It is part of a process in several stages. The first stage requires a transposition onto knowledge and works constituting tangible external realities belonging to other sciences or cultural fields. We can find such de-tours and transpositions throughout Freud's work. They make it possible to metaphorize unconscious properties and constituents of the mind con-sistent with an animistic thinking unknown to its author. The researcher is doing nothing different from the child who builds his psychic processes by means of play. It was in this way that Freud made use of the "wooden reel game", as well as electricity, chemistry, thermodynamics, medicine, sur-gery, obstetrics, not to mention anthropology, history, art, literature, reli-gions, linguistics, sociology, and so on, and of course, in 1919–1920, cellular biology.

This epistemology unsurprisingly takes up the very process of thought that is also established in early childhood until adolescence. It is this same process that is involved in the elaboration of the science of mental life. In order to elaborate the reality of mental life metapsychologically, it is neces-sary in the first instance to transpose the unconscious components onto the realities of sensory perception, to metaphorize them as contents that can be internalized, and then, in the second instance, to operate a return to abstract theorization by abandoning the infantile metaphors founded in the first stage. These metaphors continue their function of anti-extinctive restraint in the unconscious and the preconscious.

This is how many concepts of psychoanalysis are labeled by words that designate such objects of transposition. They have kept the name as a memory of the initial stage. This is the case with the expressions Oedipus complex, primal phantasies, seduction of the child by the adult, primal scene, castration by the father, murder of the father, life and death drives, and so on.

The two stages and the interval between them

This observation of a theorizing process unfolding in two stages, according to the dynamics of the process of après-coup, logically requires us to observe the respective contents of each of the two stages but also what happened during the interval. Freud does not mention the interval that separates *Beyond the Pleasure Principal* and *The Ego and the Id*, one that contains several articles that can be considered as productions belonging to the stage of psychic elaboration. These intermediate texts are *Group Psychology and the Analysis of the Ego* (1921), which deals with the collective solutions to individual trauma; *Medusa's Head* (1940), which shows the recourse to a quantitative dimension, to a multiplication with an apotropaic function that is supposed to ward off the traumatic effects of direct contact with lack; and *A Seventeenth-Century Demonological Neurosis* (1923b), a text in which the anti-traumatic solution is alienation from an institution, in this case, that of the painter Christoph Haizmann from the Church. The narcissistic needs provided by this institution, thus from outside, serve as a counter-cathexis to the traumatic regressive aspirations of the painter, who is supposed, in the form of payment, to provide this institution with images that reinforce the religious belief that is its raison d'être, a give-and-take of narcissisms. The transaction consists in each protagonist providing the other with the defenses he needs.

All these texts explore responses to the traumatic dimension and solutions to the traumatic effects of lack and to the regressive attraction (1926) to extinction associated with it. In the first stage, it is a matter of supporting a denial of the lack, then of making it possible to shatter this denial and to replace it by a work of mentalization. The second stage is, therefore, an elaboration integrating the reality of the trauma, while the first stage immobilized this quality. The interval period is a psychic elaboration without real recognition of the traumatic reality but that promotes a hallucinatory wish-fulfilment that conceals it.

These three moments, the two stages and the interval period, are the organizers of thought and desire. They constitute the process of après-coup.

This dynamic is also the one that Freud recognized as active in the approach to the difference between the sexes (1925). The inaugural denial gives way to an opening of the eyes and the recognition of the double difference of the sexes, masculine-feminine, endowed-unendowed. *Beyond the Pleasure Principle* internalized the traumatic quality and revealed the positive function of denial in the first stage.

This correlation and comparison of the two articles from 1920 and 1923 must be complemented by turning our attention to the period 1920–1923 during which Freud explored several anti-traumatic solutions. This exploration, which was necessary due to the internalization of the traumatic quality, reminds us of the importance of the contextualization of a text within the work as a whole.

Finally, this work of elaboration in the interval period brings to light new enigmas, which themselves convey the traumatic quality. These enigmas are then equivalent to the first stage of a future unforeseeable second stage. A new process of après-coup is initiated on the basis of these new enigmas. This is how the advances of psychoanalysis unfold.

Freud's work is a prototypical illustration of this dynamic not only because of its author's mental functioning as a researcher but also because it is a closed work. Nevertheless, it remained open in Freud's mind; hence, the imaginary question: What might Freud have written if he had continued to live? What are the deferred effects that could not be completed but had to be interrupted?

The chapters: reminders, differences, advances

Freud says that he will limit himself to recalling what has already been learned and that there is nothing new to be said. But he constantly introduces new differences that force him to revise his previous assertions, bringing psychoanalysis closer to a discipline of thought than to a body of compiled academic knowledge.

In Chapter 1, the new contribution is the fact that the unconscious cannot be circumscribed topographically and that it concerns the whole psyche. The existence of an unconscious ego modifies his point of view. The topographical opposition between conscious-preconscious and unconscious is to be replaced by a qualitative opposition between a coherent ego and an id that eludes all rationality. The quality of being unconscious becomes a multivocal quality and, therefore, cannot be localized.

In Chapter 2, this loss of localization, this dilution of a quality that has become diffuse, prompts Freud, on the contrary, to depict his new conception of the mind by means of a circumscribed pictorial representation. Quite untypically for him, he resorts to a drawing reminiscent of the neurological anatomy of the brain. He draws a closed mental apparatus. Inside it, he distributes the enclosed agencies on the model of areas. In 1932–1933, he took up this diagram again but opened it up to a beyond and included the superego in it. This new drawing thus reintroduces the conception of drive regression as advanced in 1920 – that is, as unlimited. The superego and the opening onto the beyond are thus linked. The 1923 diagram, on the contrary, proposes a limitation in line with his earlier conceptions of regression in which the function of the superego remained implicit. In 1900, regression is supposed to rediscover the unconscious perceptual traces of amnesia; in 1915, it seeks to reinstate the primary narcissism of the maternal bosom. The enclosed diagram of 1923 maintains such an obstacle to regression. In 1932, it is open to the void of the inanimate, to the infinite without representable content. This difference between the 1923 and 1932 diagrams tells us that an aspect of *Beyond the Pleasure Principle* is not included in the elaboration of *The Ego and the Id*. Is it not the question left open in 1920, then in 1923, and again in 1932 – that of the regressive tendency of Eros to return to a previous state along a specific path? Freud defers each time. It is thus possible to suggest that the regression of the life drive occurs in a different manner to the reductive regression that strives towards the zero of the death drive, by means of an infinite extension that also leads to extinction. This suggestion allows us to think about the clinical features of idealizations, quests, and ideologies, both manifest and unconscious, which present themselves in the form of major inhibitions and inertia and even in the form of dreadful destruction and self-destruction.

The whole of Chapter 2 is devoted to the process of becoming conscious, to the differentiation of its forms, which vary according to whether it is a question of sensory perceptions, ideas, sensations, feelings, or all the experiences coming from within the mind. The main difference concerns the role of the preconscious and the link to word-presentations and, through them, to language. Word-presentations serve as an indispensable intermediate stage between the drive thing-presentations differentiated from memory traces and consciousness. This process including the preconscious is not the same for what, coming from within, does not belong to the field of ideation. In this case, sensations, feelings, and all the experiences that account for thought processes reach consciousness directly; otherwise, they follow other vicissitudes. The "something" (1923a, p. 22) that should become sensations and feelings can follow another path than that of consciousness when it is suppressed. It is then that Freud comes closer to Groddeck and replaces the unconscious by the agency of the id, insisting on the ego's passive attitude towards the powers of the id. The allusion to the fact that "unconscious feelings" (ibid., p. 22) may undergo different vicissitudes would promote numerous studies on motor acts and psychosomatic dysfunctioning.

The path concerning ideational contents involves the ego insofar as its differentiation occurs through contact with perception by means of perceptual and memory traces, hence, the existence of two paths to becoming conscious – that of immediate consciousness due to perception and that of the long path of repression, of the differentiation of thing-presentations from the traces of the tangible sensory realities and their link to preconscious word-presentations. An implicit conception of a difference between the word-presentations derived from the preconscious and language itself, insofar as it is heterogeneous to the nature of the id, can be inferred. The question then arises as to whether language plays a part in the admission to consciousness of endogenous sensations. Hysterical conversions translate linguistic formulas (the language of the body), whereas psychosomatic disorders attest to a rupture between this "something" that should have become endogenous sensations and language.

Freud continues this chapter by introducing a modification to his conception of the ego. Its differentiation occurs not only under the influence of external sensory perceptions but also endogenous ones. His famous statement that "for the ego perception plays the part which in the id falls to instinct" (ibid., p. 25) has to be revised since the ego also arises from the influences emanating from the internal side of the mental apparatus, the id. In fact, the ego is dominated by the id, although it believes it is the master of its own house. It is at this point that Freud uses the famous metaphor of the rider and the horse. The rider/ego is very often condemned to believe that he leads his horse where he wants, when in fact, it is the id/horse that takes him where it wants to go. Freud emphasizes the ego's capacity to live in an illusion. It is this reality that leads him to study at length in Chapter 5 the dependent relations of the ego. This metaphor is related to an organized drive thrust, as in 1915, but not to the regressive tendency leading to extinction. To counter this, the horse would have to restrain its rider, to prevent him from disappearing.

Freud ends this chapter by insisting on the influence of all the endogenous sensations, in particular, those emanating from the body, thus making the ego "a bodily-ego" (ibid., p. 26), a "body-ego" (ibid., p. 27). He thus evokes, without developing the idea, the birth of a sensual ego, of a sensual body. He takes up again what he had learned from hysteria – the fact that conversion is the basis of feelings and affects but also sensuality – as well his remarks of 1914 on hypochondria and the existence of organ erotogenicity with an attracting power, that of erotic enjoyment.

And Freud makes a final remark about psychic processes taking place passively; dreams were already evidence of this since they take place while the ego is in a state of sleep. He points out that highly elaborated activities can take place passively in the ego without becoming conscious. Some of these activities are even considered as the highest on our scale of values. These are judgment, intellectual reasoning, morality, and ethics. These values can remain totally unconscious and yet have major effects on the mind – for example, producing unconscious guilt, negative therapeutic reactions, failure neuroses, and serious disturbances that can lead a subject to his own destruction.

Chapter 3 is concerned with these values and a new authority, the superego/ego ideal. Having insisted on the existence of an unconscious ego and highly valued psychological activities taking place passively, Freud turns to the existence within the ego of a function that has a major role in the organization of psychic life to the point of becoming an agency as such, namely, the ego ideal or superego. This function is involved in the process of becoming conscious. The latter constitutes the ideal of mental functioning. Just like the ego, more or less important parts of this agency can be unconscious, thus obtruding its purpose.

The development of this function is closely related to the fact that the ego does not arise from a differentiation under the influence of perception alone but under the influence of the internal constituents of the mind. The fact that the ego develops under the influence of the instinctual drives of the id, and that these strive towards extinction, introduces, quite logically, the need for another agency under the aegis of which an intrapsychic work of restraint and registration must take place, producing psychic materials reaching consciousness on its internal side or by means of transpositions on to external sensory realities, including language.

If we compare this need to carry out work under the aegis of a new agency, the superego, with reference to an ideal – that of becoming conscious – with the third step of the theory of the drives developed in 1920, we can infer that the first function of the superego is to oppose the extinctive tendencies with restraint and its second, to register drive processes within the mind on the path of becoming conscious, thus to create the drives with their thrust. The picture emerges of a superego comprised of imperatives that all have as their aim the ideal of becoming conscious: an imperative of restraint, an imperative of registration, and an imperative of orientation towards objects.

In the name of this ideal goal, the superego thus ensures that a first stage of regression is possible in order to establish a restraint and a reversal of the extinctive tendencies into registrations, then a regressive work of registration in the mind – that of the interval period – in order to complete the process of après-coup during a second stage by orienting the libidinal cathexes thus created towards the consciousness and objects. Parents advise their children to work but also to play and sleep/dream. By requiring patients to follow the fundamental rule, analysis invites them to improve their psychic regressive activities of passivity in order to obtain an improvement in their mental functioning and their libidinal cathexis of objects.

Consciousness thus appears to be two-sided: one side is turned towards the external world and sensory perception; the other is turned towards the internal world and endogenous perceptions and sensations. This two-sided nature of the screen of consciousness is illustrated by Freud in his short text, *A Note on the "Mystic Writing-Pad"* (1925). But he gives priority to stimuli from external perception and follows the path of these stimuli, with the interplay between memory and consciousness, before finally ending his text by reminding us that the mass of wax, a metaphor for the id, is not inert in the mind but produces stimuli from within that the mystic pad metaphor does not take into account.

The existence of such an agency involved in mental activity is not new. Already in *On Narcissism: An Introduction*, Freud (1914) had spoken of an ego ideal that is active in the process of desexualization grounding narcissistic libido. In *The Interpretation of Dreams* (1900), he had also envisaged such an agency, the dream censorship, which functioned while the ego was asleep, an agency regulating the dreamwork with the precise aim of preserving sleep. The ideal of the censorship is to be the guardian of sleep.

In 1923, the agency envisaged was much more general. Under its aegis, all forms of psychic work, both nocturnal and diurnal, are carried out. This agency includes dream censorship but also all the imperatives active within the mind. These imperatives apply to the instinctual drive impulses that they transform by subjecting them to operations of renunciation.

The first psychic work, discussed by Freud in 1924 at the same time as masochism, is the work of restraint and libidinal sympathetic excitation. A renunciation of extinction is thus imposed by means of a transposition onto external stimuli. The intervention of such a principle of renunciation is also active in the operations of desexualization at the basis of narcissism, as well as in the oedipal mourning founding human desire and its orientation towards objects.

The introduction of the superego in 1923 is necessary to the theory in order to explain the work carried out at the drive source, work that counters extinctive regressivity and uses it to provide a basis for registrations. This is a logical requirement within the theory, linked to advances in drive theory, that is to the internalization of the extinctive tendency as a drive quality. It is in this sense that the advent of the superego is an après-coup of *Beyond the Pleasure Principle* and of the great discovery of this period, namely, the fact that the drives, whether of death or life, are all defined by extinctive regressivity.

The mechanism of transposition proves indispensable for carrying out these forms of work and for continuing them until they become conscious: "only something which has once been a *Cs.* perception can become conscious, and anything arising from within (apart from feelings) that seeks to become conscious must try to transform itself into external perceptions" (1923a, p. 20). The model of the ordinary phobias of childhood is recognizable here. Transposition is also an essential feature of all session transference.

In Chapter 3 of *The Ego and the Id*, Freud insists on this mechanism of transposition and the part it plays in the mental work required by internal constraints to which the imperatives of renunciation are a response, with the aim of establishing an ideal mental functioning that is the first ideal of the ego. The accomplishment of the mind has an attractive force that confers on it the value of a final cause. This attraction is particularly noticeable with regard to the Oedipus complex, its deployment, and its decline. The same is true of the primary identification that Freud describes in Chapter 3, the immediate and direct identification that precedes any object-cathexis, an identification with a model of functioning based on that of the parents and persons in close contact with the child – that of the *Nebenmensch* (1950 [1895]). The mechanism of transposition is at the origin of foundational identifications.

If in Chapter 2, the transposition is envisaged by Freud as existing between unconscious elements and sensorially perceivable external realities, in Chapter 3, the transposition takes place at the level of economic transformations and provides the basis for narcissistic identifications. Part of the sexual libido of the id, of the sexual cathexes of the object and the body, is transformed into narcissistic libido through the mechanism of desexualization. The whole of Chapter 3 is centered on narcissistic identifications, on the ego-characteristics resulting from identifications linked to the loss of object, and on their stumbling blocks and defectiveness as in melancholia.

By the means of the transpositions, the two sides of the ego, external and internal, find themselves in close contact. External perceptions offer memory traces that the internal libidinal transpositions can differentiate as thing-presentations and ideas cathected with narcissistic libido. The mechanism of transposition is foundational. It is active from the beginning in the primary identification with the father (the parent) of personal prehistory.

By introducing a categorical imperative with an economy of its own, a specific, displaceable, and indifferent libido, Freud was returning to the intuitions he had when he envisaged that the therapeutic effect of becoming conscious was due to a connection with language because the latter is the bearer of a specific cathexis, a hypercathexis. The superego is thus the agency that ensures the provision of a hypercathexis. But as usual, Freud is not satisfied with this simple proposition. He had learned that "when a hypercathexis of the process of thinking takes place, thoughts are *actually* perceived – as if they came from without – and are consequently held to be true" (1923a, p. 23 [Freud's emphasis]). A hypercathexis does not suffice, therefore, for the fact of becoming conscious to have the value of a new moment of awareness. It also needs to be subjected to reality testing, which remains enigmatic. The last part of Freud's work is concerned with the play of illusions, idealizations and convictions, which can replace reality testing or rather avoid it and present themselves to consciousness as reality in place of reality testing. The enigma of reality testing remains unresolved since the place of renunciation within psychic work must be taken into account. Freud was well aware, through dreams, of the hallucinatory mechanism that consists in imposing perceptual identities from within and thus in saturating the internal side of consciousness. The latter then believes that there is only one world that created within.

This is how the interaction between the superego and the ego ideal, between the imperative to renounce and the aspiration to attain an ideal functioning, can come into conflict concerning the place and the implications of renunciation. The work of which the superego is the guarantor is guided and oriented by an ideal aim – that of the ego ideal, which may or may not refer to renunciation and, in this last case, become an idealization.

The superego is thus in the service of idealizations. It is thus possible to consider that the superego is, above all, an imperative to carry out different forms of work. These are not necessarily all linked to the principle of renunciation when the goal to be reached, attraction by the ego ideal, turns out to abandon its links with this principle and to present itself as an idealization.

After all the differentiations studied in the first three chapters, differentiations that allowed the traumatic effect of the extinction-registration difference to be diffused and the narcissism of small differences to be attenuated, it was logical that Freud should return to the drive duality through which he had introduced the traumatic difference. This is what he does in Chapter 4: "The Two Classes of Instincts". But he opts for a solution that does not fully integrate his conception of the traumatic dimension generalized to all drives. He associates this quality with the death drive alone and attributes to Eros not only an extensive but also a narcissistic conservative tendency. He thus describes an Eros that has the value of primary narcissism and promotes object-cathexes.

If life is not the prerogative of either the life drive or the death drive but results from their multiple and varied amalgams and mixtures, a question already arises. How are these amalgams made? Who manages them? What is involved in their accomplishment?

Freud prefers to envisage a simple relationship of opposition between the two classes of drive, an interplay of balance and imbalance in favor of one or the other and a tendency towards homeostasis between them. He does not bring into play the superego and its influence on what could be conceived as a work of amalgamation, of mixing-unmixing, even though he had envisaged an indifferent and displaceable libido specific to the superego and active in the process of becoming conscious. By attributing to Eros qualities of conservation that the 1920 definition of the drives did not include and that are related to narcissism, he short-circuited the involvement of the superego in the creation of libido and life.

However, he gives an essential place to the transposition of the ideal of psychic functioning onto the mental functioning of external persons who are attributed with functions of mental growth – characters (*Nebenmensch*) who attract towards them the transference of authority (parent, teachers, analyst). Here, we find intertwined the call of the superego for a work of mentalization to be carried out and a matrix promoting idealizations that escape renunciation. It is this conflict that Freud evokes through the notion of fundamental ambivalence: between foundational identifications and those that are idealizing and defective; between identifications with renunciation and those without renunciation; and between an operation of foundational murder or oedipal murder that seeks to eliminate the imperatives of the superego and their principle of renunciation. This is the work that the mind must carry out but which is targeted by this very ambivalence.

The text *The Ego and the Id* thus carries its title well. Freud introduces the superego and presents a long theoretical elaboration of the ego, with its dependent relations, its passive activities, and its mission to hold together heterogeneities and incompatibilities. He does not draw all the implications of the superego for the growth and extension of the mind, for the process of theorization and generativity. He does not develop the conflict between the infinite extension without registration of the life drive – the idealization of Eros – and the renunciation of this extension required by the superego in favor of evolutions based on the production of concrete and earthly registrations. In 1932, he defers again, but he asks:

> How the two of them [fundamental instincts] are mingled in the process of living, how the death instinct is made to serve the purposes of Eros, especially by being turned outwards as aggressiveness – these are tasks that are left to future investigation . . . The question too of whether the conservative character may not belong to all instincts without exception, whether the erotic instincts as well may not be seeking to bring back an earlier state of things when they strive to bring about a synthesis of living things into greater unities, this question, too, we must be left unanswered.
>
> (1933, pp. 107–108)

Thus, the centenary of *The Ego and the Id* is a great opportunity to reconsider these questions and to advance new proposals.

Note

1 Translated by Andrew Weller.

References

Freud, S. (1900). *The Interpretation of Dreams*. S.E., 4–5. London: Hogarth.
———. (1914). *On Narcissism: An Introduction. S.E.,* 14. London: Hogarth, pp. 69–102.
———. (1920). *Beyond the Pleasure Principle. S.E.,* 18. London: Hogarth, pp. 1–64.
———. (1921). *Group Psychology and the Analysis of the Ego. S.E.,* 18. London: Hogarth, pp. 65–143.
———. (1923a). *The Ego and the Id. S.E.,* 19. London: Hogarth, pp. 3–66.
———. (1923b). A seventeenth-century demonological neurosis. In *S.E.,* 19. London: Hogarth, pp. 72–105.
———. (1924). On the economic problem of masochism. In *S.E.,* 19. London: Hogarth, pp. 155–170.
———. (1925 [1924]). A note on the "mystic writing pad". In *S.E.,* 19. London: Hogarth, pp. 227–232.
———. (1925). Some psychical consequences of the anatomical distinction between the sexes. In *S.E.,* 19. London: Hogarth, pp. 248–258.

————. (1926). *Inhibitions, Symptoms and Anxiety. S.E.,* 20. London: Hogarth, pp. 75–174.

————. (1927). *The Future of an Illusion.* London: Hogarth, pp. 1–56.

————. (1933). Anxiety and instinctual life. In *New Introductory Lectures on Psychoanalysis: S.E.,* 22. London: Hogarth, pp. 81–111.

————. (1940 [1922]). Medusa's head. In *S.E.,* 18. London: Hogarth, pp. 273–274.

————. (1950 [1895]). Project for a scientific psychology. In *S.E.,* 1. London: Hogarth, pp. 281–397.

7 *The Ego and the Id*, and technique

Cecilio Paniagua

"We have embarked upon the analysis of the ego", wrote Freud a hundred years ago (1923, p. 36). Upon rereading *The Ego and the Id*, I thought of how many colleagues may have shared my excitement imagining the father of our profession scratching his head over the realization that the unconscious did not coincide only with the repressed and what to do about this finding. "The fact that [a] part of the ego is less firmly connected with consciousness is the novelty which calls for explanation", stated Freud (1923, p. 28). Naturally, this acknowledgement founded on clinical evidence led to modifications in his theoretical conceptualizations and the subsequent technical approaches to the mind in conflict.

The original notion of a mind divided in two portions, one repressed and the other repressing, ended becoming "not practicable" (Freud, 1923, p. 4) since it did not match well with the idea that the latter could be also unconscious; therefore, a concept of supraordinal "systems" had to be invoked. In the "Editor's Introduction" to *The Ego and the Id*, we can read that, as a consequence, "The old 'descriptive' sense of the term [unconscious] was in fact all that remained" (Freud, 1923, p. 7). In summary, the first notion of the "unconscious" was *descriptive* (*i.e.*, the recognition that part of our psychic activity was beyond awareness). Then the idea that there existed intrapsychic motives that explained why some processes were unconscious resulted in the *dynamic* point of view. Finally, the discovery that not only the repressed but also the defense mechanisms were unconscious led to the formulation of a *systematic* or *structural* perspective. In their clinical experience, all analysts can identify the validity of these abstractions as well as the existence of conflict *between* different systems and *within* systems (as in the confrontation of loyalties or the clashes between libidinal and aggressive wishes), with the ensuing compromise formations involved in the development of symptoms and character traits.

Freud struggled with the ideas of *unconscious* as adjective *versus* a substantive noun; of "unconscious" *versus* "preconscious"; the repressed *versus* the repressing; descriptive *versus* dynamic meanings; topographical *versus* structural concepts; and so on. In *The Ego and the Id*, "the last of [his] major theoretical works" (p. 4), following the *Naturphilosophie* inertia of his

DOI: 10.4324/9781003336754-7

time, Freud mixed some metaphorical and isomorphic analogies, as he had done in the past (*cf.* Paniagua, 1982), fusing figurative and literal concepts, especially in Chapter 5. Concerning *Das Ich*, Freud did not distinguish clearly between its meaning as agency with defensive attributes and the *self* as inner representation of the person's physique and personality (*cf.* Hartmann, 1950). Same was true of his ideas on the *superego* as related to categorical imperatives, morality, and the experience of *guilt versus* the *ego ideal* through which the person measures him/herself, also unconsciously, against his/her internalized self representations, more related to experiences of *shame*.

* * *

"The new terminology which [Freud] introduced had a highly clarifying effect and so made further clinical advances possible", we read in the "Editor's Introduction" (1923, p. 7). However, the "clarifying effect" implied in the concepts "id", "ego", and "superego" did not mean that the subsequent technical endeavor became easier just because it permitted the analyst to go beyond the exploration of the analysand's unconscious drive derivatives. Interpretations based on ego psychology or coined in structural terminology, *when not sufficiently addressed to the patient's preconscious availability*, end almost invariably used at the service of defense. It is well-known that patients can readily accept comprehensive-sounding interpretations, which provide intellectualizations that distract them from more complete, veracious, and painful meanings. Interpretive constructions that are not experience-near "may be convenient for [the patient's] resistance to make use of an assent . . . [that] prolongs the concealment of a truth that has not been discovered" (Freud, 1937a, p. 262). Unconsciously, analysands dread negative therapeutic reactions and cling to their "gain from illness" (Freud, 1923, p. 49). The analyst had to investigate in *close process* then what the patient feared could happen as a result of his/her repressed wishes and what strategies the mind resorted to in order to keep those under control (*cf.* Waelder, 1960). Moreover, all this is going to manifest itself in the transference of defense (A. Freud, 1936).

The problem remained thus in how the analyst should proceed to undo repression when he/she could not rely on the *repressive* constituents since these were also unconscious. How could the analyst reach a reasonable working alliance with the analysand's ego, the less irrational part of the mind, without resorting to ascendancy and suggestion? In 1920, Freud wrote that psychoanalysis, being "first and foremost an art of interpreting", had to add to this art "obliging the patient to confirm the analyst's construction from his own memory . . . inducing him by human influence to abandon his resistances". However, it became clearer to Freud that aiming simply at "what was unconscious should be conscious is not completely attainable by that method" (p. 18). Why? Because the defensive apparatus was also outside preconsciousness.

> Resistance during treatment arises from the same higher strata and systems of the mind which originally carried out the repression. . . . It is certain that much of the ego is itself unconscious. . . . Only a small part of it is covered by the term "preconscious".

The conclusion seemed then evident: a new technical approach should be developed to analyze defensive structures, starting with the "small preconscious part" (Freud, 1920, p. 19) in the clinical material manifest to both, analyst and analysand (*i.e.*, that "beacon-light in the darkness [afforded] by the word presentations [and] memory traces" [Freud, 1923, pp. 18–20] observable in the patient's free associations).

Example: An exhibitionistic patient told me of his habit to masturbate with the door open, risking that the maid saw him as she went up and down the corridor. I asked him to associate about what he expected from this lady's possible reaction to such situation. He answered that she would feel he was crazy, and he would then feel ashamed and guilty. I replied that despite the evident risk, he must have felt so intensely driven as to think that it was worth the risk. He said then that in addition to the excitement, somehow, he remembered his father beating him as a child and his dread that he wouldn't know when to stop, and as a result, he could end up actually killed, adding, "Imagine if my father had caught me doing something like this!" He recalled also masturbating in class beneath the desk as a young adolescent. Indulging in this behavior was not only a source of sexual pleasure; it represented also overcoming the threat of annihilation and a victory over his father. The memory came also to his mind of having been caught by his mother masturbating in his bedroom. She never reported it to his father, and he considered this shared secret a sign of his privileged connection with her (*i.e.*, an oedipal triumph).

These associations were totally his. Actually, I found them somewhat surprising. I think that these emotionally charged syntheses would not have manifested themselves in all their depth if *instead* of addressing manifest material and obvious reasoning, I opted for the use of content interpretations about the patient's fantasies or dynamics without sufficient respect for the readiness of his preconscious ego.

* * *

Structural psychoanalysis did not mean *only* the discovery of that which had been buried from awareness for its traumatic origins but also *how* the mind managed to maintain the effects of such material away from consciousness, thus directing our interest more towards a detailed exploration of the consequential personality traits, thence, opening the door to character analysis. Freud stated in the second section of *The Ego and the Id*, "Pathological research has directed our interest too exclusively to the repressed. We should like to learn more about the ego, now that we know that it, too, can be unconscious in the proper sense of the word" (p. 19). It is worth noting that even though Freud referred to the unconsciousness of resistances as a "new discovery" (1923, pp. 26–27), the notion of "unconscious defence [as] an attempt to repress an incompatible idea" comes from much earlier (1896, p. 162). We may wonder here, as Waelder (1967) did, to what extent was Freud aware that the "resistance against the uncovering of resistances" mentioned in his *Analysis Terminable and Interminable* (1937b, p. 239) applied also to some difficulties of his own. Gray (1982) thought that "Freud was in fact ambivalent about the trend of involving more of the patient's ego during the analysis" (p. 34). Pointedly, this author remarked, "Not long after Freud discovered that the part of the ego crucial to resistance was also unconscious, he ungraciously abandoned his colleagues to work out for themselves much of the methodology for making that unconscious ego conscious" (1992, p. 308).

It should be stressed that from 1923 on, the concept of "unconsciousness" applied not only to the works of the *ego* but also to those of the *superego*. "In our analyses we discover that there are people in whom the faculties of self-criticism and conscience – mental activities . . . that rank as extremely high ones – are unconscious and unconsciously produce effects of the greatest importance" (Freud, 1923, p. 26). And this happens to be so not just in pathological cases: "The normal man is not only far more immoral than he believes but also far more moral than he knows" (p. 52). In a well-known statement, Freud pointed out that, paradoxical as it may seem, "Not only what is lowest but also what is highest in the ego can be unconscious" (p. 27). Indeed, as most analysts can attest, "An unconscious sense of guilt [represents] in a great number of neuroses . . . the most powerful obstacle in the way of recovery" (Freud, 1923, p. 27). It is not at all unusual to come across patients who remember traumatic incidents in their childhood, whereas some anti-instinctual motivations like guilt reactions remain completely unconscious. Now I will provide an example from my own practice in which an unconscious superego compensation of intolerable feelings of imperfection and the subsequent redressing of hatred became evident:

A middle-aged patient could not derive appropriate satisfaction from her prodigal behavior. She experienced it as an unquestionable moral obligation even when, as it could be expected, she became victim of abuses. She felt that any disagreement with others, including the analyst, was invariably her fault. In treatment, she came to realize that she saw herself as naturally defective and indebted to others. She became progressively aware that ever since childhood, she felt she had to earn her parents' affection through great sacrifice and generosity, never taking for granted any measure of unconditional love from them. Analysis of her painful past and her transference reactions led to memories of her frightening dependence on her mother's moods and her guilt-provoking reactions. In the sessions, we were witnessing the consequences of the altruistic attitude she had to adopt in her formative years in order to survive psychologically in an atmosphere of poor parental care. Awareness of this in her treatment not only put her in contact with the dramas of her defenselessness and unrecognized bitterness but also filled her with feelings of shame. She had been unaware of this, as well as of the defensive nature of her indiscriminate generosity at the service of her ideal self that made her feel worthy.

This woman's masochistic lavishness represented an unconscious compromise formation between id elements (her huge need to be loved and the very strong resentment for her childhood deprivation), ego defenses (her characterological rationalizations), and her superego (her self-punitive attitude over any transgression of her unreasonable prodigality). Her protective maneuvers had kept at bay the overwhelming anxiety of her helplessness in childhood. She had been unaware of the infantile nature of her dramatic behavioral maladaptation. All elements in her peculiar behavior had been repressed or justified away. The components of this conflict and its pathological solution were *unconscious* in all three systems.

* * *

Grounded on the new structural tenets our discipline seemed more complete, reliable. and *scientific*. Let me remind here what Freud (1933) had to say in reference to this in his *New Introductory Lectures*: "I did not want to commend [psychoanalysis] as a method of treatment . . . But on account of the truths it contains, on account of the information it gives us about what concerns human beings most of all – their own nature" (p. 756–757). Indeed, the technical approaches resulting from the application of the new ego psychology seemed better suited for the research aspects of our discipline whenever its theoretical explanations corresponded reliably with the observational findings.

At present, we continue maintaining that the classical methodology is clearly indicated in the analysis of candidates and, for certain, recalcitrant character disorders in introspective patients (*cf.* Paniagua, 2021). However, I think that we ought to acknowledge that the thorough investigation of deep psychic configurations in conflict mentioned earlier usually is *not* the treatment of choice in our daily practices in a large number of cases that may benefit from "shortcuts" based on our special listening for subtexts and a sensible management of the patient's transference of authority (*cf.* Gullestad & Killingmo, 2020). Due to the nature of their psychopathology or their life circumstances, in many cases, dynamic focal *therapy* can be the most practical approach (*cf.* Dewald, 1973; Malan, 1979; Ursano & Hales, 1986; Stockton, 2005; Blackman, 2013). Let's not forget that, as Freud (1910) stated, some beneficial results can be obtained even in some "wild" treatments. We need to keep in mind that, although not optimal due to the incompleteness of their interpretations, briefer therapies, when based on our experience and benevolent ascendancy, are not devoid of effectiveness, a point already stressed by Glover (1955).

Example: A woman in her 70s was sent to me for treatment of her chronic furious behavior at home after she learned that her husband had an affair in the distant past. The domestic atmosphere was described as unbearable, and her children ended scolding her very roughly. This patient had not felt adequately loved or protected by a mother who clearly preferred her brothers. Also, her father had been distant, and she suspected that he could have been sexually involved with a cousin of hers.

Living in another province, the patient could come to sessions only once every couple of weeks. After two months of treatment, I decided to share with her my conjecture that her violent attacks on her husband were due not only to his erstwhile infidelity but also to her reliving feelings of abandonment and betrayal by her parents when she was a dependent child. Although I bypassed a detailed exploration of the conditioning consequences of her dystonic response to these early experiences, my interpretive synthesis, which had never crossed her mind, had a highly positive and lasting influence on her behavior at home.

* * *

The essential objective in the analytic study of pathological phenomena lays in the examination of their different elements in *dynamic* conflict. Since the simple categorization of these as "unconscious" did not suffice, a theory with interplaying structures needed to be formulated. In Freud's view:

> The ego [is] a poor creature owing service to three masters: the external world . . . the libido of the id, and . . . the severity of the superego. . . . The ego defends itself . . . against the instigations of the murderous id and against the reproaches of the punishing conscience.
> (1923, pp. 53–56)

How could a conceptualization like this fail to change analytic technique? This acknowledgement permitted a more effective exploration of how these psychological forces ended being articulated in particular characterological ways. The resulting understanding of conflict in the *structural* approach made possible the sequential analysis of compromise formations between elementary primitive wishes and needs, the superego injunctions, and the adaptation to external realities through the mediation of the ego agency.

This well-known evolution of concepts, however, was slow, as first indicated in the "Editor's Introduction" to *The Ego and the Id*. Moreover, it seems unfinished even today in a substantial part of the psychoanalytic literature. In his work, Freud posed the question of how the practitioner should proceed to explore the repressing forces, thus inaugurating ego psychology and its implicit techniques. According to him, this should be done "supplying *Pcs.* intermediate links through the work of analysis", adding that "the relation . . . of *internal* perceptions to the ego requires special investigation" (1923, p. 21). This "investigation" gets facilitated through the use of what Bibring (1954) described as "clarifications" (*i.e.*, interventions

in rational alliance with the analysand's preconscious ego aimed at further-
ing comprehension of manifestations on the surface material).

In a paper considered classical, Strachey (1934) summarized these developments so: "The practical lesson emerged: as analysts our main task
is not so much to investigate the objectionable unconscious trend as to get
rid of the patient's resistance to it" (p. 276). Although generally, one can
agree with Strachey's statement, nowadays, we would object to his idea
of "getting rid" of resistances, preferring Busch's (1999) better conceived
advice of defining our work as centered on "factors that can be brought
to the patient's awareness in a manner usable by the ego" (p. 191), contemplating "the patient's associations as a text to be read rather than un-
raveled" (p. 89). This is assumed to foster the analysand's self-observing
capacities in a gradual identification *not* with the analyst but with his/
her analytic function, an achievement seemingly distinctive of successful
treatments (Schlessinger & Robbins, 1983; Weber et al., 1985; Kantrowitz
et al., 1986; Falkenstrom et al., 2007). The technical point here, of course, is
how to proceed in the endeavor of clearing the patient's *own* way for a reliable acquaintance of the mechanisms through which he/she has managed
with more or less success to keep repressed wishes at bay for all his/her
conscious life. It seems pertinent to remember here Apfelbaum and Gill's
(1989) astute observation that "when Freud introduced ego analysis, it did
not constitute a more sophisticated preliminary to id analysis, but in fact
offered a new approach to id content" (p. 1073). I think one needs to remark
next that, seemingly, Freud failed to emphasize that the type of defense
analysis made possible with the application of his structural approach
could result in an *unprecedented access to particularized id manifestations not
achievable with the primitive technique* (*cf.* Paniagua, 2008).

Now, considering the previous examples, relevant questions could be
the following: Why a more complete understanding of drive derivatives,
superego demands, and the ego's attempt at reaching adaptive compromise formations between these and external reality did not displace previous theoretical approaches as expediently as could have been expected?
Why the original technique significantly based on the patient's irrational
need to honor the analyst's interpretations under the unconscious threat
of loss of love was not discarded (*cf.* Friedman, 1969)? What hindered the
necessary "change in the focus of attention" (A. Freud, 1936, p. 20) for the
analyst to grasp, in alliance with the analysand's own mentation, the unconscious workings of the ego? Why Kris's (1951) wise maxim "The interpretation concerns the warding off device, the reaction reveals the impulse
warded off" (p. 21) seemed difficult to digest in practice, when it did open
a Pandora's box of more veracious and often surprising findings (*cf.* Paniagua, 2006)? In his 1912 *Recommendations*, Freud requested his colleagues "to
be taken by surprise by any new turn . . . with an open mind free from any
presuppositions" (p. 114). How come the old topographic model continued
to prevail in technical applications? Contemporary ego psychology seems

to have contributed soundly to an understanding of the reasons why the consequences of the previous "advances" were not carried out more diligently and effectively in clinical practice (*cf.* Gray, 1973, 1982; Busch, 1995, 1999).

Waelder (1967) said, "One cannot securely repress an idea and yet be aware of having repressed it" (p. 354). Why didn't this elementary reasoning seem evident from the very beginning of psychoanalytic exploration? There seems to exist a universal resistance to assimilate certain concepts derived from the new conclusions concerning the role of the unconscious ego in the repressing mechanisms. In Hartmann's (1951) opinion, "The lag [was] on the side of technique [rather] than on the side of . . . psychological insight" (p. 143). Gray (1982) offered some explanations to account for this "developmental lag" (p. 30), adding that he found puzzling the general resistance to apply such conclusions to psychoanalytic technique, other than the natural difficulty in dealing with unaccustomed material mentioned by Freud (1933, p. 58). In Gray's (1982) view, this reluctance could be understood as consequence of our "fascination with the id; [our] predilection for an authoritative stance; [the] preoccupation with . . . the past as external reality; and [the] counterresistance to transference affects and impulses" (p. 48). Certainly, this contributes to explain the inveterate use by some practitioners of authoritative approaches to interpretive technique, contrary to the effectiveness of an examination based on the analysand's unbypassed ego functions. However, I think that not enough emphasis has been made on the narcissistic gratification analysts can experience through the display of their supposed acumen, the dismissal of our relative ignorance (*contra* Bion's essential "negative capability", 1985), the cathartic expression of countertransferential associations, and our intersubjective response to projections as though these were reliable elements on which to center interpretations (*cf.* Paniagua, 2001).

References

Apfelbaum, B. & Gill, M. M. (1989). Ego analysis and the relativity of defense: Technical implications of the structural theory. *J. Am. Psychoanal. Assn.*, 37: 1071–1096.

Bibring, E. (1954). Psychoanalysis and the dynamic psychotherapies. *J. Am. Psychoanal. Assn.*, 2: 745–770.

Bion, W. R. (1985). *All My Sins Remembered*. London: Karnac.

Blackman, J. S. (2013). *The Therapist's Answer Book*. New York: Routledge.

Busch, F. (1995). *The Ego at the Center of Clinical Technique*. Northvale, NJ: J. Aronson.

———. (1999). *Rethinking Clinical Technique*. Northvale, NJ: J. Aronson.

Dewald, P. A. (1973). *Psychotherapy: A Dynamic Approach*. Oxford: Blackwell Scientific Pubs.

Falkenstrom, F. et al. (2007). Self-analysis and post-termination improvement after psychoanalysis and long-term psychotherapy. *J. Amer. Psychoanal. Assn.*, 55: 629–674.

Freud, A. (1936). *The Ego and the Mechanisms of Defense*. New York: International Universities Press.

Freud, S. (1896). Further remarks on the neuropsychoses of defense. *S.E.*, 3.

———. (1910). "Wild" psycho-analysis. *S.E.*, 11.

———. (1920). Beyond the pleasure principle. *S.E.*, 18.

———. (1923). The ego and the id. *S.E.*, 19.

———. (1933). New introductory lectures on psychoanalysis. *S.E.*, 22.

———. (1937a). Constructions in analysis. *S.E.*, 23.

———. (1937b). Analysis terminable and interminable. *S.E.*, 23.

Friedman, L. (1969). The therapeutic alliance. *Int. J. Psychoanal.*, 50: 139–153.

Glover, E. (1955). *The Technique of Psycho-Analysis*. Madison, CT: International Universities Press.

Gray, P. (1973). Psychoanalytic technique and the ego's capacity for viewing intrapsychic activity. *J. Am. Psychoanal. Assn.*, 21: 474–494.

———. (1982/1994). "Developmental lag" in the evolution of technique for psychoanalysis of neurotic conflict. In *The Ego and Analysis of Defense*. Northvale, NJ, pp. 29–61.

———. (1992). Memory as resistance, and the telling of a dream. *J. Amer. Psychoanal. Assn.*, 40: 307–326.

Gullestad, S. E. & Killingmo, B. (2020). *The Theory and Practice of Psychoanalytic Therapy*. London: Routledge.

Hartmann, H. (1950/1964). Comments on the psychoanalytic theory of the ego. In *Essays on Ego Psychology*. New York: International Universities Press, pp. 113–141.

———. (1951/1964). Technical implications of ego psychology. In *Essays on Ego Psychology*. New York: International Universities Press, pp. 142–154.

Kantrowitz, J. L., Paolitto, F., Sashin, J. et al. (1986). Affect availability, tolerance, complexity, and modulation in psychoanalysis: Follow-up of a longitudinal prospective study. *J. Amer. Psychoanal. Assn.*, 34: 529–559.

Kris, E. (1951). Ego psychology and interpretation in psychoanalytic therapy. *Psychoanal. Q.*, 20: 15–30.

Malan, D. H. (1979). *Individual Psychotherapy and the Science of Psychodynamics*. Woben, MA: Butterworths.

Paniagua, C. (1982). Metaphors and isomorphisms: Analogical reasoning in "Beyond the pleasure principle". *J. Amer. Psychoanal. Assn.*, 30: 509–523.

———. (2001). The attraction of the topographical model. *Int. J. Psychoanal.*, 82: 671–684.

———. (2006). Técnica interpretativa y la sorpresa del analista. *Revista de Psicoanálisis*, 63: 163–178.

———. (2008). Id analysis and technical approaches. *Psychoanal. Q.*, 77: 219–250.

———. (2021). In F. Busch (ed.), *Dear Candidate*. New York: Routledge, pp. 84–87.

Schlessinger, N. & Robbins, F. P. (1983). *A Developmental View of the Psychoanalytic Process, Follow-Up Studies and Their Consequences*. New York: International Universities Press.

Searl, N. (1936). Some queries on principles of technique. *Int. J. Psychoanal.*, 17: 471–493.

Sterba, R. (1953). Clinical and therapeutic aspects of character resistance. *Psychoanal. Q.*, 22: 1–20.

Stockton, W. J. (2005). *Now It All Makes Sense*. Charlottesvile, VA: Free Will Pub.

Strachey, J. (1934). The nature of the therapeutic action of psychoanalysis. *Int. J. Psychoanal.*, 50: 275–292.

Ursano, R. J. & Hales, R. E. (1986). A review of brief individual psychotherapies. *Am. J. Psychiatry*, 143(12): 1507–1517.

Waelder, R. (1960). *Basic Theory of Psychoanalysis*. New York: International Universities Press.

———. (1967). Inhibitions, symptoms and anxiety: Forty years later. In S. A. Guttman (ed.), *Psychoanalysis, Observation, Theory, Application*. New York: International Universities Press, pp. 338–360.

Weber, J. J., Bachrach, H. M. & Solomon, M. (1985). Factors associated with the outcome of psychoanalysis: Report of the Columbia Research Project. *Int. Rev. Psychoanal.*, 12: 127–141.

8 The fate of the ego in *The Ego and the Id*

Fred Busch

In *The Ego and the Id*, Freud's monumental work, he presents a totally revised metapsychological framework, based primarily on *clinical* findings. It is a demonstration of his psychoanalytic acumen and his uncompromising honesty with himself and towards the theory he founded. However, it is my impression that some of his most important findings were never accepted, even by those who claimed allegiance to Freud.

Foundational to Freud's new theory was his proffering the ego as a structure and the discovering of unconscious resistances emanating from the unconscious ego. While Freud considered the *analysis of the unconscious ego's resistances as the cornerstone of a psychoanalytic cure*, our understanding of the concept remains somewhat confused, now 100 years later. One hears it referred to far too rarely in clinical discussions, while published papers dealing with the topic most often fluctuate between its pre- and post-structural meanings and the technical implications inherent in these positions. As Schafer (1983) stated, "Certain things about resisting which ought to be well known and are said to be well known and sufficiently appreciated and applied, are in fact not known well enough and not consistently attended to in practice" (p. 66). Gray (1982) charitably calls this muddled understanding of one of Freud's basic concepts a "developmental lag", while reminding us that our understanding of theory informs our clinical stance. Paniagua (2001) described what he called the attraction of topographic technique, pointing out that while most analysts are aware of the changes in Freud's theory, they still return to thinking topographically in their clinical approach. Thus, it is a curious thing that one of the major changes Freud made to his model of the mind, based upon a clinical fact, which had immediate clinical consequences, was and continues to be ignored by the majority of the psychoanalytic world. *Freud's clinical insight hasn't been proven wrong or dismissed for lack of clinical evidence; it is simply treated as if it never existed.*

The reasoning behind the importance of analyzing resistances is straightforward. If we still believe the centrality of building preconscious representations of what was unconsciously motivating patients to self-destructive behavior as the cornerstone of a psychoanalytic cure and if

DOI: 10.4324/9781003336754-8

we still believe there are unconscious resistances against these unconscious motivations from becoming preconscious, then it seems clear that
analyzing unconscious resistances are a necessary part of any analysis.
It is important to remember these unconscious resistances are based on
greatest fears one can imagine, and sometimes, we cannot even imagine
them.

But what does it mean to analyze an unconscious resistance? First, it is
necessary to identify it and help the patient to see them. It is not so easy for
the analyst to identify them, as they usually appear as part of the *process*
rather than the *content* (Busch, 2013). The process is the music that accom-
panies the words. For example, there are innumerable ways for a patient
to tell and associate to a dream (e.g., I'm telling you this dream, but I don't
believe dreams have meaning; The patient always views external events
as the cause of the dream; You think you're so smart, so let's see if you
can figure this out, etc.). These are not conscious thoughts, as the patient
thinks he is doing what a patient is supposed to do in analysis (i.e., bring
in dreams). There are other more obvious resistances like when a patient
is talking about something in an emotional way, and suddenly, there is a
change in her voice to a more stilted way of talking or when the patient
falls silent.[1]

A history of unconscious resistances

Freud (1895) recognized the existence of resistances very early on and returned to the subject many times (1914, 1915–1916, 1923, 1933, 1926, 1937a,
1937b, 1940). The significant difference between his first and second model
of the mind was that in *The Ego and the Id*, the clinical technique for analyzing resistance was now based on the view that "the ego is indeed the
locus of anxiety itself" (1923, p. 57). "The earlier conception was not far
from considering the libido of the repressed impulse motion as the source
of anxiety; according to the new conception, it was instead the ego that
was to bear the brunt of this anxiety" (Freud, 1926). Based upon this new
model, analyzing the *causes* of the ego's anxiety would lead to the unconscious factors playing a role in the patient's symptoms. In contrast, his
first theory led to *interpretation of deep unconscious conflicts* as a way of free-
ing the libido that supposedly was dammed, leading to anxiety. *Yet till the
end of his life, Freud remained ambivalent towards applying his second theory of
resistance analysis* (Busch, 1992). Paniagua (2001) pointed out that even in
Freud's last work, he was still making statements such as "the ego struggles against our instigation, while the unconscious, which is ordinarily
our opponent, comes to our help" (1940, p. 179), seemingly forgetting that
that ego, which "struggles against our instigation", is also unconscious
(Paniagua, 2001, p. 61).

It is striking how some of the most prominent theorists in Europe after
Freud (Bion, Klein, Winnicott) almost never quote *The Ego and the Id*, and,

therefore, do not see resistance analysis as a consistent part of technique. Klein (1932) seemed to hold on to Freud's first theory, when she states:

> An interpretation which does not descend to those depths which are being activated by the material and the anxiety concerned, which does not, that is, *attack the place where the strongest latent resistance* is and endeavour in the first place to reduce anxiety where it is most violent and most in evidence, will have no effect whatever on the child, or will only serve to arouse stronger resistances in it without being able to resolve them again.
>
> (p. 52, italics added)

Klein, Bion, and Winnicott seemed to stay close to Strachey's (1934) ambivalently[2] held idea of the analyst as a benign superego to *overcome* resistances. Even then, he saw resistances as needing to be destroyed rather than analyzed, as seen in his statement, "But how are we to set about this task of *demolishing* the resistance?" (ibid., p. 130, italics added).

Even those early European analysts who grasped the importance of analyzing unconscious resistances showed some fundamental misunderstanding. For example, in the first part of his book on *Character Analysis*, Wilhelm Reich (1933) gives some excellent examples of how to analyze unconscious ego resistances. However, Reich is not consistent in applying this perspective and later in the same book reverts to militaristic metaphors to show how the resistances need to be broken through, as if they were based on motiveless stubbornness.

In Anna Freud's (1936) earliest work on ego psychology, while championing the investigation of the ego as a necessary component of a psychoanalytic investigation and pointing the way to the study of unconscious defenses, does surprisingly show some ambivalence about the necessity of investigating ego resistances. She describes "abolishing" and "destroying" the ego resistances as a way station to analyzing the id. It is a view of the resistances as something to be attacked in order to get to the real work of id analysis.

After 1936, sporadic articles would appear on resistances, with the same ambivalence towards Freud's structural theory, until the 1950s when Loewenstein (1952, 1953, 1966) started writing about the clinical application of working with the ego in analysis. There is much to be praised in his writings, but there was a subtle modification in what was to be analyzed in working with resistances that led away from analyzing the feelings that led the unconscious ego to establish resistances. That is, he viewed resistances as against the instincts, rather than the feelings of threat or danger generated in the unconscious ego. This resulted in the analyst, once again, trying to bring forth the instinctual derivatives, rather than the feelings of danger the unconscious ego was responding to. This was then evident in Greenson's (1967) voluminous work on analyzing resistances.

What Fenichel wrote in 1951 is also indicative of the situation in American psychoanalysis over the next four decades:

> The development of what is called 'analytical ego psychology' was fostered by the recognition that the analysis of resistance should be considered the effective therapeutic agent. It was also found that this analysis is conditioned above all by the complete study of the chronic attitudes of resistance anchored in the character of any individual. Again, the number of works relating to this newly acquired psychological knowledge is incomparably greater than the number of articles in which the authors seek to make use of this new data for the advancement of the analytical technique.
>
> (1951, p. 106)

Although I've come to disagree with him on numerous points,[3] the renaissance of interest in resistance analysis started with the work of Paul Gray (1973, 1982, 1986, 1987, 1990), who, like Freud, placed resistance analysis at the center of the psychoanalytic process, with the unconscious threat to the ego as the crucial component. In his view, the work of analysis involves identifying the resistance and analyzing the threat for the purpose of allowing thoughts greater access to consciousness. He developed a method for analyzing unconscious resistances. However, it may not have been sufficiently emphasized that understanding resistances might take a slightly different type of listening on the analyst's part. In most case reports, one hears the analyst listening to the *content* of the associations for the derivatives of the unconscious fantasies (see footnote 3). Listening for the resistances sometimes requires greater attention to the *process* of associations or the music accompanying the words (as noted previously). Thus, the heart of Gray's clinical technique revolves around listening for the moment in the psychoanalytic process when a resistance is in operation. He calls these moments "breaking points" (1990), where there is a change in voice. "It may be a blatant, dramatic, a sudden difference from what occupies the moment before; or it may be an exceedingly subtle alternative" (p. 1087). A typical example of this type of resistance is a patient who was complaining about her roommate and, after a brief pause, says, "Well, she really is a nice person". A Gray-like intervention would be "I noticed that after you complained about your roommate, you seemed to need to undo these feelings by saying she's a really nice person.[4] It seems to me like expressing your complaints made you feel uncomfortable".[5] The analyst then waits to see if the patient's association sheds light on the discomfort or whether she still needs to ward off the feelings of annoyance with her roommate.

At other times, one can hear the resistance in an analysand's "consistency of voice". Take, for example, the patient who rushes from topic to topic or the analysand who keeps spaces between topics so they do not touch. At these times, the analyst may listen primarily for the meaning of *how* the analysand is associating, rather than to the meaning of the associations themselves. The associations may be in the action of associating. For example, a patient comes rushing into the office and starts talking even before she gets on the couch. She continues to talk in a rushed tone, leaving little space for the analyst to say something. After this goes on for a while, I say, "It's my impression that today, from the moment you came into the office, you're not leaving any space for me to think or talk". Her response was "I hate your voice". She then went on to say that when I speak, it reminds her of the sexual fantasies she's had about us, which she was afraid to talk about, fearing/wishing that I would get excited and force her to have sex with me.

For various reasons, Gray's perspective eventually lost favor in the United States, where his perspective had gained many followers. One factor was the narrowness of his view. He seemed to believe that one only had to practice resistance analysis, rather than helping the patient represent unconscious fantasies and conflicts. He also didn't believe in the analyst using his countertransference to understand the patient when appropriate. He also tended to downplay the necessity of being supportive with patients at specific times or the effect of the analyst's way of being on the treatment.

While discovering Gray's method of analyzing resistance helped me understand clinical technique in a new way, ultimately, I found it necessary to expand my approach. Based upon my understanding of the ego, I've elaborated on the role of the preconscious, the importance of building representations,[6] understanding the child's way of thinking (i.e., language action), the use of clarification, working *within* the transference and countertransference, and so on (Busch, 2009, 2013, 2015, 2022).

Clinical vignette

My thoughts about the clinical material will be in italics.

The patient is a 60-year-old man, who is in management at a large, multinational corporation. He felt stuck in his inability to rise any higher in the corporate world. He's in a second marriage of twenty years. I've worked with him, four times per week, for approximately two years. He had a long analysis in his late 1940s, which seemed to be helpful with his anxiety and depression at that time. The impression he gave of this analysis was that it was supportive, and he felt the analyst steered him into doing things he later wasn't so sure of (e.g., divorcing his first wife).[7]

He came to see me after hearing that his previous analyst was in declining health. The vignette I will talk about includes what I believed was stimulated by an unconscious fantasy leading to a conflict he was dealing with in and outside of the treatment. He wished to be close to a man who would guide him, direct him, and make him into a "real man". Due to some inappropriate nudity on the part of his mother, and some intrusive behavior, his desires often became sexualized. Thus, as soon as he started to feel close to me, an unconscious fantasy of being raped by me developed, leading to starting an argument or becoming more distant.

PAT: I had a dream last night. There was this guy who was walking in front of me, and I wanted to talk to him, and it looked like he didn't want to talk to me. So I think, obviously, this guy was you, and I was the other guy. I think this probably goes back to my mother and father, both of whom I felt were angry with me. (Pause.)

FB: As we've talked about before, it's my impression that in dealing with the dream, you sometimes come up with answers rather than seeing what you may find, as if letting your mind.
          Here, I'm attempting to bring an enacted unconscious transference resistance to awareness while also using an analyst-centered (Steiner, 1994) clarification (Bibring, 1954;Busch, 2013,2015).

Patient: I know we talked about this before, but this is what's coming to mind.

FB: I appreciate that, and now it seems important why that way of thinking about the dream came to mind rather than another.

Patient: (Brief pause and then he talked about how the previous evening, he sent his sister an email suggesting that if she wanted to see a therapist, he would pay for it.)
          I remembered that he offered this to his sister numerous times, along with other money, and this usually angered her.

FB: It was my impression that when you offered this in the past, it often made her angry. (He agrees.) Making someone angry comes up as a thought in response to why you may be interpreting dreams in the way you do.

Patient: (He first talked about the rational reasons he offered help to his sister – i.e., she's not eating, previous anorexia, and several others. Then he said that when he previously talked about his sister and her problems and he thought about suggesting therapy and he decided against it, he remembered me asking, "WHY?" He thought I was suggesting that he should have offered it.)
          I had no memory of asking this question and tend not to ask "why" questions (Busch, 2013). I wondered to myself if this was one of those times he needed to see me as pushing something on or into him.

Patient: I remember when I was about 13 or 14, and I had this great counselor who played soccer in college. He was really cool. He was also the soccer coach. There was this one game where we played against another, much bigger camp. I was amazing. And we beat them. I have always had the thought that Harvey that caused me to be so amazing. He did something, like he gave me a special incentive or told the other players to give him the ball but doesn't remember.
          I then remembered a story he told me earlier when he became a star soccer scorer in high school. He thought his father had done something, like

talked to the other coaches or referees to make it happen. Yet he remained angry and demeaning towards his father through most of his life.

Patient: The previous day, I was thinking it would be nice to take a walk with Molly (his wife) and imagined some things we could talk about. It was a pleasant thought. A little bit later, she came into my study and suggested they take a walk, and I got pissed. I felt she was taking over (said with a lot of anger).

This is a constant theme in the marriage.

FB: If we follow your thoughts, it seems like a part of you longs for someone to guide, support, and ease the way for you. Yet when that happens now, it makes you angry and you feel intruded upon.

Patient: When I was in analysis with Jack, I thought he was suggesting I do certain things, like getting married and having children or going to the institute. I went along with it, but after, felt I was being too passive. That's why I could never go back to him.

Over time, we could understand how the early overstimulation with his mother's nudity became confused with his longing for someone to take over and direct his life, leading to an unconscious homosexual fantasy of being raped and the attendant anxiety it aroused. This led to a constant longing to be taken over and the resultant anger of what was being done to him.

Final thoughts

How do we understand most analyst antipathy towards incorporating Freud's views on the unconscious ego into their clinical technique? Kuhn (1970) noted the difficulty of accepting paradigm changes, and this may explain the reluctance in accepting Freud's second topique by the generation of analysts writing at the time Freud published his paper. They believed Freud's topographic model served them well. Further, Freud's ambivalence in using his own model must have caused confusion in what it meant to follow Freud's ideas.

The beginning explorations of the dimensions of the ego by Hartmann, Rapaport, and others were not clinical in nature but instead turned towards the development of the ego, its autonomous functioning, and especially developmental tasks in conjunction with the environment and their effect on the ego. This line germinated a rich harvest of data, which ultimately have enriched our clinical work. However, the more strictly clinical investigations into the work of the ego, especially the unconscious ego suffered from benign neglect. The result was that the knowledge of the resistances stagnated.

Then there is the issue of tribal politics that play a greater role in the formation of an analytic identity than we give credit to. If there is a strong adherence to a particular theoretical perspective in an institute, it serves the young analyst best in her professional advancement to follow this perspective. As I mentioned previously (Busch, 2015), it is my impression that for too long, each "school" has tended to guard the purity and effectiveness of its own position. For practical and transferential reasons, we find it difficult to leave our home base, and to try to do so is sometimes interpreted as an attack. This would require what Bolognini (2011) suggested that we have to come out of our own "shadow zone", where we hold on to excessive simplification of the theoretical field. "The symptom of this shadow zone is precisely the incapacity for an interchange with the 'non-self,' which is unconsciously feared as dangerous and too disturbing" (Bolognini, 2011, p. 11).[8]

Notes

1 I've demonstrated how many analysts treat silence as an epiphenomenon, rather than an indication that something important has happened in the patient's mind that has led her to stop talking.
2 Sometimes Strachey seems to indicate that this has limited effect and, at other times, presents it as the main factor in making the unconscious conscious.
3 I differed with Gray on a basic point. I've focused on the danger that leads to the resistance, while Gray focused on the unconscious content that led to the fear. It's my belief that the analyst needs to analyze these frightening dangers to the ego, which then makes analysis of the unconscious fantasies, conflicts, and so on possible because the fears are not so fearful. I have other differences elaborated later.
4 We often think the patient is aware of this switch, but most frequently, this is not the case and why it is important to bring this shift to the patient's attention as a first step in analyzing a resistance.
5 I am using here a variation of Steiner's (1994) analyst-centered approach, which I've described elsewhere (Busch, 2013).
6 Reading the work of French analysts (e.g., Aisenstein, Donnet, Green, Marty) helped me in this regard.
7 At least partially, this seemed based on an unconscious fantasy explained later. In our work, he often interpreted something I said as encouraging him to act in a particular way, although it was far from my intention.
8 In a forthcoming publication, Homayounpour (In Press) pointed out an important oddity in *The Ego and the Id*. While Freud devoted a major section of the article proposing a new formulation of the unconscious superego, it isn't mentioned in the title or in the drawing where he depicts this new model of the mind.

References

Bibring, E. (1954). Psychoanalysis and the dynamic psychotherapies. *Journal of the American Psychoanalytic Association*, 2: 745–770.
Bolognini, S. (2011). *Secret Passages*. London: Routledge.
Busch, F. (1992). Recurring thoughts on unconscious ego resistances. *Journal of the American Psychoanalytic Association*, 40: 1089–1115.
———. (2009) "Can you push a camel through the eye of a needle?" Reflections on how the unconscious speaks to us and its clinical implications. *International Journal of Psychoanalysis*, 90: 53–68.

———. (2013). *Creating a Psychoanalytic Mind: A Psychoanalytic Method and Theory.* London: Routledge.

———. (2015). Our vital profession. *International Journal of Psychoanalysis*, 96: 553–568.

———. (2022). *A Fresh Look at Psychoanalytic Technique.* London: Routledge.

Fenichel, O. (1951). *Problems of Psychoanalytic Technique.* New York: Psychoanalytic Quarterly.

Freud, A. (1936/1966). *The Ego and the Mechanisms of Defense.* New York: International Universities Press.

Freud, S. (1895). Studies in hysteria. *S.E.*, 2.

———. (1914). Remembering, repeating, and working through. *S.E.*, 12.

———. (1915–1916). Introductory lectures on psychoanalysis. *S.E.*, 15 & 16.

———. (1923). The ego and the id. *S.E.*, 19.

———. (1926). Inhibitions, symptoms and anxiety. *S.E.*, 20.

———. (1933). The dissection of the psychical personality. *S.E.*, 22: 57–80.

———. (1937a). Analysis terminable and interminable. *S.E.*, 23.

———. (1937b). Constructions in analysis. *S.E.*, 23.

———. (1940). An outline of psychoanalysis. *S.E.*, 2.

Gray, P. (1973). Psychoanalytic technique and the ego's capacity for viewing intrapsychic activity. *J. Am. Psychoanal. Assoc.*, 21: 474–494.

———. (1982). "Developmental lag" in the evolution of technique for psychoanalysis of neurotic conflict. *J. Am. Psychoanal. Assoc.*, 30: 621–655.

———. (1986). On helping analysands observe intrapsychic activity In A. D. Richards & M. S. Willick (eds.), *Psychoanalysis: The Science of Mental Conflict: Essays in Honor of Charles Brenner.* Hillsdale, NJ: Analytic Press.

———. (1987). On the technique of analysis of the superego: An introduction. *Psychoanal. Q.*, 56: 130–154.

———. (1990). The nature of therapeutic action in psychoanalysis. *J. Am. Psychoanal. Assoc.*, 38: 1083–1098.

Greenson, R. R. (1967). *The Technique and Practice of Psychoanalysis*, 1. New York: International Universities Press.

Homayounpour, G. (In Press). The ego and id and . . . the *superego*. In F. Busch & N. Delgado (eds.), *The Ego and Id: 100 Years Later.* London: Routledge.

Klein, M. (1932). *The Psycho-Analysis of Children.* Int. Psycho-Anal. London: The Hogarth Press.

Kuhn, T. S. (1970). *The Structure of Scientific Revolutions.* Chicago: University of Chicago Press.

Loewenstein, R. (1952). Some remarks on the role of speech in psychoanalysis. In *Practice and Precept in Psychoanalytic Technique: Selected Papers of R. M. Loewenstein.* New Haven, CT: Yale University Press, pp. 52–57.

———. (1953). Some remarks on defense, autonomous ego, and psychoanalytic technique. In *Practice and Precept in Psychoanalytic Technique: Selected Papers of R. M. Loewenstein.* New Haven, CT: Yale University Press, pp. 40–51.

———. (1966). Defense organization and autonomous ego functions. In *Practice and Precept in Psychoanalytic Technique: Selected Papers of R. M. Loewenstein.* New Haven, CT: Yale University Press, pp. 40–51.

Paniagua, C. (2001). The attraction of topographical technique. *Int. J. Psycho-Anal.*, 82(4): 671–684.

Reich, W. (1933/1949). *Character Analysis.* New York: Farrar, Straus & Cudahy.

Schafer, R. (1983). *The Analytic Attitude*. New York: Basic Books.

Steiner, J. (1994). Patient-centered and analyst-centered interpretations: Some implications of containment and countertransference. *Psychoanalytic Inquiry*, 14: 406–422.

Strachey, J. (1934). The nature of the therapeutic action of psycho-analysis. *International Journal of Psychoanalysis*, 15: 127–159.

9 Modern ego psychology

The new ego

Eric R. Marcus

Freud's 1923 paper, *The Ego and the Id*, changed everything. I will discuss the profound changes in psychoanalytic theory that unfolded. I will discuss its implications for concepts of ego, self, structure, processes, affect, representation, adaptation, psychic reality, and technique. I will then comment on the perhaps-future development of ego theory.

Freud's 1923 paper changed the meaning of the word ego from self to a group of processes. He thereby broadened his descriptive theory of mind from a theory about emotional content to a descriptive theory of how the mind works. He began to describe the mind at work.

He began to understand that the mind at work requires not just an understanding of the content of motivation but also how meaning is constructed. This idea led him inevitably to the concept of structure. The emotional life has not only stable contents but also stable organizations and relationships. How the mind of the individual constructs and organizes meaning is part of the experience and structure of meaning. Once the idea of structure emerged, as a developmental aspect of psychic reality, relatively fixed but also plastic, one could consider the ongoing developmental and adaptational relationship between emotional experience and reality experience.

Freud (1915) had already described two processes of mental organization, the primary process organization of emotional information and the secondary process of cognitive information; the secondary process based on logic and the primary process based on affect. His 1923 shift to focus on the ego's processes allowed a more careful focus on how the two organize the experience of meaning. In attributing these processes to a separate agency, the ego, he gave these processes a place in his mental topography that was unconscious, preconscious, and conscious. It was why topography, the unconscious, was not sufficient for a theory of mind. Now all levels of topography played a role in meaning as did the new agencies.

The ego now became an organizer of experience: emotional experience, cognitive and reality experience, conscience experience, relationship experience, and object relations experience. Freud described the ego as beholden to the three agency and reality masters. As a result, the ego was both the

DOI: 10.4324/9781003336754-9

seat of anxiety and the organizer of compromise of the conflicts. The ego is now both the seat of anxiety and the mastery organ of anxiety.

One could also look more specifically and carefully at the processes that do the organizing. Thus was Hartmann (1958) inspired. He described the ego's processes. These processes organize reality experience and the mind's adaptation to it. We now have a complex, open system, a structured mental organization of contents and processes both consistent and plastic at the same time. This structure opens both to unconscious emotional experience and to the external world in reality. Ego processes synthesize the two together in a psychic reality of meaning experiences.

Meaning is the emotional meaning. Motivation and meaning were now more complex than just drive motivation meaning. Modern ego theory understands that meanings are not just drive produced but produced in relationship to all the agencies. It isn't only the id that provides motivation. The superego does also. The ego does also. Conflicts and their combinations do also. Motivation is also driven by reality and the adaptation produced. Adaptation is not only to emotional conflict, id, ego defenses, and superego but also to the real world.

We now have more than drive discharge. We have meaning satisfaction, meaning as a motivator. Meaning satisfaction is a strong motivator. Meaning satisfaction is the concept of emotional and cognitive adaptation to reality exigencies that permit emotional meaning satisfaction. The satisfaction is to be had in the alterations of reality experiences, in the emotional adaptation to reality, and in the growth and development of changes in yearnings. Their relationship appears in a compromise in psychic reality.

Because the ego became so complex, psychoanalytic theory also became more complex, as it now looked at not only neurosis in the emotional life but also the secondary process, cognition, and other autonomous ego functions. Freud, thereby, took a gigantic step towards making of psychoanalysis a general psychology, one of his great hopes. This also allowed the application of psychoanalytic work to widened spectrum cases (Stone, 1954) of patients with psychiatric illnesses.

These ideas about what was going on in the mind changed the focus of psychoanalytic work from drive conflict and conflicts of drive with reality to conflicts within the mind. Now it wasn't just about drive conflict. It wasn't just about conflict between drive and reality. It became conflict between the organized mental agencies and their structures. The affect dynamic meanings of psychodynamics were now illustrative of the agency conflicts and their compromises.

The compromise is a meaningful adaptation. This is why modern ego theory looks not just at the conflict but also at the compromise. Compromise is not just a vector sum. It is a synthesis. Compromise is now the ego's job. The ego accomplishes this through certain synthetic processing capacities left to later writers to explicate: Arieti (1976), Blank and Blank (1986), Hartmann (1958), Marcus (1999), Schafer (1968), Shill (2022), and

Winnicott (1971). After 1923, Freud's daughter Anna (1956) was then able to describe the defensive functions in the preconscious. Defensive functions, because they opposed drive, could not be explained by the unconscious drives alone. The concept of the ego described an agency function to which the defensive functions seem naturally to belong. She described defense functioning in the preconscious, which is clearly within the ego's purview.

This broadened the view of the preconscious function from its role in latent dream thoughts and from its function in making the unconscious conscious to its role in personality function. The idea of processes allowed her to describe defensive processes that were more than just repression or projection. This allowed for a more detailed characterology because the defenses were not just resistances but rather, ego styles of resistance that are characteristic of the personality. Later, ego psychologists would describe these personality defenses as attitudes (Fenichel, 1954) or styles (Shapiro, 1965). This broadens the concept of personality from a derivative of the sexual drive and its different libidinal phases to general character attitudes, which organize adaptation and its experience and which influence behavior. These attitudes of personality are what happens when temperament meets experience. These personality attitudes influence the experience of human sexuality and provide the fantasy framework of sexual attraction and behavior (Marcus, 2023).

Anna Freud (1965) then, because she was working with children, noticed the developmental processes of the mind. She saw that all the mental faculties and agencies had their own developmental lines. The synthetic capacity of the ego to organize and synthesize those different faculties also has its own line of development. Inherent in Anna Freud's line of development concept is its application to the concept of structure. Normal structure, unlike neurotic personality structure, is not rigid and fixed. It grows and develops. Developmental means gradual growth change according to an inherent plan of unfolding. Growth means gradual change according to adaptation to external stimuli and ecology.

Understanding structure as a line of development in and of itself allows one to understand mental growth in a more accurately complex and nuanced way. The ego is flexible, adaptable moment by moment, flexible and plastic at its outer edges, derivatives, applications, and meanings.

Her work catalyzed the growth of child analysis when she applied her ideas of lines of development to the treatment of children, whose dynamic structures develop with the developmental processes of cognition and other ego apparatus functions like the symbolic function and abstraction. In sharp contrast to Melanie Klein, who looked only at the contents of the unconscious id's objects, and even then, mostly aggression, Anna Freud looked at the holistic mind, its organizing processes, as well as its dynamic contents.

And because she worked with children, she could notice the evocation, growth, and development of these ego functions not only in relationship to their neuro mental unfolding but also to adaptation to reality and the emotional challenges of reality. One can see how Hartmann naturally grew out of this work, elaborating Anna Freud and expanding to include all ego boundary and integration processes. The adaptation function of the ego, its growth and development, is an important topic that only an ego metapsychology can describe.

Anna Freud added to the complexity of structure. She added defenses. She added lines of development. She added adaptation to reality. She added development. This was a modern description of mental function, all of mental function. Hers was the beginning of psychoanalysis as a general psychology.

An advantage to the concept of structure was that it focused on enduring patterns of mental experience. It could be applied to the repetitive structures of experiences. It could be applied to the idea of character neurosis, where structured attitudes are rigid and repetitive. It could be applied to the concept of repetition compulsion in which the fixed paradigm is repeated over and over, adapting now not so much to reality, which can evoke it, but to past emotional experience, which requires it.

It allows for a technique of interpretation: of defenses, structure conflict, adaptational failures, and stable mediating character structures of personality. This was Anna Freud's technique, described by Couch (1995) as eclectic in the sense that it paid attention to all agencies and to reality. In fact, her view of technical neutrality is often misquoted in that it refers not only to midway between the agencies but also to reality. Bringing back reality to the equation reminds the analyst about the adaptation issue. It brings trauma back into the field of classical psychoanalysis, which seemed to have dropped it when Freud switched from actual seduction to the fantasy of seduction. Either-or could now be both.

Waelder's definitive paper (1936) described the exigencies and complexities of conflict and compromise. The conflict and compromise were complex. He called compromise over determined and multi determined. He meant many elements go into it and repetition of theme is part of it. Arlow and Brenner (1964) applied Waelder's ideas to technique. Brenner elaborated this in the body of his work (1982).

But Brenner (1982) in his conflict theory focused only on conflict and, thereby, took the structure idea to reductions of mind. The first reduction was that psychoanalysis was only about neurosis, primarily neurotic symptom, and its conflict and compromise structure. In fact, psychoanalysis was and is always more than that. The second reduction was that Brenner's theory was about conflict, not compromise. Therefore, the second reduction was that the compromise itself was merely a vector sum of the conflicts and, therefore, only an obfuscation of the deeper conflict dynamics. It had no emotional meaning in itself. It had no adaptation significance in and of itself. Generated from conflict, it had no tertiary or quaternary autonomy. This is too bad because it made analysis of personality neurosis problematic. He then introduced a third reduction to mind as only fractal layers of conflict. He dismissed Hartmann. The fourth reduction occurred in technique, in changing the emphasis of treatment to interpretation only of structural conflict elements.

Left out is the creativity and dynamic meaning of the compromise itself and the organizing processes that produce it. No longer was psychoanalysis able to contemplate creativity nor secondary autonomy and change in function. Therefore, and more importantly, it misunderstood the adaptational function of the ego and also of one of the functions of the unconscious itself.

We break compromise down too quickly to our peril. If dreams are affect representations, then they are meaning makers. Then their manifest content is also meaningful and not just obfuscatory. To ignore the compromise risks losing the meaning of the compromise and then instead of music, with its emotional meanings, you get notes and can no longer tell the difference between Mozart and *Row, Row, Row Your Boat*.

Left out also or diminished was the idea of affect as crucial motivator and crucial meaning maker. Structure gains its significance in mental life not just because of regularities and predictability but also because it organizes meaning experiences of emotional importance.

Thus, the excesses of conflict and compromise ego psychology and what it left out. Why was self psychology, interpersonal, intersubjective, privileging of countertransference, invented and popularized? Where did they all come from and to what were they responding? They came from psychoanalysts responding to the demotion of affect in the old conflict and compromise ego psychology. Object relations theory brought back intense affect units of self representations and its effect link to the corresponding object representations. Self psychology brought back the meta-organization of self-experience and I's self-esteem affect states. Relational psychoanalysis brought back the object relations constructions of affect relational experiences of whole relationships. Intersubjective psychoanalysis brought back the affect states of meaning in all experience.

But every revolution goes too far and spurs its counterrevolution. The self and interpersonal revolution against a mechanistic ego resulted in the discarding of ego function and structure in turn catalyzing the present modern ego return to structure and function. The revolution was against technique, a valid criticism. It didn't require a turning away from structure. We cannot have a theory of the human mind without a descriptive theory of its structure.

The construction of structure is the organized result of ego processes of organization, which organize the basic units of all human structure, symbolic representation. Symbolic representation is the organization product of affect meanings. Object relations theory describes a certain type and content of symbolic representations. Self psychology describes experiences of the self and use of the self as a symbolic representation. Interpersonal uses the relationship, the ego organized experience of the real relationship, to understand and separate these experiences from their symbolic representation components of object relations in personality attitude. Intersubjective takes as a given that strong internal affect experiences are multi-determined symbolic representations in their emotional meaning.

Affect and, therefore, dreams, self-symbolic representations, are not just coequal with other elements of conflict and compromise. They are the meaning maker representations. Affect representations are called symbolic representations because their product symbolizes affect meaning. They have a special place as motivational experience. They are motivational. They are explanatory. The structure, in a sense, exists because of and for them.

Therefore, modern ego theory studies the phenomena of affect representations, their iconography, and the organization of the experiences of iconography in symbolic representations in its different forms. The different forms of symbolic representations of emotional reactions include the important symbolic alterations of reality and symbolic alterations of the body.

It probably is then no wonder that after Waelder (1936) came Hartmann (1958). Hartmann did look at ego processes. He understood that the mind, the ego, has processes as well as structures. Those processes organize structures. Those processes organize reality experience, emotional experience, and their relationships.

He understood that the making of meaning must have a process of meaning making. He described ego-organizing processes as neuro-mental apparatuses directed towards organizing the mind and adapting to reality. Examples are logic, memory, category organization, synthesis, and therefore, creativity, among others. These are ego functions. They are aspects of the secondary process.

Arieti (1976) pointed out that they are also, at times, combined with the primary process to form a creative tertiary process. This is the ego mechanism that organizes Winnicott's (1971) creative transitional area of experience. The tertiary process is a transitional process organizing an intermediate zone between fantasy and reality. We can now see some of the organizing mechanisms of psychic reality, the name we give to the experiences of the integrated and organized relationship between emotional experience and reality experience.

Recent advances in cognitive neuroscience and in applied techniques, like dialectical behavioral treatment and cognitive behavioral treatment, use the idea of ego dysfunction and techniques. They are based on Hartmann's ideas without ever knowing it or acknowledging it. The modern view of the ego is as an information-processing organ. Serious psychiatric illnesses are illnesses of the ego and deform, delay, and use ego functions in characteristic ways. DBT and CBT deal with these specific ego dysfunctions to educate the person about their malfunctions and train those functions to do a better job.

Hartmann also brought the concept of adaptation within psychoanalytic theory. There are crucial ego capacities that organize the relationship between emotional experience and reality experience to further adaptation. Symbolic alterations of reality are some of the stable structures of what happens once the out gets in. Symbolic representations, their different types and combinations and state changes, their autonomous uses for adaptation, and their relationship between emotional experience and reality experience, these are all constructions of the ego.

To understand adaptations to reality requires an understanding of the mind's interactions with objects in reality and the structural result. Schafer (1968) described the internalization process of reality and its development from introjection to identification. He, thereby, expanded Freud's idea of the growth of the ego due to identification with a lost object. Schafer added the idea of growth due to identification, a change in the self representation based on an experience of the internalized object representation. This means that the ego grows and develops not just through loss, identification with lost objects, as Freud first said, but also, through ongoing identifications with living objects. Schafer also maintained complexity by pointing out that the internalization involved not just the object in reality but also the fantasy in the self representation and in the object representation, creating a real object experience that is an amalgam of fantasy and reality called psychic reality.

The relationship of the object in reality to the real object experience of the mental simulacrum and the object representational emotional reactions to reality are different object experiences. They influence identifications in the self representation differently. How those interact in symbolic representations, especially symbolic alterations of reality, are at the frontier of research in how the ego adapts.

Schafer described identifications. Winnicott (1971) described the mental process and the experience of it and use of symbolic alterations of reality of the object in reality in his transitional object discovery. He furthered his observational research in his paper on the use of the object by which he meant the real object. He described the creative process of integration of internalizations from reality that Schafer's identification term labeled.

The modern ego is not just a collection of processes. It functions not just as an inhibitor of discharge. It is most crucially a synthesizer, a creator. The human ego synthesizes the three different modalities of information reception: the sensory, the cognitive, and the emotional. The ego takes temperament as it interacts with experience, joins it with endowment capacity, and builds a complex mental experience, reality and fantasy, using affect representations of different types as its core experience of emotional meaning and reality meaning. The ego builds symbolic representations in various forms into complex tertiary experiences of organized structures and then into state-changed, autonomous, adaptational composites called personality. Meaning, complex-layered conscious, preconscious, and unconscious meaning, is the cause and the result.

Hartmann said that in the normal human, ego processes achieve relative autonomy from dynamic conflict and, therefore, can be used more impartially than pure emotion for adaptation to reality. We have come to see how important these functions are in also organizing emotional feelings and emotional adaptations to reality (Marcus, 2022).

Hartmann was criticized because his secondary autonomy seems to alienate these processes from the emotional life. It was Schafer who pointed out the dynamic experience of these processes and later, Arieti, who pointed out the contribution of the primary process to even supposedly, at times, logical solutions of adaptation to reality. You could say that secondary process provides the reality day residues for the evocation of emotional meaning organized by affect associations in the primary process, like the dream. Together, with secondary processes organized by tertiary processes, they provide the compromise formations of psychic reality and its adaptations.

Thus was born the modern ego. It had to be born because with a widening scope of psychoanalysis, to child observation and to work with sicker patients, came observations about ego growth and development and its failures and dysfunctions. These define the more serious illnesses. The different illnesses leave their signature on the ego and its functions. Jacobson (1971) began to apply the idea of differential ego function to sicker patients. All these efforts were powerfully generative for the growth and development of a modern ego psychology and its organizations.

Kernberg (1975) applied this method, the description of ego organization, to narcissistic and borderline patients. Bellak et al. (1973) described specific ego dysfunctions of the psychotic illnesses. Marcus (2017) then described the ego structure of psychosis and its characteristic symbolic representations.

When you look at these command-and-control ego functions of categorization, organization, synthesis, and symbolic forms, you observe that they are on a spectrum. Each ego function and its results are on spectrums of organization and uses. The spectrums involve the relative mix of primary and secondary process, of reality testing, of type of organizational forms, and of coherence and usability of symbolic forms. These involve varying relative capture of objects in reality and varying relationships to the internal real object.

This leads to the technique idea, which is treatment specific to specific ego dysfunction. It allows for a more integrated spectrum of technique. It can provide a rationale for different types of treatments within the eclectic approach. The type of treatment depends on the ego function of the patient. This allows a mental organization approach to psychotherapy, psychoanalysis, and medication.

Meaning

The meaning maker is affect. Affect can be free-floating but tends to form representations. The basic building blocks of human experience are affect representations, the smallest units of meaning. Affect representations are inherently symbolic representations. Affect representations are called symbolic representations because their product symbolizes meaning in the iconography of their representations. Object representations theory looks at the affect validity to be found in fantasies about self and object and the affect experience that links them. Self psychology uses the affect validity of the self, particularly its self-esteem emotional experience, which seems so valid and so important to patients with neurotic and narcissistic self-esteem organization. Relational psychoanalysis looks at the affect organization inherent in relationships and in their enacted behavior. Intersubjective psychoanalysis focuses on the internal affect experience of each of the participants in the psychoanalytic couple.

Story

The continuity of affect representation meanings forms a structure. One name for this continuity is story. Story expresses both the meaning in the structures and the meaning in the experiences of the structures. These then become part of the structure. It's one of the ways the structure grows and develops, the meaning of the experiences of meaning, themes. This continuity is part of its personality and its sentience. The analysis of these themes, organized in personality attitudes, is what the psychoanalysis of personality analyzes. When the story is preconscious or unconscious, we call it fantasy. Freud called it that. Arlow (1969) agreed.

One of the differences between Mozart and *Row, Row, Row Your Boat* is the complexity of the story they tell. The structure of the music, like the structures of the mind, organize meaning. Structure must also include the idea of narrative structure. Narrative structure has a beginning, middle, and conclusion. Story shows their relationships, their growth and development, and their integration. There is a pre-story and an after story. There is a context to the story. It is true of all stories and their narrative structures.

Stories have different organizations. Some complex narrative structures are sequential. Some complex narrative structures are circular. Some start in the middle and then reveal their beginning and end. In the primary process, major aspects of the story are simultaneous. But stories they are. Stories are organized by ego processes.

Self

We need a modern ego psychology approach to self and to person.

The self is a synthesized and synthesizing, experiential, observational capacity of endowment. It is there from birth (Stern, 1985), and it grows and develops to varying degrees throughout the lifetime, maturing and growing more complex. The growth and development of the self involves the growth and development of the complexity of representations and their experiences. A crucial aspect is the growing and maturing of complex synthetic ego function.

Psychoanalysts must understand that self is a synthetic product with a validity and veracity of its own. It has not only a conflict structure, not only an object relations structure, not only a relational or self-object need. It is not only a compromise structure. It is larger than personality, one of its attributes. It is all these and more. It is larger than the sum of its parts. The self is a thing in itself. It is an influenceable but autonomous structure. The experience of this autonomy is the experience of a strong self affect validity. It isn't cogito ergo sum (I think, therefore, I am) but rather, affectus ergo sum (I feel, therefore, I am). The self has strong affect validity. It is perhaps one of the reasons it emerged. It is needed as an observer, to use affect validated information, information that has a meaning, for adaptational purposes.

And it is a creative synthesis. The most valued human experiences are creative syntheses. Music, love, attachment bonding, and self-esteem are self-state syntheses. Winnicott wrote about them. They are constructions for which there is a process and, therefore, have a process description. Love is, therefore, a verb and a noun. It is a process experience, not just a product experience. And there is the dynamic experience of ego processes. This dynamic experience is organized as personality and used by the self for adaptation, to emotions, and to reality.

Meta-theory

Meta-theory is an overarching theory of psychoanalysis. If there is to be a general psychology of psychoanalysis, the different metapsychologies would each have to be a part of it. Interestingly, none claims to be a general psychology. Most are theories of technique with no or limited theory of mind. Some have single or limited factor views of mind and of etiology.

Because the ego is a synthesizing capacity of the human mind, it may help us in synthesizing our various metapsychologies. If so, it makes of modern ego psychology a meta-theory. (Marcus, 2018; Eagle, 2022). This is consistent with the goal of psychoanalysis as a general psychology.

One can see from differential ego function that each metapsychology covers a cluster of patients with a similar ego function profile. Technique is often geared towards ego function. Those with psychotic illnesses need help with reality testing and observing ego. They need help with the boundaries between concept, percept, and affect. Those with behavior-oriented personality disorders, who immediately enact their dynamics into the relationship, may do especially well with relational therapists regardless of whether they are borderline or neurotic. Those patients who either feel intense affect resonance in their relationships or are frozen and feel nothing may do well especially with intersubjective analysts. Fragile, higher-level narcissistic patients, whose self-esteem is both grandiose and fragile, without overt aggression, may do especially well with Kohutian self psychologists. Borderline and sicker narcissistic patients with conscious and preconscious envious aggression may do well with Kernberg analysis or TFP. Patients who need intensity and protection from face-to-face interaction in order to connect with their emotional life, reconfigure affect validity in language and concepts, and feel better and more in control when they can view their illness or personality problems from the point of view of their own self-observation may do especially well in more classical psychoanalysis.

In the previous section is a differential therapeutics based on ego function. It is given as an example of the integrating power for theory that a modern understanding of the ego has. Each metapsychology seems to describe a different group of patients more amenable to a technique that immediately engages the ego organization and level of their affect validity. Affect validity is the feeling that what they are feeling is true to themselves. It may be felt in different modalities according to ego function and types of ego organization. This is a description of what is called ego style (Shapiro, 1965) and is a characteristic of the ego's organization of personality experience.

This has been a modern ego psychology view of the ego. A guess at the future of modern ego psychology is that it must explore the unity a complete description of mind can bring to our splintered psychoanalytic theories.

References

Arieti, S. (1976). *Creativity: The Magic Synthesis*. New York: Basic Books, Inc.

Arlow, J. (1969). Unconscious fantasy and disturbances of conscious thinking. *Psa. Q.*, 38(1): 1–27.

Arlow, J. & Brenner, C. (1964). *Psychoanalytic Concepts and the Structural Theory*. New York: International Universities Press.

Bellak, L., Hurvitch, M. & Gediman, H. (1973). *Ego Function in Schizophrenics, Neurotics, Normals*. New York: Wiley.

Blank, R. & Blank, G. (1986). *Beyond Ego Psychology*. New York: Columbia University Press.

Brenner, C. (1982). *The Mind in Conflict*. New York: International Universities Press.

Busch, F. (2014). *Creating a Psychoanalytic Mind: A Psychoanalytic Method and Theory*. London and New York: Routledge.

Couch, A. S. (1995). Anna Freud's adult psychoanalytic technique: A defence of classical analysis. *Int. J. Psycho-Anal.*, 76: 153–171.

Eagle, M. (2022) *Toward a unified psychoanalytic theory: foundation in a revised and expanded Ego Psychology*. New York: Routledge.

Fenichel, O. (1954). *The Collected Papers*. Second Series ch 14. New York: W. W. Norton.

Freud, A. (1956). *The Ego and Mechanisms of Defense*. New York: Routledge.

———. (1965). The writings of Anna Freud, Vol. Six. *Normality and pathology in children: assessments of development*. Chapter 3, p. 62–91. The Concept of developmental lines. Conneticut: IUP.

Freud, S. (1915). The unconscious. In *The Standard Edition of the Complete Psychological Works of Sigmund Freud*, London: Hogarth Press. 14. pp. 166–175.

———. (1923). The ego and the id. In *The Standard Edition of the Complete Psychological Works of Sigmund Freud*, London: Hogarth Press. 19(1).

Gilmore, K. J. & Meersand, P. (2014). *Normal Child & Adolescent Development: A Psychodynamic Primer*. Washington, DC: APA Press.

Hartmann, H. (1958). *Ego Psychology and the Problem of Adaptation*. Trans. D. Rappaport. New York: International Universities Press.

Jacobson, E. (1971). *Depression: Comparative Studies of Normal, Neurotic and Psychotic Conditions*. Madison, CN: International Universities Press.

Kernberg, O. (1975). *Borderline Conditions & Pathological Narcissism*. New York: Jason Aronson.

Marcus, E. R. (1999). Modern ego psychology. *Journal of the American Psychoanalytic Association*, 47(3): 843–871.

———. (2017). *Psychosis & Near Psychosis: Ego Function, Symbol Structure, Treatment*, Revised 3rd edition. London and New York: Routledge.

———. (2018). Psychoanalytic meta theory: A modern ego psychology view. *Psychodynamic Psychiatry*, 46(2): 220–239.

———. (2022). Dreams and adaptation: The waking work. *Psa. Inq.*, 42(3).

———. (2023). *Modern Ego Psychology & Human Sexual Experience: The Meaning of Treatment*. London and New York: Routledge.

Schafer, R. (1968). *Aspects of Internalization*. Madison, CN: International Universities Press.

Shapiro, D. (1965). *Neurotic Styles*. New York: Basic Books, Inc.

Shill, M. (2022). Adaptation, affect, and the ego: Some thoughts on Hartmann. *Psa. Inq.*, 42(3): 204–216.

Stern, D. N. (1985). *The Interpersonal World of the Infant*. New York: Basic Books.

Stone, L. (1954). The widening scope of indications for psychoanalysis. *JAPA*, 2: 567–594.

Waelder, R. (1936). The principle of multiple function. *Psa. Q.*, 5: 45–62.

Wallerstein, R. S. (2002, Winter). The growth and transformation of American ego psychology. *JAPA*, 50(1): 135–169.

Winnicott, D. W. (1971). *Playing & Reality*. London: Tavistock Publications.

10 A generative paradox

The subject who is the unconscious master in his own house

H. Shmuel Erlich

Psychoanalysis dwells in the realm of the immaterial, the insensible or at least not easily sensible. It resorts to "common sense", in Bion's sense as evidence from two or more senses, and uses the words and language of patient and analyst to gain meaning (1963, pp. 10–11). On another level, though, it deals with the ineffable and immaterial that is psychic reality and the unconscious (Freud, 1900), which is largely inaccessible to common sense. In this further "sense", it is also the realm of the paradoxical, where opposites exist without mutual contradiction, as in Freud's description of the unconscious (1915c). Psychoanalysis thrives on transforming such contradictions to produce "compromises", which are novel creations.

In many ways, this is the essence of Freud's psychoanalysis and those who follow, expand, and reshape it. In this sense, it is easily distinguishable from psychoanalytic approaches that rely on "common sense", on what is available through the data of the senses and consciousness, while shying away from aspects that do not fit the common sensical view. The most telling feature of such approaches, which distinguishes them from a Freudian perspective, is the place and value assigned to consciousness. It is the theme of consciousness and its relatedness to that of subject in Freud's view that I wish to trace from its inception to its culmination in *The Ego and the Id* (1923).

Freud's uncommon attitude to consciousness and his treatment of it can be traced all the way to his *Project* (1895), which predates his self-analysis and *The Interpretation of Dreams* (1900). It represents a detour from his and Breuer's earlier revolutionary declaration that "hysterics suffer mainly from reminiscences" (1893–1895, p. 7, original emphasis). That pioneering effort built upon the role of events and sense data that, having been relegated to a "second consciousness", could still become subject to regular (commonsense) consciousness and be abreacted. Freud the physician and clinician here employed the data of consciousness in the service of understanding the etiology of the malady to achieve its healing. In essence, it is the model of trauma and its "real" psychic impact, which nowadays is vigorously regaining prominence. Yet only two years later, in the *Project*, we see Freud, the unrelenting explorer of the psyche, construct a different

DOI: 10.4324/9781003336754-10

model of the mind to create a "scientific psychology", a project that is to become his overriding preference and preoccupation. Significantly, this new and ingenious approach does not start from the data of consciousness, neither his own psyche nor his clinical experience, but from his neurological base: the structure and function of the neuron (newly discovered and researched, including by Freud himself) and the "laws of motion", referring to physics and reflecting his Helmholtzian underpinnings.

What is immediately striking about this approach is the groundwork laid down: the *Project* conceives of the mind (mental apparatus) as two incompatible systems, responsible, in turn, for admitting and transferring sense data (perception) and storing the residues obtained from these inputs (memory). It is notable that these two systems are necessary and sufficient for the operation of the mind without the assistance of consciousness. The *Project* (never published or discussed and apparently destroyed by him) contains no dynamically conceived unconscious and refers to drives as "quantities of excitation" stemming from within the organism, and the role of consciousness amounts to an *additional component* of the mental apparatus, responsible for the invaluable capacity for differentiating "qualities", but not as the mind's primary foundation or condition. Primacy belongs to perception and memory, functioning and operating regardless of consciousness. In this, Freud laid down one of his most significant assumptions about the mind and its functioning: the mind is greater than the data of consciousness and, in many ways (though not all), essentially independent of them. It represents Freud's evolutionary perspective in which man evolves from his animal heritage, which remains the basis of his mental functioning, as exemplified by the role of drives and unconscious operations, with consciousness as a meta-achievement that separates him from his unconscious and animal heritage. It is a fundamental theme that prevails and is traceable, through certain vicissitudes, all the way to *The Ego and the Id* (1923) and beyond.

What then is the place and role of consciousness? First, though not spelled out, consciousness is closely associated with what constitutes the subject and sense of "I". Secondly, the answer to this question, as for many of Freud's theoretical assumptions, depends on the periodic context under discussion, and it is further obscured by issues of translation. "Ego" is Strachey's term for what Freud consistently calls "the I" (*Das Ich* in German). Its continual use by Freud can be divided into three distinguishable meanings that are prominent at different periods (Kernberg, 1982; McIntosh, 1986). Briefly, these different usages alternately refer to the "I" as the *subject* initiating mental and volitional action; as the *object* of mental and actual action, which may be termed "*the self*"; and as the *character* of a person, referring to the stable association of various features that describe him. In the period 1914–1918, for example, in *On Narcissism* (Freud, 1914), the term *Das Ich* (translated as "ego") refers to the "I" as object, or self, which can be and is invested (cathected) with drive intensity.

There is yet another important meaning or usage of the term "I", which refers to a stable *psychological structure*, invested with its own energy to be minimally affected and vulnerable to swift changes and upheavals. It is, of course, the meaning received or bestowed on it in *The Ego and the Id* (1923), which earns it its description as the structural model. But in this precise sense, the "I" is already defined and described in the *Project* (1895, pp. 322–324) in physical, neuronal terms, whose main purpose is the *inhibition* of the primary processes, allowing for volitional, adaptive, and reality-oriented action. This physical description easily transformed into psychological meaning once Freud made this switch in *The Interpretation of Dreams* (1900). Clearly, from the very start, though left unelaborated and unexplained, Freud's use of the term "I" included this structural meaning as the fundamental functional condition, which enables other psychological functions to emerge and take form.

Summing up what we have so far: From the very beginning, Freud uses the term "I" in a variety of intertwined, complementary meanings. The "I" is treated phenomenologically as encompassing the ideas of subject, object (self), and character (personality). It is also a structure within the mind, charged with containing (inhibiting) impulses to enable and safeguard adaptive, volitional, and goal-directed action, both internally and externally. It is the structural component of the mental apparatus that allows and maintains directionality, realistic achievement of goals, and the actual (rather than phantasmatic) satisfaction of needs and desires. In Freud's view and usage, all these meanings co-exist and are relegated to the "I", and he allows himself to wander between them freely, according to the prominently addressed aspect, since they are facets of a whole. Admittedly, this freedom was not always available to those who came after him, leading to confusion and obsessional attempts to make sense of the term, assigning it to one component or another in a limiting and restrictive manner.

What seems missing in this conceptualization is the place, role, and contribution of consciousness. But is it absent? Is this an oversight, or are we faced with an implicit basic assumption? The immediate next step in the development of the model of the mind suggests the latter. The very last heading of the final chapter (Chapter 7) of Freud's monumental *The Interpretation of Dreams* (1900) reads, "The unconscious and consciousness – reality" (p. 610). Although its focus is on the unconscious, it makes the distinction between conscious thought and communication and underlying unconscious processes. The overriding question is perhaps philosophical and epistemological: What is the nature of reality, and how do we cognize it?

Freud's Kantian answer delineates the limitations of consciousness: Reality (internal as well as external) is essentially unknowable and grasped imperfectly through the senses. Consciousness is the special sense-organ humans have developed, which provides a limited, inaccurate, and potentially misleading picture of both internal and external reality. Our dependency and reliance on consciousness leads to its overvaluation and idealization, creating the erroneous presumption or illusion that its data are synonymous with mind. Hence, the discoveries made by psychoanalysis:

> that the life of our sexual instincts cannot be wholly tamed, and that mental processes are in themselves unconscious and only reach the ego and come under its control through incomplete and untrustworthy perceptions – these two discoveries amount to a statement that *the ego [Das Ich] is not master in its own house.*
>
> (1917b, p. 143; original emphasis)

The resistance and hatred directed at psychoanalysis is attributable to this psychoanalytic blow to human narcissism. It is also one of the reasons why the natural place of psychoanalysis should be at the periphery and not the object of fashionable social acceptance (Erlich, 2013).

A careful reading of Chapter 7 of *The Interpretation of Dreams* elucidates the place and role of consciousness. This chapter presents the foundation of the topographical model that held sway until it was (more or less) superseded by the structural model in 1923. Of its numerous important features, the topographical model is particularly interesting and relevant to our discussion regarding the place and role of consciousness. The diagram Freud provides in this chapter contains an arrow running from left to right, from perceptual inputs through memory traces and unconscious impulses towards the preconscious and eventually to consciousness. This directionality typifies normal daytime functioning. It reverses its course at night and during sleep, running right to left, from day's residues and evoked unconscious ideas and impulse to finally reaching the perceptual level (which is why dreams are typically visual experiences), thus introducing the concept of *regression*.

What does this model tell us about the place and role of consciousness? It is situated, like the perceptual end, on the boundary with external reality. Taking a playful liberty, we may take the page with the diagram and fold it so that the two ends meet and consciousness (Cs) meets perception (Pcpt.), which is exactly Freud's point in beginning the discussion in *The Ego and the Id*. Consciousness, as said earlier, is essentially the sense-organ to perceive and apprehend internal and external reality; hence, Pcpt.-Cs. together are the nucleus of the development of the ego (1923, p. 23). But this is not all.

The dynamics of the psyche are expressed in the arrows Freud draws under the diagram of 1900, expressing the motion inherent in this mental apparatus. It is not a static or passive entity but one that strives towards dynamic action. The unconscious, too, is a formidable dynamic entity since it is where the drives are transformed from their somatic origins into psychological events defined as representation imbued with intensity. The unconscious part of the mental system continuously strives for expression and fulfilment. Yet whereas the unconscious is open to *receiving* external input, it is unable to reach and act upon external reality directly. Why is this, and what does it imply?

We come here upon Freud's presumption, as expressed in the topographic model, that volitional, directional, and adaptive action in the real world must be channeled through consciousness and performed by it. Consciousness (including the preconscious) acts and performs according to the secondary processes, which are logical, realistic, and adaptive. Unconscious action, on the other hand, is guided by the primary processes, geared to immediate release and satisfaction, regardless of its actual adequacy. Consciousness is situated on the boundary with external reality and is responsible for volitional, directed, and realistic action and performance, and unconscious impulses must seek expression and satisfaction in external reality through it. As Freud put it, consciousness oversees motility (i.e., action).

But the assumption goes even further and deeper and has definite therapeutic implications. Freud has equated consciousness with two other related concepts: *subject* and *I*. In effect, he assumes that the only way "I" can be said and expressed is through consciousness, and there is no way to express it unconsciously. And if the "I" can only be expressed consciously, so is the subject, the prefiguration of the I. Essentially, therefore, these three are one: *consciousness* is the seat and expressive means of the *subject-I*. Moreover, this trinity is unified by its characterization as containing the rational, realistic, logical, and adaptive aspects of the psyche. The three-that-are-one represent the only part of the psyche that can apprehend and comprehend reality in adaptive, realistic, and rational ways.

There are fargoing implications to this assumption, which guide and characterize Freud's work in the years leading up to *The Ego and the Id*. Probably the most important among them is its therapeutic implication and application. "Making the unconscious conscious" forms the backbone of the therapeutic endeavor of this period, and it is easy to understand why. Symptoms (like dreams) represent the distorted ways in which unconscious impulses find their expression in external reality while remaining essentially repressed. The therapeutic working hypothesis, grounded in the topographic model, aims to allow the unconscious material to reach consciousness so that it will be perceived by the conscious-subject-I, who is mature, rational, logical, and adaptive. The expectation is that such a rational and mature subject-I, when confronted with the repressed, will be able to see it for what it is – unrealistic early childhood memories, conflicts, and wishes that are totally out of line with present reality and have little or no place in it. This subject-I would undoubtedly see such impulses for what they truly are and abandon them, achieving psychic unburdening, equilibrium, and freedom from symptoms. The work of therapy follows the dictum of "making the unconscious conscious" because it expresses the belief and faith in an enlightened, intelligent, consciously aware, and rational subject. If we see in this faith the residues of the Enlightenment, soon to be challenged and displaced by more dystopic insights, we will probably not be wrong. In many ways, it is a view of consciousness *cum* subject that still persists nowadays and finds expression in economic theories and certain political orientations, perhaps even those underpinning liberal democracy.

A corollary of this view of the subject and consciousness is the attitude taken towards the drives and their part in human functioning and, consequently, of the role of repression. Repression, the powerful dynamic need for expelling and distancing what may be threatening or painful to consciousness, is the psychic bulwark against drives, and it makes no sense without them. Far from being equated with mere forgetting, neglecting, or even disavowing, repression is the psychological action that safeguards the conscious-subject-I from having to suffer the pain and unpleasure produced by conflict that stems from intolerable drive impulses. As Freud put it, its only effect is the removal of the obnoxious impulse from consciousness, nothing more (1915b). Once the conscious-subject-I is formed and in place, it can experience the pain and discomfort of conflict. It is, therefore, in need of protection against such experiences, which probably it would have been spared if such awareness had not developed.

It is this insight that led Freud to state in several ways that repression proceeds from the ego (the "I"). It is understandable, even necessary and predictable, that the ego-I (*Das Ich*) is the agency that is endangered since conflict produces psychic discomfort and pain for it, precisely because of its equation with consciousness. It needs to be stressed that in this sense, the ego is not defending itself against depletion and being restricted and undermined. In fact, it is employing repression to safeguard its freedom to act and perform. Yet by instituting repression to guard itself, it may well be allowing such harmful effects, which are repression's side effects and collateral damage. But if we ask ourselves the question, which Freud seems to have put aside until *The Ego and the Id*, namely, Who is the psychic agent that is in charge that determines the course of action (as in the *Project*)? The answer would have to be this: it is the ego, the sense of I, the subject who acts in the world and who does so based on its capacity to be conscious and initiate volitional choice and action. It is an obvious assumption yet one that Freud seems to either have ignored or taken for granted. As we have seen, he did not really ignore it since by assigning the place of choice and volition to consciousness, he implicitly included what needed to have been spelled out: the *subject* and the *I*, which were one and the same for him in his continuous usage of the term *Das Ich*.

Several intermediate works demonstrate this underlying unity as well as pave the way to the transformation of *The Ego and the Id*. I will mention only a couple of the most outstanding ones, out of the conviction that many more can be found and pointed to. Perhaps the earliest one concerns Freud's description of the pleasure-ego and the reality-ego: "Just as the pleasure-ego [*Das Lust-Ich*] can do nothing but wish, work for a yield of pleasure, and avoid unpleasure, so the reality-ego [*Das Real-Ich*] need do nothing but strive for what is useful and guard itself against damage" (1911, p. 223). The two principles are cast as two differing *I-qualities* or *stances*, which wish, perform, and work, as the I-subject does indeed. The attached footnote, quoting Bernard Shaw, makes this even clearer. The superiority of the reality-ego over the pleasure-ego has been aptly expressed by Bernard Shaw in these words: "To be able *to choose* the line of greatest advantage instead of yielding in the direction of least resistance". (*Man and Superman*) (*Ibid.*, my emphasis).

Discriminating and exercising choice is unquestionably the province of the conscious-subject-I.

Another example:

> Under the dominance of the pleasure principle a further development now takes place in the ego. In so far as the objects which are presented to it are sources of pleasure, *it takes them into itself, "introjects" them . . . ;* and, on the other hand, *it expels whatever within itself becomes a cause of unpleasure.*
>
> (1915a, p. 136, my emphasis)

This notion, of taking pleasurable object "into itself" and expelling "whatever within itself" becomes a source of unpleasure, points to the aforementioned fact that in this period (1911–1917), the "I" (*Das Ich*) refers mainly to one's own self as distinguished from others, encompassing both psyche and soma. In other words, it refers to the ego-"I" as subject, or in present terminology, one's self.

In this sense, it is used in *On Narcissism* (1914), where the *"I"-subject* becomes the original and primary *object* of the sexual drives, in what may be rendered as "self-love", or loving oneself:

> that in their later choice of love-objects they have taken as a model not their mother but their own selves. They are plainly seeking themselves as a love-object, and are exhibiting a type of object-choice which must be termed "narcissistic".
>
> (1914, p. 88)

The revolutionary discovery introduced in *On Narcissism* is that the subject ("I") can take itself as an object, indeed does so before it chooses or is able to relate to others as objects. The initial and primary "I" includes oneself as subject and object joined together by erotized love.

That this is the actual meaning of the newly introduced narcissistic development is made abundantly clear when the question of differentiating narcissism from autoerotism is addressed: "a *unity* comparable to the ego cannot exist in the individual from the start; *the ego has to be developed*" (ibid., p. 77, my emphasis). The subject-I is a "unity" that depends on psychological growth and development to evolve, together with the consciousness attached to it. The narcissistic investment of the self is essentially an *object relation*, albeit with oneself as the object. This is not the case with autoerotism: "The auto-erotic instincts, however, are there from the very first" (ibid.). Autoerotism represents direct pleasure derived from a stimulated organ; it is not an object relation. Freud concludes that "there must be something added to auto-erotism – a new psychical action – in order to bring about narcissism" (ibid.), namely, the development of the conscious-I-subject.

The last example that illustrates the use of the "ego" in the sense of subject-I comes from *Mourning and Melancholia* (1917a). This important work introduces further differentiation and complexity in terms of the inner world and psyche in which new concepts play significantly, mainly the role of identification and of splitting. To illustrate the theme developed here, it is sufficient to quote the following: An object relation with a (real) person came to an end, and the libido invested in it was freed. Rather than being invested in another person, this occurred:

> it was drawn back into the ego . . . [and] served to establish an *identification of the ego* with the abandoned object. Thus the shadow of the object fell upon the ego, and the latter could henceforth be judged by a special agency, as though it were an *object*, the forsaken object. In this way an *object-loss was transformed into an ego-loss* and the conflict between the ego and the loved person into a cleavage between the critical activity of the ego and the ego as altered by identification.
>
> (1917a, p. 249, my emphasis)

It is worthwhile to remind ourselves once again that in all the previous instances in which "ego" is used, Freud's term is "I" [*Ich*]. Furthermore, the growing theoretical complexity evidenced here introduces relatively new terms and concepts, like splitting, a critical agency, and an "I" that seems to evolve gradually towards what will shortly become the structural ego-I. My point is that the term "I" here still serves the meaning of referring to oneself – as subject and conscious-I. It is evidenced by the phrase "the shadow of the object fell upon the ego" and the reference to identification. Through identification, the melancholic's I-subject assumes the mantle, so to speak, of the lost-other. It implies the transformation of the subject's "I" to be "reshaped" and take on the identity of the lost object. The response to the object-loss has turned into an ego-loss since the ego has succumbed to abandoning and curtailing its autonomy and independence.

This brings us finally to the *The Ego and the Id* (1923). Since the unity, or trinity, of consciousness-subject-I was essentially subsumed in all of Freud's theorizing up to this point, two questions present themselves: What moved him to undertake a further theoretical shift and introduce a new metapsychological model? And is it truly new, in the revolutionary sense, or a restructuring and reshaping of the existing model?

It is relatively easy to answer the first question since Freud supplies the answer to it, though as I want to show, there is something misleading about it. The theoretical shift that required an altered conceptualization of the mind (mental apparatus), Freud tells us, was necessitated by the phenomenon of *resistance*. Resistance implies that while the subject-I is consciously working in the analysis and doing all it can to improve, it is unconsciously working against such change, improvement, and healing that analysis can potentially provide. This resistance, of which the subject is unconscious, must be attributed to the ego and emanates from it, and therefore, there must be a part of the ego – "and Heaven knows how important a part" (1923, p. 18) – that is unconscious.

What is, of course, peculiar is that resistance has been intrinsically embedded in Freud's clinical and therapeutic work from the very start. There are the well-known methods he first employed to overcome it, including admonition to recall and pressure on the forehead, not to mention the influence of hypnosis. The methodological shift to free associations following *The Interpretation of Dreams* (1900) is well-known, but resistance as a critical phenomenon remained a critical key concept. Let me illustrate this with two quotes out of literally many dozens, which also demonstrate the close relation between resistance and the conscious-subject-I: "We can lay down no general rule as to what degree of distortion and remoteness is necessary before *the resistance on the part of the conscious* is removed" (1915b, p. 150, my emphasis). Or the following:

> Psychoanalytic work shows us every day that translation of this kind [of the unconscious into conscious] is possible. In order that this should come about, the person under analysis must overcome certain resistances – the same resistances as those which, earlier, made the material concerned into something repressed by rejecting it *from the conscious*.
>
> (1915c, p. 166, my emphasis)

The existence and importance of resistance is, therefore, nothing novel. So is also its intrinsic negative relationship to consciousness, along with repression.

What is novel and revolutionary is, therefore, not the phenomenon of resistance. What has been radically revised is the trinity *subject-I-consciousness*. Freud abandons his earlier understandable yet also somewhat naïve notion of the equation of these three. It is notable that, with all his debate and controversy with "the philosophers", he had adopted their view that equates the subject-I with what is conscious. In this sense, *The Ego and the Id* represents a deeper psychoanalytic understanding that, indeed, like many of his previous insights, does not sit well with philosophy.[1]

The starting point of *The Ego and the Id* is a review of the role of perception and its relation to consciousness, which forms the nucleus of the ego. A basic characteristic of the ego (*Das Ich*), one that correlates well with its bodily origins ("the ego is first and foremost a bodily ego", 1923, p. 26), is around consciousness as the perception of one's internal and external worlds. The *subject-I* is indeed a creature of somatic, perceptual, and conscious experience. The discussion proceeds, however, to elucidate the changed view of *consciousness* and its effect on the subject-I:

> We must admit that the characteristic of being unconscious begins to lose significance for us. It becomes a quality which can have many meanings, a quality which we are unable to make, as we should have hoped to do, the basis of far-reaching and inevitable conclusions.
>
> (1923, p. 18)

Of the numerous implications introduced by the revised model of the mind (which the French refer to as the "second topography"), it is the displacement of consciousness that strikes me as the most outstanding. Consciousness was always perceived and treated by Freud as a necessary, but far from sufficient, component of the mind. For a long time, and for good reason, he concentrated his efforts on dispelling the notion of *mind = consciousness* in order to provide the basis for his discovery of the unconscious and its major role in human psychology. In so doing, he consistently relegated the role and function of rationality, reality testing, logical thinking, and general adaptiveness to consciousness, the manifest, inclusive, and defining determinant of the subject-I. Therapeutic success was to be achieved by making the unconscious conscious and allowing the conscious subject-I to experience, assess, and evaluate the unconscious wishes and conflicts to be repudiated and rejected by the subject-I. Resistance, while always identified and acknowledged, meant that the subject-I was as yet unprepared to allow this to happen, as if it needed further persuasion.

What changed this understanding? Most probably a complexity of factors but a major one is the previously introduced dual drive theory (Freud, 1920). The presence and impact of the death drive elucidated phenomena characterized by self-destructiveness much more severe than simply resistance. Thus, the negative therapeutic reaction, attributed to the death drive and motivated by unconscious guilt feelings, makes its appearance in the present context. The readiness of the subject-I to act in a way that is not simply or merely irrational but outrightly self-destructive must have led to a revamped view of the subject-I. The fact that part of the ego-I (*Das Ich*) is willing and ready to work towards its own ruin and devastation throws new light on the nature of the subject. Indeed, throughout *The Ego and the Id*, the role of the newly discovered and conceptualized dual drives is clearly manifest. It is present in the attempt to integrate the dual drive theory with this new model of the mind. It is even more in focus in the various ways in which aggression and destructiveness can be directed against the self, as in the negative therapeutic reaction, and even more so in the newly introduced superego that can lead to the subject's own demise and represents "a pure culture of the death instinct" (1923, p. 53).

The new division of the mind into three "instances" or agencies that are constantly in a state of actual or potential tension with one another, not to mention outright conflict, deeply alters the notion of the subject, the "I" (*Das Ich*) that not only is no longer master in its own house but is also often set to destroy it. Consciousness can no longer be the hallmark of this subject. The trinity of consciousness-subject-I is broken up and abandoned, to be replaced by the new trinity, id-ego-superego.

What has become of the subject in this new model? Translation and its tendency to distort original meanings, though not the main cause, has contributed to the obfuscation of the issue. Suffice it to point out that in Freud's terminology, the three agencies or aspects of the mind all relate to the "I": the German terms are *Das Ich, Das Es*, and *Das Über-Ich* (i.e., The I, The It, and the Over-the-I). The "It" is related to the "I" as the part of itself, which the subject regards as "not a subject" (as in: "It is raining outside"). The "superego" is not a "superior I" but an id-component that, due to its special meaning and the identifications involved, assumes a posture in relation to the "I" as being over it (in a controlling sense) while maintaining its id-characteristics.

The most telling fact regarding the subject is what happened to both consciousness and the "I". *Das Ich* is no longer entirely synonymous with consciousness, and part of it is indeed unconscious. This suggests a double implication: Consciousness is now a quality or dimension of mind that may or may not extend to various parts of it. It is no longer the condition for adaptive, rational action. The subject-I, liberated from this imposed equation, can now be seen as split, perhaps even fragmented. It no longer exists or is synonymous with a special part of the mind since it can be both conscious and unconscious.

But here we must ask: What is the meaning of an unconscious subject? Is it not an outright contradiction? It is unquestionably paradoxical, yet at the same time, it is also true. It represents Freud's newly gained insight, guided by the expanded dual drives theory, into the nature of the subject. The subject is no longer the enlightened rational aspect of mind and person. The fact is that the subject is larger than its conscious-rational aspect. It encompasses its own irrationality and self-destructive tendencies, which it must own if it wants to survive. It is the culmination of Freud's assertion that the mind is larger than consciousness. Once consciousness and the I are separated from each other, the I is larger than itself, so to speak, since it can be both conscious and unconscious. The "unconscious subject-I" presents a newer, deeper, and much wider psychological horizon that encompasses both its rationality and irrationality as intrinsic aspects.

The therapeutic message changes as well: it is no longer sufficient to become aware, in the sense of making conscious what was unconscious. The therapeutic endeavor faces a much more difficult challenge: to be able to own, accept, and integrate hateful and destructive aspects of oneself, as well as despised or forbidden ones, as making up the subject-I, as being important aspects of what one essentially "is". The unconscious subject is the source of newly found creativity and realism, much beyond idealized and simplistic awareness. It becomes the hallmark of what maturity and clear-minded existence in the world can be. It also represents the advance of psychoanalysis to a more mature stance, one that, if understood, is not necessarily pessimistic or optimistic but realistic and potentially accepting of the subject with all its frailties and riches. Allowing the subject to expand beyond its conscious aspects and embrace its unconscious ones puts the Freudian project on a far more encompassing level, characterized by a full 360 degree perspective. It achieves Freud's original effort to circumscribe the importance of consciousness and, simultaneously, to offer an expanded view of ethics and moral responsibility by assuming into oneself-as-subject those parts one may not directly know. In this renewed sense, it represents much more than a restructuring of the mind. It presents us with a fully revamped reading of the subject and subjectivity, one that allows the subject to take its rightful place beyond the couch and pathology, as an actor fully present and engaged in social, political, and ethical human life. All this is made possible by the realization that it is not a subject that has an unconscious but a subject that is inherently both conscious and unconscious. The central issue and theme for humanity is not mere awareness, which can be gained and dismissed, but responsibility.

In summary, I have tried to trace the place and different meanings of the subject-"I" (*Das Ich*) in its relation to consciousness. Throughout the early and middle periods of Freud's theoretical development, the emphasis was on the subject-I as intrinsically conscious and of consciousness as expressing the subject-I and its ability to act rationally and adaptively. *The Ego and the Id* introduced a radical reworking of this conceptualization, severing the bond between the subject-I and consciousness. From here on, the subject is paradoxically both conscious and unconscious, possessing varying qualities and parts that co-exist in tension states. While this may not be a commonsense view of the subject, this very paradoxical nature expands its psychoanalytic understanding in creative ways. It changes the therapeutic focus from making the unconscious conscious to owning and assuming responsibility for intrinsic components of the subject that are destructive and unethical. This larger and more encompassing understanding of the subject-I has direct bearing on its place and action on the personal as well as the larger social scene.

Note

1 For a fuller discussion of this see Cavell (1991) and Kirshner (1991).

References

Bion, W. R. (1963). *Elements of Psychoanalysis*. London: Karnac.
Breuer, J. & Freud, S. (1893–1895). Studies in hysteria. *S.E.*, 2: 1–251.
Cavell, M. (1991). The subject of mind. *Int. J. Psycho-Anal.*, 72: 141–152.
Erlich, H. S. (2013). *The Couch in the Marketplace: Psychoanalysis and Social Reality*. London: Karnac.
Freud, S. (1895). Project for a scientific psychology (1950 [1895]). *S.E.*, 1: 281–391.
———. (1900). The interpretation of dreams. *S.E.*, 5: 339–621.
———. (1911). Formulations on the two principles of mental functioning. *S.E.*, 12: 218–226.
———. (1914). On narcissism: An introduction. *S.E.*, 14: 73–102.
———. (1915a). Instincts and their vicissitudes. *S.E.*, 14: 117–140.
———. (1915b). Repression. *S.E.*, 14: 146–158.
———. (1915c). The unconscious. *S.E.*, 14: 166–204.
———. (1917a). Mourning and melancholia. *S.E.*, 14: 243–258.
———. (1917b). A difficulty in the path of psycho-analysis. *S.E.*, 17: 135–144.
———. (1920). Beyond the pleasure principle. *S.E.*, 18: 7–61.
———. (1923). The ego and the id. *S.E.*, 19: 13–59.
Kernberg, O. F. (1982). Self, ego, affects and drives. *J. Amer. Psychoanal. Assn.*, 30: 893–917.
Kirshner, L. A. (1991). The concept of the self in psychoanalytic theory and its philosophical foundations. *J. Amer. Psychoanal. Assn.*, 39: 157–181.
McIntosh, D. (1986). The ego and the self in the thought of Sigmund Freud. *Int. J. Psych-Anal.*, 67: 429–448.

11 Melancholia as a clinical and metapsychological agent

A look over the ego/superego

Ignácio A. Paim Filho

Introduction

According to *The Ego and the Id* (Freud, 1923/2007a), which is celebrating 100 years, there are two main reasons for selecting melancholia as a clinical and metapsychological agent in order to explore the ego and the superego. Firstly, I find indicators signaled by Freud in his work regarding his peculiar aptitude for listening, perceiving, feeling, and reflecting on the task of identifying the intricacies by which we constitute ourselves as individuals inserted in a cultural order. Here, once again, we have psychopathology producing narratives to also access the structural. Second, I find evidence in clinical work and in our contemporary culture of a circumstance that evokes reflecting on melancholia, as a narcissistic condition and as something that is in the register of an incandescent self-destructiveness, which leads to thinking about the relationship, especially, between the ego and the superego. Our discontent, our psychic suffering, is in the order of the lethality of a death drive insufficiently tamed by the libido, in its different compounds. It is time to consider this organization, which hangs over the ego. What can we do when we are doomed to suffer from a need of punishment, often lived but not felt?

The melancholic human being, or even the contemporary human being, in his various presentations, often promotes his melancholic misery through the transformation into its opposite and the return of it onto himself. If we understand that melancholia is caused by a pathology of ideals, some questions arise: What are the ideals that permeate our time? Are they ideals of becoming something which is under the register of incompleteness or ideals of an idealization compromised by an idea of completeness? These questions lead my reflections towards the performance society, which flows into the burnout society, conceived by Han (2017a). The first is characterized by subjects immersed in the insane search for an impossible success – self-imposed imposition – driven by the motto of "where there's a will, there's a way". The failure to carry out this deadly mission shapes the universe of the burnout society – "the exhausted and depressive performance subject of today" (Han, 2017b, p. 53).

DOI: 10.4324/9781003336754-11

Looking at this composition, I raise a speculative hypothesis postulating that narcissistic neuroses, with their equivalent of melancholia, are for the 21st century just as historical neuroses, in particular, hysteria, are for the 20th century. Let's see how we can configure this proposition taking Freudian thinking as a delineated guide by this observation:

> What follows is pure speculation . . . you can take it into consideration or despise it. Otherwise, it is an attempt, driven by pure curiosity, to explore an idea to the end, just to know how far it can take us. (Freud, 1920/2006b, p. 149)

Revisiting the vitality of the Freudian legacy

The theme of melancholia has a long history in the development of Freudian thought, as exemplified in draft G: "It would not be so bad, therefore, to start from the idea that melancholia consists of mourning over the loss of libido" (Freud, 1894/1986, p. 99). Following this same tune, he then makes an analogy regarding this interminable mourning as a hemorrhage, a result of a wound, which produces a hole in the psyche. This proposition of a libidinal impoverishment, a loss without mourning, will be presented twenty years later, when he will write the famous paper *Mourning and Melancholia* (Freud, 1917/2006a), a moment which places this clinical theme at the center of his concerns and that will accompany him over the years to come. I believe that melancholia, from Freud to our time, occupies a similar place as the historical neuroses, a stimulus to advance in the metapsychological understanding of how we constitute ourselves as subjects. In this direction, Freud points out the importance of melancholy with its narcissistic identifications, as an access route to a better knowledge of hysterical identifications: "clearly the narcissistic being is older than the hysterical one, and it is through it that we can have a better understanding of hysterical identification, studied less thoroughly" (Freud, 1915/2004b, p. 109). This conception is ratified and amplified in this calling, which I hear as a summoning to contemplate *the oldest* – that is, our origins – having melancholia as a guiding thread and as a guide to the labyrinths of the soul: "let us pause for a moment on what the melancholic's being affection reveals to us about the constitution of the human Ego" (Freud, 1915/2004b, p. 107).

As we stop, just for a brief moment, we contemplate the intriguing ideas forged in the metapsychological texts of 1914–1915. We find two unique and challenging narratives, within our intent on reflecting about the issue of melancholia as exposing the darkest intimacy of the superego in its visceral relationship with the ego: *On Narcissism* (Freud, 1914/2004a) and *Mourning and Melancholia* (Freud, 1917/2004b). I understand that the first will provide theoretical subsidies to reflect on the universe of narcissistic identifications, a condition that is hypertrophied in melancholic episodes, especially those resulting from the first cathexis of parental figures, which create the universe of primary narcissism, the ego ideal: the identified being – "product of the first identification that took place at a time when the ego was still feeble" (Freud, 1923/2007a, p. 56). Note the importance of this fragile ego indispensably requiring the object to be present in an adequate way, which provides the likely to be autonomy. We cannot forget that this identification is captured by the superego when it splits from the ego, giving the first a particular power over the second: remnants of a frail ego in the face of this identification that is within the scope of narcissistic plenitude, alluding to the "father of its own personal prehistory" (Freud, 1923/2007a, p. 42). In this process, Freud announces that, in a second stage, the creation of the ideal ego takes place as a consequence of the development of the identification process; it is no longer a question of being identified but of identifying with . . . , presence of the symbolic inscription of castration linked to being "heir to the Oedipus complex" (Freud, 1923/2007a, p. 56). This component will have the function of hosting our ideals – a condition for emerging from repression – and equating moral conscience, mechanisms that are involved in the composition of the superego. I understand that the text on narcissism introduces more emphatically the problem of the ego and its multiple semblances in the work of Freud. This picture, at that moment, in terms of the ego ideal and the ideal ego and its unfolding in the definite reality ego (Freud, 1915/2004b). Following this script, it is important to emphasize and reaffirm that the ideal of ego is the immediate precursor of what will become the superego in 1923, with its functions of self-observation – moral conscience and ideal harboring.

The ideas postulated in this text from 1914 have direct resonances in the 1915 paper: narcissism theory, mourning, and clinical melancholia. Revealing and instigating clinical advances in freudian metapsychological thinking, the topic of 1900 (Freud, 1969c) centered on the dialectic between the repressed unconscious versus the preconscious suffers one of its first clashes. The ego attains dynamic and economic prominence but lacks a topography. Freud (1914/2004a) emphasizes that it does not exist from the beginning, that it must be developed. The mention of a "new psychic action" is spawned (Freud, 1914/2004a, p. 99) in order to give rise to the ego and the narcissism. Such action evokes the consideration of the need for the intervention from the other, as for the occurrence of psychic life, beyond the "initial real-ego" (Freud, 1915/2004b, p. 159), along with the belief that it takes place through primary identification. These two texts, in their complementarity and interaction, determine a new place for the primary objects within the constitution of the subject: from supporting actors to protagonists (Paim Filho, 2014). These instituted prerogatives, in a circumscribed way, will propel the turning point of the tying and untying of freudian thinking from the twenties, which, among other destinations, will culminate in the second topography (Freud, 1923/2007a), topography which will shelter the possibility of structuring a way of thinking beyond the historical neuroses. This thinking is consistent with the principle that announces identification as prior to object choice, as Freud would say, the "oldest affective bond with another person" (Freud, 1921/2020b, p. 178) – being as a condition for working in search of having. Thus, in *Mourning and Melancholia* (Freud, 1915/2004b), he continues to weave the elements that will support such conceptions, including the initial speculations about the original passivity of the human offspring, propelling speculations from the one who interrogates, spawned in 1920, about the relevance of the existence of a primary masochism and a secondary sadism: "there could also be a primary masochism evolving from the Ego" (Freud, 1920/2006b, p. 175). This inference, in a potential state, gains body and soul in the text of "The economic problem of masochism" (Freud, 1924a/2007b) – important acquisition to be contemplated, in addition to the sadism of the superego, the masochism of the ego, and the prominent interaction in melancholia. This is stated in the "categorical imperatives" (Freud, 1923/2007a, p. 45) of the superego, in its coercive position with the ego, which can be summarized in the following expression: "You must be like this (like your father)" (Freud, 1923/2007a, p. 44). And at the same time, the prohibition: "You cannot in such manner (like your father), that is, you cannot do everything he does, some things remain his prerogative" (Freud, 1923/2007a, p. 44). The impossibility of equating these mandates, in melancholia, determines that the ego is treated as an object of the imperative superego. This condition makes the ego a prisoner of the thought – "You must be like this" – in a narcissistic identification with the father. On the other hand, the "you cannot" loses its condition of recommendation, to be lived under the dictate "You must not be like your father" – the failure of the oedipal identification with the father, agent of symbolic castration – impediment in recognizing the prerogatives that are exclusive to the father, record of alterity, destiny to live on the margins of one's own desire, impossibility of carrying out the symbolic parricide. Following this proposition, I understand that in melancholia, we have staged the happening of the alienating filicide (Paim Filho et al., 2017, p. 80): "He will have his alterity and his individuality dead. In the name of upholding the non-castration of the mother and the non-interdiction of the father, he will surrender his own life to them".

When uttering likenesses and differences between the process of mourning and melancholia, Freud establishes a fruitful dialogue, which allows highlighting the importance – structural and psychopathological – of the work of mourning versus the work of melancholia. The first will be associated with the work of psychic change, which will imply elaborating the losses inherent from the reality of castration. This one gains expression within the knowledge of transience – fear of death, fear of moral conscience – liberating knowledge from narcissistic ties, a precondition to be followed, with a certain degree of autonomy, in the search for new emotional investments, guided by logic: that we never renounce, we only negotiate (Freud, 1908/1969b). The acquisition of such a position allows the advancement of endogamous mandates, committed to the idealization of ideals, in favor of exogamous mandates, committed to non-idealized ideals. The importance of mourning, loss of the object, in the construction of an identification complex guided by the search for greater instinctual freedom is set.

Regarding the second one, the work of melancholia, it means being submitted to the logic of the "eternal return of the same" (Freud, 1920/2006b, p. 147), imprisonment in endogamous mandates, a universe of idealizations in which the primary object marks all its might, which is explained by the freudian sentence: "Thus, the shadow of the object fell on the ego" (Freud, 1917/2006a, p. 108). The aforementioned shadow, already in that text, marks reference to a place that observes and judges the ego from its ideals. This place – which takes the ego as an object – does not have a topography as well. It is constituted by an inference built from a clinical demand, which melancholia exposes it in a deeply engraved way. Being taken as an object by this component is the way in which Freud structures his thinking about the self-destructive lethality present in melancholia: "Let us add that in the two opposite situations, extreme passion and suicide, the ego, although through totally different ways, ends up being subjugated by the object" (Freud, 1917/2006a, p. 111). It should be noted that Freud (1920/2006b) sought to substantiate this destructiveness without the concept of death drive. Process characterized by the self-depreciation of the ego in which, according to Freud, reveals the unconscious attacks on the object, or rather, on what is left of it, as an identification with the abandonment of object within the ego by ideals: regression of the object choice for identification. Reflecting on this proposition, I recall the freudian idea from 1895, which speaks of a psychic hole in melancholia, or even an open wound. Analogy that tells us to think about abandonment, a genuine libidinal hemorrhage, the impossibility of a psychic life in the absence of the object, the fragility of the identifications, which constitutes the ego are exposed, in the face of "grandiose objects" (Freud, 1923/2007a, p. 56). In this sense, we confirm that we have here the inaugural event of melancholia as a spokesperson, par excellence, of the critical instance, which will be taken by the superego, with its exacerbated rigor over a weakened ego.

Freud (2016), in 1924b, in *Neurosis and Psychosis* – a complementary text to *The Ego and the Id* – will explicitly say that melancholia in particular is a byproduct of the conflict between the ego and the superego. Due to this specificity, melancholia is called narcissistic neurosis, unlike other psychoses, which present a conflict between the ego and the external world, as well as neurosis referring to a conflict between the id and the ego. The proposition of neurosis calls to attention: Why such a name? Would the loss of reality in this neurosis be similar to that of psychoses? Yes and no. I think we have, in favor of the idea of neurosis, a primordial factor mentioned by Freud (1917/2006a, 1921/2020b) at least twice – the melancholia revolt of the ego in relation to the superego – which presents itself as submission but, at the same time, reveals a character of unconscious rebellion, frustrated attempts to break ties with narcissistic hegemony, ascending to oedipal triangulation, coming to carry out the path from alienating filicide to symbolic parricide.

However, the enigmas of the constitution of these components will demand further work from Freud, a work that summonses him to start dealing with human destructiveness – in oneself and/or in the other – through a vertex that transposes the restrictive nexus of the empire of libidinal development, in its relationship with the self-conservative, or yet, the interests of the ego. Considering the duality of death drive versus life drive, in 1920, Freud opens the door to the reflection about the existence of other territories, which are beyond the pleasure principle. Trauma resulting from the excesses from the external world reappear through traumatic dreams. The compulsion to repeat claims thinking about early traumas, the world of the unrepresentable, with its non-desiring sexuality, cries out to be heard. This broad context – characterized and led by the intense and intriguing concept of the destruction drive – will be the determining factor in favor of the need for a new model of psychic apparatus, device that can contemplate the complexity in which involves the unrepresentable, demands that are beyond the conflict ruled by the principle of Nirvana. The universe of the unrepressed unconscious signals, in a forceful way, the need to enlarge the psyche apart from a topography, a dynamic and an economy centered exclusively on the logic of desiring sexuality. The postulate that the ego is largely unconscious is announced straight away.

Within the construction of his thinking in this text, which implicitly inscribes the symbolic birth of the second topography, Freud (1921/2020b) offers us the narrative of child's play, a structural compulsion to repeat: "fort-da" game (p. 141). He perceives it as linked to the reenactment of the presence/absence of parental figures. This game consisted of making objects disappear and reappear, playing a toy on a reel of strig – the narcissistic fantasy that controls the object – in a repetitive way. The question that emerges from this play is, Why should the disappearance of the object be repeated? Such process of disappearance contradicts the logic of the pleasure principle (i.e., the quest to relive the experience of pleasure) and advocates a non-pleasant repetition (i.e., the quest to relive the experience of pain). These circumstances lead Freud to postulate the need for this repetition as a form to connect what is not connected: master the traumatic situation, which the absence of parental figures represents, search for the creation of a symbolic universe.

The demands of the culture and the clinic taken in by Freud, mainly in the first and the second decade of the 20th century, allowed him to work in building a new path, designing new territories for the psyche, now in the light of the unprecedented duality: death drive versus life drive. In this sense, it is important to observe the words that Freud explicitly initiates the text from 1923:

In this paper, I will continue the reflections started in "Beyond the Pleasure Principle" (1920/2006b). . . . Attending to them with an attitude of benevolent curiosity, as if observing how far it would reach . . . the hypotheses must be related to strictly psychoanalytic pictures (Freud, 1923/2007a, p. 27).

Regarding this pretension, crisscrossed by a *benevolent curiosity*, let us see how we can relate the instinctual enigmas, enunciated in 1920, with a more accurate psychoanalytic look, and the tripartite conception of the psyche in id-ego-superego. I believe, once again, that melancholia can be a good indicator for guiding us through these new grounds, which show through psychopathology, with their intensities, the scope of the constitution of new psychic structures. Intending to confirm the reasoning of the importance of the pathological considering the structural, I recall the words of Freud (1933/1969a):

On the other hand, we are well aware of the notion that pathology, by making things cruder, can draw our attention to normal conditions that would otherwise elude us. "Where it points to a breach or a rent, there may normally be an articulation present" (p. 77)

As we know, in the work of 1915, the self-destructiveness of melancholia was thought of exclusively through the critical component of the dialectic, together with sadism, the latter being an exclusive tributary of the libido. Now, in the twenties, we have in the superego the possibility of reflecting its coercive action over the ego, from its link with death drive, in its different degrees of fusion with libido. This picture challenges us to understand the emblematic Freudian phrase: "To live, for the ego, means to be loved, to be loved by the superego" (Freud, 1923/2007a, p. 65). What happens when the ego is not loved? The ego succumbs to worthlessness, the destructiveness resulting from the idealizations of the superego – an ego ideal disguised as the ideal of the ego, product of its identifications, together with its desexualizations, which implies to release a quantum of death drive not entwined, spilled over the ego. In this direction, Freud points out that, in melancholia, there is a scenario in which the "superego prevails pure death instinct" (Freud, 1923/2007a, p. 60). This instinct of destruction will act on the ego, in a sadistic way, as a need of punishment.

In order to establish bridges between the text of 1920 and the one from 1923, I return to the disturbing situation – actively repeating what was passively lived – performed in the game of the thread spool (Freud, 1920/2006b) that insists and persists in repetition. On this matter, I make an association with two possible destinations of this traumatic experience and its implications for the constitution of the ego and the superego, taking the work of mourning and the work of melancholia as references, to equate a way of thinking about our time. The first, as indicated earlier, refers to the process of playing as a mechanism, which enables a way to seize the object, the repetition committed to the elaboration and the symbolic acquisition, via the identificatory dynamics, which allows the transit of passive identifications to active ones. In this scenario, we have been operating the work of mourning, supporting the loss of the external object and internalizing it as an identification model. Let us remember: "the ego is formed to a great extent out of identifications which take the place of cathexes abandoned by the id" (Freud, 1923/2007a, p. 56). Therefore, we are in a territory, which creates conditions for the development of the ego, crisscrossed by castration, in better conditions to negotiate with the demands from the superego – the one who is operating, above all, in favor of the ideals fed by the current of tenderness, resulting from the resolution of the oedipal conflict.

Reflecting on the second reference in regard with the work on melancholia and its relationship with the play of "fort-da", I understand that in this one there is an impediment on living this process: the traumatic is reissued in a repetition compulsion, controlled by the disruptive force of a Nirvana principle. The act of playing as the initiator of the process of elaboration and appropriation of primary objects, as an exercise to come to detach oneself from them in the external world and relocate them in the ego, as nonalienating identifications, is suspended. The primary objects, invested with their narcissistic power, explained in the conception of a petrified primary narcissism, do not allow the necessary conditions for the rupture of the narcissistic pact to happen. Following this way of thinking, the superego, since its tributary origins to the id, determines an imprisonment to its mandates and a nonexistence in the absence of the object.

Freud, busy in structuring his ideas and moved by the desire to broaden the understanding and effectiveness of the postulates formatted from the duality exposed in 1920 and the new conception of the psyche from 1923, leans upon, as previously commented, in 1924, on the enigmas of masochism. The clinical and theoretical issues regarding the interaction between the ego and the superego are updated in the light of a new paradigm: primary masochism, secondary sadism. Self-destructiveness precedes the destructiveness of the other. The ego's need for punishment, so noticeable in melancholia, receives new contributions resulting from the destructive relationship that occurs in the interconnection between the masochism of the ego versus the sadism of the superego. In the analytical process, the negative therapeutic reaction (i.e., falling ill at the best) is shown as an improved presentation of the destructive force of moral masochism (i.e., guilt in search of punishment): "The ego, facing the perception that it fell short of the demands postulated by its ideal – by the superego – will then react with a feeling of fear" (Freud, 1924a/2007b, p. 112).

Continuing his goal of legitimizing the new context of his metapsychological propositions in progress since 1920, Freud (1933/1969a) will write the *New Introductory Lectures on Psycho-Analysis* – an opportunity to explain, with greater precision, the complexity of the second topography, leaving clues to enter the territory of the unrepressed with more expertise. In view of this inference, I highlight the XXXI Lecture, returning to the theme of melancholia, now in a position to combine it, among other elements, with the theme of masochism, reconfigured in 1924. In the context of the 1930s, we have the opportunity to integrate in the constitution of the ego and the superego, the fates of primary and erotogenic masochism. This is understood by Paim Filho and Terra Machado (2021) as the first destination of the drive, the founding matrix of the psyche. From this matrix of the soul, we will have female masochism, linked to the ego, and moral masochism, linked to the superego, which is externalized through its sadism over the unprotected ego. Therefore, in melancholia, we will also have the conjunction of these two aspects of masochism at work:

> The superego applies the most rigid moral standard to the defense-less ego that is at its mercy; it represents, in general, the demands of morality, and we immediately understand that our sense of guilt is an expression of the tension between the ego and the superego. (Freud, 1933/1969a, p. 79)

The ideas elaborated in this lecture brought along records of freudian thinking in respect to the relationship between these structures, the duality in the drive for life and death, and the *Civilization and Its Discontents* (Freud, 1930/2020a). Discontent due to the need to deprive humans of discharge, with no mediation, of their destructiveness into the external world. What is prevented from this discharge returns to the superego and potentiates its moral conscience, which, in turn, exacerbates its aggressiveness towards the ego: "We call guilt consciousness the tension between the severe superego and the ego which is submitted to it; it manifests itself as a need for punishment" (Freud, 1930/2020a, p. 377).

So once again, we have melancholia making its appearance and calling us to think about it as a good clinical and metapsychological agent for acknowledging the ego and the superego in the light of our time.

Developments of the Freudian legacy: reflecting on narcissistic neurosis as a model for thinking about psychic suffering

In a previous article (Paim Filho et al., 2018), we discussed the idea of melancholia as something more than a pathology with the intention and the idea of maybe producing something regarding the Freudian legacy on the origins of drive/object. Taking into consideration the freudian "melancholic complex" (Freud, 1917/2006a, p. 111), we intended to place this proposition as a basic structure of the psychic apparatus. We comprehend that the human psyche, with its relationship with its primary objects, always maintains a non-elaboration quantum of this loss of origins. The yearning for this always forsaken object, yet never renounced, follows through one's whole life. Therefore, the melancholia of the origins is based by the never-ending search for a reencountering of a meeting that has never happened in its plenitude: If the ego is constituted from the other, the ego is always missing, always yearning. In nostalgia, we find the essence of the missing absolute object that constitutes us, an unfathomable essence. The soul's yearning guzzles life's unlimited transience.

We infer that nostalgia stands for this melancholic state as the feeling of missing something is for mourning. Starting from the melancholic state's structural reference, we carry the idea that the generating principle that composes the melancholia versus mourning by which we transit between what is able to be elaborated and what urges to be elaborated, without being strictly tied to clinical melancholia. On that account, following such a proposition, we will be able to equate the different vicissitudes of this complex in our daily lives.

Pursuing this path, as an example, I remember Han's depressive subject proposition on *Burnout Society* (Han, 2017a). Here, it is necessary to highlight that Han understands, in his dialogue with Freudian thought, depression disassociated from melancholia. Therefore, he does not witness the presence of the prohibitive superego action within depression. Trailing his thought, I understand that Han's theorized depression justifies the differentiation towards classical melancholia. However, rereading his thoughts under a new perspective, I believe that we can utilize melancholia, with its immanent narcissism, as a possible gateway to the field of depression, allowing us to reflect on how it establishes its relationship with the ego and the superego. Both of them carry, with its own differences, the fickleness of a deathly narcissism, allowing us to ponder about them within the universe of narcissistic neuroses.

Utilizing this proposition as a signal, we will follow up our narrative with the intention of working upon possible articulations, as Freud would tell us: "Where it points to a breach or a rent, there may normally be an articulation present" (Freud, 1933/1969a, p. 77). Within melancholia and, perhaps, depression, we witness a reference to reflect upon the different manifestations of narcissistic neurosis, with its intricate relationship with the melancholic complex. Freud's classical statement from 1915, with all its dramatic instances placed on the one which is overshadowed by the object, the superego, destituting the ego from its singularity, bisected by ambivalent feelings, where becoming is prominent; on the other hand, we have the remaining presentations, which remit to emptying out the ego and its libidinal reserve, however, within different intensities and dynamics. In this segment, we ponder, for instance, about a spectrum that exists between the psychopathologies of daily life until the many variations of depression. Having that in mind, I reaffirm that I understand this condition of depression as one of the vicissitudes of the melancholic complex, beyond classical melancholia, beyond the conflict, where ambivalence doesn't reign, and because of that, there is no melancholic rebellion to happen but a self-rebellion. Within this scenario, there's a radical distancing from a prohibitive superego and, at the same time, a tangling of a superego invested on the demands from an ego ideal: distinguishing both instances are done in a precarious fashion. Under these conditions, the imperatives from the superego are lived as self-imperatives. Territory that takes us back to a solid identification with the horde's father, the one from full pleasure and with a promise of immortality. It is a calling for one to return to living within a narcissism that satisfies itself autoerotically: "the superego becomes positive on the ego-ideal" (Han, 2017a, p. 100). Within this context, we notice the elements that constitute the subjects of a performance society with its belief in its own creed of people being rulers of themselves.

However, for these subjects – exhausted within themselves – the burnout society does not take long to present itself: "from the gap which opens between the real ego and the ego-ideal spawns the auto-aggressiveness" (Han, 2017a, p. 100). Therefore, we come across a splintered ego in its unattainable ideals, subjugated by the idealizations belonging to a superego that led the ego into believing that, during the time pursuing a narcissistic full performance, it would be possible for the ego to reach it. When such project is not effectuated, the ego succumbs into a logic of just living – self-rebellion – when no invigorated objective that would imply recognizing castration finds an addressee: "whoever *survives* becomes like a *living dead*, which is way too dead to live, and way too alive to become dead" (Han, 2017a, p. 52). I understand that, guided by the previous point, melancholia's work, as a counterpoint to the mourning's work, operates in a more significant manner in our times – operation which happens due to an impossibility of fulfilling the idealizations of the superego that in turn comes from a culture that seeks fulfillment under the guise of absolute self-sufficiency. At the same time, the structure from the ego-definite reality subjugated by unattainable realities, by itself, will suffer from its pain, lived, but not felt, of keeping itself on the sidelines of the culture's demands, many times succumbing to a sense of death in life. I remember that in Freud's posthumous work, between many elements, the reaffirmation of presence within the superego, the demands of social order: "Of course, not only the parents' personal identity acting in the parental influence, but also the family's traditions, race and kin transmitted by them, as well as the social demands represented by them" (Freud, 1940/2014, p. 21).

In times of narcissistic pathologies from an ego tangled in alienating identifications, prisoners of the superego's idealizations, I believe that the universe of narcissistic neuroses – vulnerability of mourning – can provide better ways of understanding the culture's and the subject's own discontent, discontent that brings along the prominence of melancholia, intensity of a drive of destruction that refers to a thought over the death of desire, or even *The Agony of Eros*, in the words of Han (2017a): "In the hell of sameness, which brings society further into equalization, we can, therefore, no longer find the erotic experience. Such experience foreshadows asymmetry and exteriority in the other" (p. 8).

References

Freud, S. (1894/1986). Carta 17/12/1894. Rascunho G: Melancolia. In J. Masson (org.), V. Ribeiro (trans.), *Correspondência Completa Freud-Fliess, 1887-1904*. Rio de Janeiro: Imago.

———. (1900/1969c). Interpretação dos sonhos. In J. Salomão (trans.), *Edição Standard das Obras Psicológicas Completas de Sigmund Freud*. Vol. 6. Rio de Janeiro: Imago.

———. (1908/1969b). Escritores criativos e devaneios. In J. Salomão (trans.), *Edição Standard das Obras Psicológicas Completas de Sigmund Freud*. Rio de Janeiro: Imago.

———. (1914/2004a). À guisa de introdução ao narcisismo. In L. A. Hanns (trans.), *Escritos da Psicologia do Inconsciente*. Vol. 1. Rio de Janeiro: Imago. (1914). On narcissism: An introduction. The Standard Edition of the Complete Psychological Works of Sigmund Freud, 14. London: Hogarth Press.

———. (1915/2004b). Pulsões e destino da pulsão. In L. A. Hanns (trans.), *Escritos da Psicologia do Inconsciente*. Vol. 1. Rio de Janeiro: Imago.

———. (1917/2006a). Luto e melancolia. In L. A. Hanns (trans.), *Escritos da Psicologia do Inconsciente*. Vol. 2. Rio de Janeiro: Imago. (1917) Mourning and Melancholia. The Standard Edition of the Complete Psychological Works of Sigmund Freud. 14. London: Hogarth Press. 14

———. (1920/2006b). O além do princípio do prazer. In L. A. Hanns (trans.), *Escritos Sobre a Psicologia do Inconsciente*. Vol. 2. Rio de Janeiro: Imago.

———. (1921/2020b). Psicologia das massas e a análise do Eu. In M. R. S. Moraes (trans.), *Cultura, Sociedade, Religião: o Mal-Estar na Cultura e Outros Escritos de Sigmund Freud*. Obras Incompletas de Sigmund Freud. Belo Horizonte: Autêntica.

———. (1923/2007a). O Eu e o Id. In L. A. Hanns (trans.), *Escritos sobre a Psicologia do Inconsciente*. Vol. 3. Rio de Janeiro: Imago.

———. (1924a/2007b). O problema econômico do masoquismo. In L. A. Hanns (trans.), *Escritos sobre a Psicologia do Inconsciente*. Vol. 3. Rio de Janeiro: Imago.

———. (1924b/2016). Neurose e psicose. In M. R. S. Moraes (trad.), *Neurose, psicose, perversão – Obras Incompletas de Sigmund Freud*. Belo Horizonte: Autêntica.

———. (1930/2020a). O mal-estar na cultura. In M. R. S. Moraes (trad.), *Cultura, Sociedade, Religião: o Mal-Estar na Cultura e Outros Escritos de Sigmund Freud*. Obras incompletas de Sigmund Freud. Belo Horizonte: Autêntica.

_____. (1933/1969a). A dissecção da personalidade psíquica (Conferência XXXI). In J. Salomão (trans.), *Edição Standard Brasileira das Obras Psicológicas Completas de Sigmund Freud*. Vol. 22. Rio de Janeiro: Imago.

_____. (1940/2014). Compêndio de psicanálise. In P. H. Tavares (trans.), *Compêndio de Psicanálise e Outros Textos – Obras Incompletas de Sigmund Freud*. Belo Horizonte: Autêntica.

Han, B. (2017a). *Sociedade do Cansaço*, 2a edição ampliada. Petrópolis, RJ: Vozes.

———. (2017b). *Agonia de Eros*. Petrópolis, RJ: Vozes.

Paim Filho, I. A. (2014). Totem e tabu: um proêmio ao narcisismo. In CEPdePA. *Para uma Introdução ao Narcisismo: Reflexos e Reflexão*. Porto Alegre: Centro de Estudos Psicanalíticos de Porto Alegre.

Paim Filho, I. A. et al. (2017). Filicídio nosso de cada dia: estrutura, alienação e ato. In I. A. Paim Filho & G. Borges (eds.), *Sobre o Filicídio: uma Introdução*. Porto Alegre: Sulina.

———. (2018). Complexo melancólico: o anseio da alma. In *Percurso: Revista de Psicanálise/Instituto Sedes Sapientiae*. Ano XXXI, n. 61. São Paulo.

Paim Filho, I. A. & Terra Machado, A. P. (2021). Masoquismo destino das pulsões – origem do sujeito. In CEPdePA. *Pulsão de Morte: a Inegável Existência do Mal*. Porto Alegre: Centro de Estudos Psicanalíticos de Porto Alegre.

12 Consequences of the new structure of the mind

Claudia Lucía Borensztejn

The Ego and the Id manuscripts

In order to begin writing this text to honor the 100th anniversary of the publication of *The Ego and the Id,* a search in the database of the Argentine Psychoanalytic Association (APA) and a consultation in its library led me to the discovery of a singular book edited in 2011 by Juan Carlos Cosentino titled *The Ego and the Id,* whose subtitle announces unpublished manuscripts and published version. It collates the manuscripts of the draft that Freud began to keep from 1914 onwards because someone warned him that they might have an economic value for his grandchildren. These manuscripts are preserved today in the Sigmund Freud Collection Library of Congress in Washington, USA.

In the first instance, there were notes of the work that Freud took to his London exile. The drafts were the second stage of the birth of the Freudian texts and then they went into the clean copy. The manuscript of the draft of *The Ego and the Id,* which has some rearrangements and changes in the clean copy, is preserved. In Freud's draft, at the bottom of page 31, dated August 9, 1922, the phrase "so far I have finished" appears, although he later adds another page dated August 13 and 30 with ideas, comments, and crossings out (Cosentino, 2011, p. 21).

On August 4, five days before the concise statement that closes the last page before "so far I have finished", he writes to Otto Rank:

> I am about to write an article entitled The Ego and the Id. The draft has progressed a great deal but, on the other hand, it awaits a state of mind and certain ideas without which it cannot be completed.
>
> (id, p. 21)

Freud wrote *The Ego and the Id* in a little over two weeks from July 23 to August 9.

Cosentino's book is the fruit of an exhaustive research comparing texts with a personal translation from the German carried out within the framework of the University of Buenos Aires, UBACyT (science and technique

DOI: 10.4324/9781003336754-12

project, 2004–2007) under the title *The Redefinition of the Unconscious from 1920* – available only in Spanish under the title *La redefinición del inconsciente a partir de 1920*. On p. 23, it reads:

> there is no doubt that there is in Freud a certain uneasiness with this new structure of the psychic apparatus that he is proposing. The draft shows traces of multiple corrections: deletions, rearrangements, additions of paragraphs, notes on sheets or fragments of supplementary paper. . . . It is almost the last great theoretical work that preserves so much innovative and structuring force as to separate in fact the whole psychoanalytic literature into a before and an after at the moment when the dissymmetry between the repressed unconscious and the unconscious material that remains unrecognized is born . . . Freud begins to write the clean copy as soon as he finishes the draft. It took him less than a month; the distance between the draft and the clean copy is eloquent since the first is not a skeleton of the second, nor an x-ray, it is rather a quantity of raw blocks not classified or structured until the moment of the production of the published version.

There is innovation and reformulation, but with prudence, as is evident from the numerous deletions that remain, urged by distinctions between the repressed unconscious and the unconscious with a capital Icc., Freud continued to correct until the galley proofs (Cosentino, 2011, p. 189).

The final version by Freud appeared in the third week of April 1923, and this writing wishes to be a humble tribute to the 100th anniversary of what became known as the second Freudian theory of the mind id-ego-superego.

The synthesis of each chapter can be read in the introduction by Fred Busch, who has called for, and stimulated, the writing of these texts, celebrating the 100th anniversary of its publication, resulting in an invitation for reflection and rereading of *The Ego and the Id* while considering the enormous consequences of the new structuring of the psychic apparatus: placing the ego in a different situation and in a central position, after having united it to the consciousness, discovering that a significant part of it is unconscious and that this unconscious part is constituted mostly by the defense mechanisms.

In his introduction, Strachey (Freud, 1923, p. 4) also points to *The Ego and the Id* as the last of Freud's major theoretical works in which he offers "a revolutionary description of the mind . . . all subsequent writings bear the mark of its effects, at least as far as terminology is concerned".

Strachey says that the traces of this scheme go back first to the *Project*, then it follows in the *Interpretation of Dreams*, and in 1915, in the *Metapsychology*.

The mechanism of repression had been the basis of the mental conception of an unconscious repressed part and a repressive part that left the ego on the side of the conscience (Cc), and this changes in the new formulation.

The reformulation of the ego

The Dictionary of Psychoanalysis (Laplanche & Pontalis, 1967, p. 476) in the entry on the term "ego" says:

> psychoanalytic theory attempts to explain the genesis of the ego within two relatively heterogeneous registers, either by considering it as an adaptive apparatus differentiated from the "Id" by virtue of contact with external reality, or by defining it as the result of identifications leading to the formation within the person of a love object charged by the "Id".

In other words, the ego can be considered as an internal object within the psychic apparatus, a conception that will be the axis of the Kleinian development.

Another conception of the ego in relation to its functions and in respect to the ego drives, as well as those of the superego and reality, is as a mediator in charge of the interests of the totality of the person. On p. 476 (Laplanche & Pontalis), it reads:

> Certainly no one is unaware that Freud spoke of the ego from his earliest writings, but he generally did so in a rather unspecified way, as it is argued, designating then this term the personality as a whole. . . . On the other hand, the 1920 turn cannot be limited to the definition of the ego as the central instance of the personality. . . . Finally, we do not think it desirable to attempt a clear distinction between the ego as person and as instance, since the articulation of these two meanings forms precisely the core of the problematic of the ego.

The post-Freudian schools have tried to clarify this double meaning and have brought complexity with new ideas such as the self, the person, and the subject as opposed to the object. Freud not only finds and embraces the classical meanings by opposing, for example, the organism to the environment, the subject to the object, and the interior to the exterior, but he also applies the term "Ich" to these different levels and even takes advantage of the ambiguity of its use, which indicates that he does not exclude any of the meanings from his field.

In the section on the ego, Laplanche's dictionary takes up again the turn of the twenties:

> However, it is not possible to deny Freud's own testimony about the essential change that then took place. It seems that if the second topic makes the ego an instance, it is above all because it has to adapt itself to the modalities of psychic conflict better than the first theory

of which it can be said schematically that it took as its main axis two types of mental functioning: primary and secondary process.

(p. 485)

The parties involved in the conflict are elevated to the category of instances: the ego as the agent of defense, the superego as the system of prohibitions, and the id as the drive pole. The Cc is placed at the core of the ego, as well as the recognized functions of the preconscious. But what is important is that the ego is now largely unconscious, especially the resistances to psychoanalytic treatment, which are a manifestation of the force of the repressed and which present a compulsive, repetitive nuance.

The new positioning of the ego was the starting point for new developments in psychoanalytic theory, beginning with its three main arteries: that of the psychology of the ego, that of Lacan's subject, and that of Melanie Klein's object relations, which, consider the ego in their respective lines, present differences in the clinic and in technique.

Other questions in relation to the ego pointed out by Laplanche and Pontalis (p. 489) refer to Freud's formulations on the bodily ego:

the ego derives from bodily sensations, mainly those originating on the surface of the body . . . This indication invites us to define the instance of the self as based on an operation of the organism in the psyche.

The mechanisms that participate in the constitution of the ego are diversely described according to the different theories, as identifications, introjections, narcissism, mirror phases, good or bad objects at its core, theories of the primitive development of the self, and from there, derive the different techniques aimed at the ego, or the self, or the internal objects, or the subject, always with the premise of the unconscious at the foundation of the psychic and of motivation of acts and behavior that defines psychoanalysis.

The superego: Post-Freudian views

The superego is described in *The Ego and the Id*:

for the first time, highlighting its critical function as an instance that separates itself from the ego and dominates it. We see how one part of the ego opposes another, judges and criticizes it and, so to speak, takes it as an object.

(Laplanche & Pontalis, 1967, p. 440)

For Freud, the superego emerges with the decline of the Oedipus complex and is the result of a primary object relationship that becomes identification with the parents by internalizing the oedipal prohibition.

For Melanie Klein, this occurs much earlier, in the oral stage in which sadism predominates, which gives this formation its character of cruelty, and she notes, according to Freud, that the child's superego is not formed in the image and likeness of the parents but on the image of their super-ego and is transmitted along the generations (Laplanche & Pontalis, 1967, p. 442). Klein even points out that the severity of the child's superego may be inverse to the kind or tolerant upbringing of the parents.

According to Hinshelwood (1989, p. 130):

> while Freud presented the unconscious feeling of guilt as a central conflict between the Ego and the superego, Melanie Klein, in the analysis of Rita, described guilt feelings in a 15-month-old girl, which led her to antecedent this feelings to the early Oedipus complex.

The concept of the superego intrigued Klein at a time when she was in analysis with Abraham, and he in turn was exchanging with Freud about his ideas on the evolution of the libido at different stages. Klein came to the conclusion that what Freud described was the end of a process and that in the beginning, it was the successive introjection of experiences that made up the internal objects. She inferred them while playing with children through mechanisms well described by her, such as externalization and personification, as the expression of masturbatory fantasies (Klein, 1929). Then these fantasies were nominated as unconscious fantasies. The theoretical status of the term unconscious fantasy acquired legitimacy when Susan Isaacs presented her paper in the controversial discussions and the term "masturbatory fantasies" disappeared. They were its prolegomenon. They represent the mental conflict derived from the id and the ego and superego, which are internal objects and also good or bad images according to their function and the kind of instinct that provides them with the energy from the id. The unconscious fantasy is the mental expression of the instinct (Isaacs, 1943).

On page 140, Hinshelwood continues:

> Klein elaborated more systematically in 1933 (The early development of the Cc in The Child) the theory of the origin of the super-ego from the death instinct. She based her ideas in Beyond the pleasure principle (Freud, 1920) and, came up with the proposition that the first function of the Ego is to project the death instinct to the outside, onto an object in the external world, thus giving birth to the Ego. And at the same time this defensive process of the ego is constitutive of the Super-Ego.

By thus projecting the origin of these instances at birth, she takes for granted the existence of a mind in the infant from the beginning of life, a mind that performs complex psychic operations.

It was this idea that aroused the greatest disagreement between the positions of Anna Freud and her followers and those of Melanie Klein and her group in the famous controversies that took place in the British Psychoanalytic Society between 1942 and 1943.

Once these discussions have come to an end, Melanie Klein's interest in psychic instances declined, and she focused more on the idea of internal objects resulting from constitutive intersections of the ego and the superego, which gave her the possibility to move forward in her research towards the theory of the positions with the description of the partial and total ego as an essential characteristic of each, schizo-paranoid and depressive position respectively.

The whole of Melanie Klein's work starts from the 1920s turn in Freud concerning the second theory of the mind, the second theory of the drives, and the second theory of anxiety. In her exchanges with Jones, Melanie Klein reproaches him for having welcomed Freud in London, when he had to flee from Nazi persecution (see *The Freud-Klein Controversies 1941-45*, Pearl King & Richard Steiner, 1991, p. 222) and also for having chosen Glover as his successor in the British society, knowing how much he attacked her, followed by her daughter, Melitta. Klein regrets her role in this struggle since she found it difficult to progress in her ideas about the depressive position because of the attacks received. She wrote to Jones:

> my greatest experience in this respect was with the works Beyond the Pleasure Principle and The Ego and the Id, and what an experience it turned out to be. . . . I saw my own work in a new light. . . . In particular when I began to understand it in relation to aggression, reparation and the part it plays in the structure of the personality and in human life in general.
>
> (ibid., p. 224)

During the controversies, the article that took the longest time to discuss was precisely *The Nature and Function of Phantasy* by Susan Isaacs, finally in charge of presenting the concept of unconscious fantasy. Hinshelwood (ibid., p. 322) points out that in the debates about unconscious fantasy as a psychic expression of the drive, *The Ego and the Id* is quoted many times, and he also recalled that according to Freud, the self is first and foremost a bodily self. In the subsequent discussion, it is Clifford Scott who says the following:

> we want to know more about what the body means in unconscious phantasy whether we speak of the self or of other persons as total or partial objects, of the core of the self, of its integration or disintegration, of the organization or disorganization of the subject's functions as opposed to the object, this may be of less importance than the way in which we describe new contents of experience.

Then the discussion continues with Ronald Fairbairn (ibid., p. 328):

in my opinion I believe that the time has come for us to replace the concept of phantasy by that of internal reality with the self and its internal objects. These should be contemplated as an organized structure with an identity of its own, an endo-psychic existence and an activity as real in the internal world as that of any object in the external world. Attributing these characteristics to internal objects may be surprising to some but they are after all characteristics that Freud had attributed to the super-ego. It just so happens that the super-ego is not the only internal object. The activity of internal objects like that of the self is of course derived from drives originating in the Id. Nevertheless, these objects must be contemplated as possessing an activity of their own. Internal activity becomes the setting for situations involving the self and its internal objects.

Further, on page 337, it reads: "The ego will show everything experienced in early situations in the transference and it will be the function of the analyst to help the patient to express them in words when they appear".

After four meetings held over three months, Paula Heinman's article "Some functions of projection and introjection in early childhood" began to be discussed and then the subject of psychic structure is addressed more directly. She says (ibid., p. 451):

we contemplate the psyche as composed of three main parts differentiated by their functions. The id is the reservoir of drives and therefore the source of energy of all psychic activity, the ego is the interpreter or intermediary between the various parts of the psyche and the external world. The super-ego is the internalized representative of the most important objects of the individual: the parents.

In his work *The Ego and the Id* (ibid. p. 453), Freud stated that when he explained the disorder of melancholia (1917) through the concept of introjection, this process and its importance in the formation of the ego and its character, which contains the history of its object relations, was not known. This is widely confirmed by Melanie Klein. She points out that introjection is also a decisive factor in the formation of the superego (ibid., p. 455), and it is the earliest form of object attachment. Paula Heinmann continues: "The role of the processes of projection and introjection referred to the psychic system acquires more meaning when the influence of the life and death drives is considered" (ibid., p 456).

Acceptance of the death drive hypothesis implies a focus on the manifestations of destruction and the interplay of love and hate (ibid, p. 457) and both drives the libido and the destructive drive seek to extend their goals in bodily activities . . . and psychic functions derive from them as described by Freud.

As drives are psycho-bodily processes, the psychic experiences occur together with the bodily drives, and there is a psycho-emotional relation towards the object that gratifies or frustrates. In the same text, Heinmann states: "no chapter in the intricate book of human affairs has been so enriched by Melanie Klein's research as that concerning the relationship of the individual to his objects" (ibid., 460).

According to Freud, the ego is a sedimentation of resigned object investments, so we have reasons to believe that the object aspect of the drive requires close scrutiny in Freud's work. Marjorie Bierley (Hinshelwood, ibid., p. 461) says:

> It is precisely this close scrutiny to which Melanie Klein has devoted herself and which has highlighted the enormous significance of object investments from the beginning of life. According to Freud the autoerotic phase is consecutive to a period in which the infant's libido is attached to an external object: the mother's breast. Freud left unresolved the question of what happens to this intense and fundamental relationship when the child enters the autoerotic phase. For Freud these first introjections form the basis of what is called identification.

The formulation of the second theory of the mind has given psychoanalysis the basis for the different lines that derive from it. The psychology of the ego, that of the self, the one of object relations, the intersubjective theory, the intra-subjective, the interpersonal, are in the common basis of many implicit theories that we unconsciously use because we implicitly consider the concept of ego and superego alternatively as mental structures, as internal objects, and as parts of the complex structure of the personality, of the relations of the subject with himself, with the other, and with the environment.

The consequences in the Argentinean School of Psychoanalysis

The Argentinean School of Psychoanalysis, with its roots in Freud, Klein, and American ego psychology, was unanimous in the acceptance of the second theory of the mind. The ideas of Arnaldo Rascovsky on fetal psychism are an example. He presents the hypothesis of a fetal ego that is initially a double of the id and its object (Borensztejn ed.; Diccionario de Psicoanálisis Argentino, 2015, p. 221).

Garma et al. (1983) developed his conceptions about the superego, making it a central axis of the theory of technique: to diminish the strength of the superego and the consequent feeling of guilt that originates from its action is for him one of the fundamental goals of psychoanalysis.

In a paper titled "The super-ego and the reality in neurosis and psycho-sis", his collaborators state that "In 1932, the Internationaie Zeitschriit für Psychoanalyse published a paper by Angel Garma on schizophrenia". Fifty years later, concepts supported in this work would be rediscovered as new findings. The ideas enunciated by Angel Garma are still remarkably valid and deserve to be highlighted. According to Freud, neurosis and psychosis appear as opposite types of reaction to solve psychic conflicts. In psychosis, the ego would put itself at the service of the id and, for this purpose, would lose its contact with external reality, and in neurosis, it would submit to external reality and repress the id.

Garma considered that schizophrenics do not seek the primitive satis-faction of their libidinal desires. They have returned to the oral digestive phase of sexual development and present intense feelings of guilt. Their identification has the character of a union of the ego with a persecutory ideal; the ego loses its limits as a consequence of the attacks of the superego and of the repression of libidinal instinctive impulses. The schizophrenic loses contact with external reality because he rejects the id and not because he satisfies it.

Aslan (1978) in his studies on mourning describes the steps of the altera-tion of the ego in the mechanisms of incorporation, introjection, and iden-tification. Aslan says it would be possible to establish a series of degrees of "ego alteration", ranging from the most partial and transitory introjection to the most permanent and total identification. Perhaps a brief comment on the energy used in identifications is in order. Freud has given us two alternatives – the first, better known, in *The Ego and the Id* (1923, p. 54):

> The super-ego comes from an identification with the father taken as a model. This identification has the nature of a de-sexualization, or even a sublimation. It seems now that when such a transforma-tion takes place, there occurs at the same time an instinctual de-fusion: after sublimation the erotic component no longer has the power to bind all the destructiveness that was combined with it, and this is released in the form of an inclination to aggression and destruction. That is to say, it is the life instincts that are employed in identification.

On the subject of technique, it is undoubtedly Racker who makes an essential contribution to it with his investigation on countertransference. This is highlighted in a paper by Stefana et al. (2021). There, the authors point out:

> In September 1948, he presented the paper A Contribution to the Problem of Countertransference in which he recognized countertransference – defined as the set of images, feelings and impulses towards the patient – as an important tool for analytic practice. More specifically,

he argued that countertransference is instrumental in bringing [the analyst] to notice a psychological fact about the patient.

(ibid., p. 323)

And it allows him to identify intellectually with and potentially understand the patient. (He would later call this concordant countertransference.) This presentation was published in the *International Journal* in 1953, but references to articles on countertransference appearing in the intervening five years were recorded in footnotes. Hence, in Argentina, Racker is considered the pioneer on this subject. In the notes, he quotes Paula Heinmann, but she never quoted him, even though his paper had been published in English.

Although in the 1950s, the term "countertransference" was usually restricted to complementary countertransference, also concordant countertransference should be considered as an integral part of the overall phenomenon of countertransference. Racker reported a common situation that illustrates both concordant and complementary identifications.

> The analyst identifies himself with the patient's id and ego and with the patient's dependence upon his superego; he also identifies himself with this same superego – a situation in which the patient places him-and experiences in this way the domination of the superego over the patient's Ego. The relation of the Ego to the superego is, at bottom, a depressive and paranoid situation; the relation of the superego to the Ego is manic insofar as this term can be used to designate the dominant, controlling and accusatory attitude of the Superego towards the Ego.

(Stefana et al., 2021, pp. 116)

In addition to complementary and concordant identifications, Racker describes direct and indirect countertransference. The former is experienced when the object of this countertransference is the patient, whereas indirect countertransference occurs when it stems from an object other than the patient (such as the supervisor or other colleagues). It is easy to see how these ideas come from a conception of the patient as a person and the external world in relation to the analyst.

Finally, Racker divided countertransference experiences into "thoughts" and "positions". The former are the thoughts that the analyst suddenly discovers in himself, without being able to find a rational connection with the patient and the material he has brought. Countertransferential positions, or rather, "roles manifested or behaviorally enacted, which may lead to persistent role-taking and/or acting-out on the part of the analyst", often involve deeper conflicts and greater disturbance. One sees here how much Racker had anticipated the conceptions of enactment that emerged after Sandler's paper about role responsiveness (Sandler, 1976; Borensztejn, 2009). Racker relied not only on the structural model of the mind but also on the model of internal object relations.

In this contribution, I hope to have fulfilled the objective of paying homage to Freud's work that has developed the best theory of the mind and its functioning not yet comparable to any other to this day and complemented and enriched in its development because this theory has opened the study of the instances of the mind – that of the person as a whole and his relations with the world around him, as well as to the clinical approaches and theories of treatment that provide the necessary technical instruments to relieve human suffering. So far, I have finished.

References

Aslan, C. M. (1978). Un aporte a la metapsicología del duelo. *Revista de Psicoanálisis,* 35(1): 19–60 (only in Spanish [A contribution to the metapsychology of grief]).

Borensztejn, C. (2009). El enactment como concepto clínico convergente de teorías divergentes. Revista de Psicoanálisis. *APA,* 66(1): 177–192 (only in Spanish The enactment as a convergent clinical concept of divergent theories).

Borensztejn, C. L. (ed.). (2015). *Diccionario de Psicoanálisis Argentino volumen II,* K-Z.-- Buenos Aires: APA Editorial (only in Spanish).

Cosentino, J. C. (2011). *Freud Sigmund, El yo y el Ello: manuscritos inéditos y versión publicada.* 1a edición. Buenos Aires: Mármol-Izquierdo Editores.

Freud, S. (1923). The ego and the Id. *SE,* 19: 3–63. London: Hogart Press.

Garma, A., Allegro, L. A., Arbiser, A., de Arbiser, S. Z., Lustig de Ferrer, E. S., de Garma, E. G., Gioannini, F. A., Schlossberg, T., Weissmann, F., Winocur, J. & Yampey, N. (1983). El superyo y la realidad exterior en neurosis y psicosis. *Revista de Psicoanálisis,* 40(3): 497–503.

Hinshelwood, R. D. (1989). *Diccionario del pensamiento Kleiniano.* Buenos Aires: Amorrortu Editores. (Diccionary of Kleinian Thought. R. D. Hinshelwood, London).

Isaacs, S. (1943) *The nature and Function of Phantasy. Spanish translation in Desarrollos en Psicoanálisis. Melanie Klein. Obras completas.* Tomo III. Buenos Aires: Paidos Horme, 1978.

King, P. & Steiner, R. (1991). *The Freud- Klein Controversies 1941–1945.* The New Library of Psychoanalysis. David Tuckett (ed.). In association with the Institute of Psychoanalysis, London.

Klein, M. (1929). *La personificación en el juego de los niños en Contribuciones al Psicoanálisis. Obras Completas tomo II.* Buenos Aires: Paidos. Horme. (Spanish translation of Contributions to Psychoanalysis. London: Hogarth press).

Laplanche, J. & Pontalis, J. B. (1967). *Diccionario de Psicoanálisis.* Barcelona: Editorial Labor SA (Spanish translation from the French).

Sandler, J. (1976). Countertransference and role responsiveness. *Int. Journal of Psychoanal,* 3: 43–47.

Stefana, Alberto, Hinshelwood, R. D. & Borensztejn, Claudia Lucía. (2021). Racker and Heimann on countertransference: Similarities and differences. *The Psychoanalytic Quarterly,* 90(1): 105–137, DOI: 10.1080/00332828.2021.1851136 to cite this article) To link to this article: https://doi.org/10.1080/00332828.2021.1851136

13 The legacy of complexity

Raúl Tebaldi

Introduction

A review of *The Ego and the Id* now, a hundred years after its publication, invites us to adopt a historical perspective that may encourage us to explore in depth the genial foresightedness of Freud's proposals. Their theoretical-clinical influences are clear not only in subsequent papers in his works but also in the investigations of other authors up to the present.

In this paper, I highlight the epistemological viewpoint since I view *The Ego and the Id* as an example of Freud's model, anticipating modern epistemology, and oriented his thinking long before the formal enunciation of the epistemology of complexity.

Psychoanalysts in the 21st century, concerned with suffering in contemporary clinical work, cannot dispense with the humanistic character of Freudian thought.

Its methodology is built as a foundation, perhaps not so noticeable and yet important for our understanding of the current theoretical and clinical standing of this core paper of the second "topic". An initial appraisal enables us to observe how its metapsychological concepts are presented both precisely and flexibly, forming a network with multiple possible interrelations devised to explain both normal and pathological psychic phenomena.

In *The Ego and the Id*, an expression of Freud's scientific thinking, his methodology also reflects his characteristic creativity. To what extent is Green's statement earlier a product of his observation and preservation of this methodology? Should the contemporary epistemology of complexity declare its origin in Freud?

Actually, the issue of complexity is the very quality that discourages all attempts to summarize the contents of *The Ego and the Id* if we aspire to avoid the pitfall of simplification.

Although Freud's paper may admit certain pedagogical classifications, especially in its well-known schema, when we examine the construction of these hypotheses, complexity inevitably emerges, also because it is the only way to address the reality of mental functioning and clinical work with "limit" conditions.

DOI: 10.4324/9781003336754-13

We recall that Freud presented this paper as a continuation of *Beyond the Pleasure Principle* (Freud, 1920) and that its reception in the psychoanalytic group succeeded in overcoming resistances among the colleagues that had accompanied its 1920 predecessor, as contemporaries noted. Consequently, I begin with *Beyond the Pleasure Principle*, discussing the importance of its hypotheses in relation to clinical work and epistemology.

As an example of the application of the second "topic", I take up a less well-known but perhaps quite significant later moment in his self-analysis (Freud, 1936). Finally, I present some comparative observations between current clinical work with "limit" functioning and Freud's self-analysis.

The epistemological break

We would do well to remember that post-Freudian theoretical-clinical developments show that simplification has often won the day, sometimes because the starting points of their investigations were based on a patient population restricted to certain categories and other times due to the predominance of a theory at a given moment in the history of a school of thought.

Green says:

> I vindicate the richness and technical power of Freud's thought. In my opinion, none of the theories that have attempted to surpass it . . . succeeded in doing so. And what is worse: they all fell into some type of reductionism.

He adds that "my relation with the works of Freud involves neither Talmudism nor any religious adhesion to their letter" (Green, 1994, p. 47).

Now then, in what way is Freud's theory unsurpassable? What does reductionism mean in psychoanalysis?

As I said, the answer lies in the paradigm of complexity that organized his thinking, of which he was the pioneer or creator, having recognized that it suited the ordering of psychic functioning.

We need to go back over well-known background material in order to understand the logic accompanying the development of his ideas. From our present vantage point and familiarity with his works, it is difficult to imagine the impact produced by *Beyond the Pleasure Principle*, when Freud turned all his attention to clinical work with negative phenomena, formerly untreatable by analysis and not integrated into the theory. Until 1920, Freud himself had resisted the thought of an independent drive that would account for destructivity. His disciples' irritation, apparently in relation to the universal character attributed to the death drive, should more likely be attributed to its broader questioning of what had hitherto become instituted and accepted as the theory, technique, and objectives of psychoanalysis.

His paper confronted these colleagues with other realities perturbing therapeutic success: negative therapeutic reactions, masochism, neurosis of fate, traumatic neuroses, and character disorders (Jones, 1953).

At present, the current "limit" states or functioning confirm the anticipatory value of his assertions regarding the influence of trauma, repetition compulsion, and their relation to destructiveness, which cannot be explained simply by repressed sexuality. In this way, the new proposal overturned the hegemony of repressed sexuality as the genesis of conflicts.

It also explained negative phenomena producing resistances different from those described previously, phenomena which shifted the ego's position and proposed its complexity. In the early treatments, resistances often seemed to be the product of an ego unwilling to remember, an ego driven by narcissism, whose resistance could arrest the progress of analysis.

In his new proposal, the tendency to dissolve psychic tension through discharge is imposed upon an ego presented as being weak in the face of traumatic assaults by reality, the drives, and feelings of guilt. This view creates the need to recognize the ego's unconscious aspect, its defenses, and as he does in 1923, to investigate the dependent relationships of the ego, which lead it to participate in the repetition of unpleasure.

Whereas in the first "topic", psychoanalysis aimed at the deconstruction of a frontier – repression – it was now required to construct dams for liberated or very silent forces, the latter far more lethal. As of 1923, this deconstructive work also had to aim at identifications forming the defense barriers of character and those participating in the genesis of guilt feelings and imperative idealizations oppressing the ego.

Methodologically, this is the theoretical moment when Freud evades the trap of wanting to place the obstacles he finds in clinical work onto a Procrustes's bed of theory. In other words, he avoids excluding human suffering unexplained by theory, thereby avoiding an epistemological obstacle (Bachelard, 1948).

In terms of complexity, Morin points out: "Our systems of ideas . . . are not only subject to error but also protect the errors and illusions that are inscribed in them" (Morin, 2015, p. 22).

The presentation of *Beyond the Pleasure Principle* responds fully to this central principle. It even questions the predominant technique in use until that time, derived from the first "topic", centered upon the interpretation given by a neutral analyst but insufficient when faced with the new phenomena.

Psychoanalysis is consequently freed from the totalizing threat of the first "topic". Not in itself lacking in complexity, the first "topic" continues to form the basis of a large part of "orthodox" psychoanalytic technique.

It is important to highlight that this transformation is a model of theoretical integration, vitally necessary for the enrichment of contemporary psychoanalysis and for addressing the complexity of current clinical work. The first "topic" never disappears since it is always present as part of a new and broader unit.

Morin considers: "The paradigm of simplification (disjunction and reduction) dominates our culture today, and it is today that the reaction against this undertaking is starting" (Morin, 2015, p. 110).

Freud's refusal to accept the simple cause-effect relation has explicit moments, such as his famous argument against Rank's idea of centering analysis of the patient's anxiety on the analysis of birth trauma anxiety (Freud, 1926). Morin continues: "If we join cause and effect, the effect will return to the cause retroactively, and the product will also be a producer. We are going to differentiate these notions, and at the same time we will bring them together" (Morin, 2015, p. 110).

Freud's modifications to the initial trauma theory, and of course, transference theory as well, were soon translated into hypotheses responding to this paradigm. In fact, we detect a clear allusion to a posteriori resignification when he describes how the dynamics between the two scenes of the trauma are activated by pubertal sexuality (Freud, 1895). Freud logically persists in this line, when he constructs *The Ego and the Id*, since he continues to think in terms of these dynamics of complexity, especially when he returns to a point of greatest personal interest: the ego's relation with reality.

The second "topic" and Freud's self-analysis

Epistemological complexity would be unimportant if it were limited to creating a logical frame in which to support hypotheses. However, as we have been showing in relation to Freudian developments, it is the clinical field of psychoanalysis that demands the orientation of complexity. Today's "limit" states and functioning still require this orientation if we are to construct clinical work based on metapsychology (Vertzner Marucco, 2014).

In *The Ego and the Id*, when Freud promotes reality to the status of a psychic agency, he describes it as "pulsating". This quality, which may refer to the inherent instability of the external world, is joined by the influence of the internal world and its drives. The distortions perception undergoes in the present also depend on childhood experiences and drive-activated identifications from the traumatic past.

As we see in his 1936 letter to Romain Rolland, the loss of reality is a product of the dynamics of conflictive and drive-compromised frontiers. He also shows how self-recognition, based on the acknowledgment of the self, fluctuates in close relation with the reality principle. By that time, he had already discussed the defenses in relation to traumatic reality: disavowal and splitting of the ego.

Thus, analytic attempts to restore the reality principle and the self-esteem should be constructed by contemplating both the ego and the complexity of psychic functioning as described in the second "topic".

The servitudes of the ego show that the boundaries between the agencies, potentially virtual and dynamically mobile, are modified in consonance with the drive component mobilized in the conflict. The id and its potential defusion from the drive, guided only by the pleasure principle and capable of reaching discharge, threatens the frontiers between the agencies, this movement being the product of a variable balance between the stability of the psychic structures and the potency of the drive. Traumas of the past, as bequests affecting the ego that include identifications derived from pathological links, are central to these dynamics.

In our terminology, the category "borderline patient" is applied to psychic functioning showing an alteration of the ego-not-ego frontier, which is the relation with perception and reality, and constitutes a painful oscillation between psychosis and neurosis. However, Freud's concern is to show that loss or distortion of reality, in differing degrees, is part of all psychic functioning, according to his integrative frame of complexity.

His 1936 letter shows profound interest in continuing to explore his unconscious in search of a meaning for a significant, chronologically distant experience: his "memory of the Acropolis".

In the description of his experience, he reconstructs the effects of the conflict in his ego, compromised at the intersection of superimposed scenarios: between external reality and the internal world, their boundaries hazy, his ego negotiating with these two powers. In this way, he distinguishes two co-existing readings of reality that indicate the splitting of the ego or, as he adds, of the personality itself.

Whereas one aspect of himself recognizes the existence of the Acropolis, another aspect creates doubts about this realistic perception through a type of negative hallucination that both affects perception and also disturbs his old wish to be there – to the point that he is surprised when he is not moved by the view of a place that had been a source of admiration when he was a student. He links these estrangements with depersonalization, alienation, and hallucination.

By way of association, his analysis arrives at childhood complexes interfering with his once-strong desire to visit and enjoy the Acropolis. His mind goes back to the poverty of his childhood and of his father, who could not afford that trip and also had limited cultural interests.

He considers that recognition of these realities at some point determined the transformation of childhood narcissistic idealization into disillusion with the father figure. He understands that this de-idealization unconsciously signifies an aggression against his father, to which he attributes the consequent onset of guilt.

The whole conflict persists structurally in the internal world through identifications as a conflict between the ego and the superego; the latter harbors the aggression and blames the ego.

According to his descriptions, the superego is so powerful that his long-held hope to be in Athens was significantly perturbed, to the extent that he could find no incentives to take the trip. He attributes to childhood experiences with his brother the idea that the latter had also been going through the same unconscious conflicts. Finally, guilt and displaced aggression had led to their quarrels.

As we see, repressed sexuality does not occupy the central position he assigned it in the first "topic" but is instead replaced by aggression. Not even the origin of this aggression is attributed directly to oedipal rivalry but rather, to its narcissistic aspect, whose expression is de-idealization, less closely linked to fantasy than to memories of experienced reality.

Perhaps this genesis centered on narcissism and realistic experiences configures an important point of contact with the way we understand the functioning of current "limit" organizations.

Considering that this brother is the figure he associates with Rolland – since he mentions that they are the same age – provides us with the signifying transference detail, sustained in this letter in which he expresses the possibility of restoring tender fraternal affection, now free of oedipal conflicts, and transferred in his missive onto Rolland.

In Freud, the entire episode has operated over time as a question, a door inviting him to an analytic exercise as he displays the force of his life drive and allows us to glimpse the pleasure of sublimation it involves, which he shares with the reader.

His depersonalization is a product of transitory and characteristic "limit" functioning, which involves several boundaries. In line with the proposal of *The Ego and the Id*, we can define "limit" conflict as an isolated or extended moment of lost differentiation between the drive, the object, and the ego, in this case, inherent to neurosis, under tremendous oppression by the superego.

From a different viewpoint, important for current clinical work, Freud's self-analysis assumes psychic functioning that is the product of a certain "efficacy in the resolution of the Oedipus complex". We infer it by qualitatively evaluating the configurations and functions of the different psychic agencies, the way they participate in the conflict, and the ego's symbolic and associative wealth. This episode is, therefore, presented as a "limit" conflict typical of neurosis, with all the participant weight of the post-oedipal ego ideal-superego.

As a complement, when we observe another boundary, that of narcissism, we see that the regressive aspirations of narcissistic ideals are limited. This limit is not unrelated to Freud's ability to tolerate and work through childhood narcissistic wounds – a possibility that requires great tolerance of psychic pain, indispensable to complete the realistic de-idealization of the parents of childhood and to recognize his own aggression. We appreciate other qualities of his ideal, such as his "adult analytic ideal", which seeks to clarify these unconscious issues.

Paradoxically, the importance of this "oedipal efficacy" does not free the psyche from conflicts between superego and ego, although as long as the agencies preserve their organization and operate in a differentiated way, they function as a limit against more severe narcissistic problems. As a corollary, we, therefore, have an ego able to undertake working through introspectively by aiming to investigate the participation of its internal world in conflicts. We could say that the ego of neurosis, even when compromised by disavowal and splitting of the ego, is capable of perceiving its alterations and then attempts to restore the affective state in which it recognizes itself.

In Freud's crisis, although pleasure is disturbed, nothing indicates that this event might stem from repetition compulsion beyond the pleasure principle. This distinction is more than evident in his estrangement, the alteration of his character, since the ego notices the absence of subtle affects related to aesthetic pleasure and tenderness in the fraternal link. Affective subtlety does not usually participate in "limit" conflicts beyond neurosis since they are more "drive-like".

In any case, many reasons determine the restricted scope of a self-analysis. We cannot know whether his constructions were sufficient or whether conflicts at other limits were participating at the moment of the crisis and, therefore, remained inaccessible to analysis (Tebaldi, 2019). However, my intention is to highlight the complex conception of the conflict Freud shows us, which is fundamental for our advancement in contemporary clinical work.

Other limits: reality in contemporary clinical work

The limits that contemporary clinical work requires us to explore and theorize upon owe much to the paths Freud pointed out, particularly in *The Ego and the Id*. The imperative destructivity in "limit" states motivated a critical review of the death drive and also of its connection with deficiencies in symbolization and the ego's capacity for working through.

Identification, conceived as memory traces of vicissitudes of an introjected link, opened the way to resolving the solipsism of the death drive. The power of primary identification and preverbal trauma was reconsidered as determining drive destinies (Freud, 1939; Green, 1993). Consequently, a new boundary entered the scene: the frontier between the non-represented and the represented.

This field of the scantily represented is recognized by Freud in relation to the pre-oedipal maternal link (Freud, 1931) and preverbal trauma. Here, all his contributions to originary psychic development acquire value and come together: experiences of pain and satisfaction in the *Project* (Freud, 1895) and the origin of the nucleus of the ideal in narcissistic identification with unrealized parental wishes (Freud, 1914).

Freud understands that the delicate foundational processes of the ego's capacity to represent and symbolize depend on the baby's playful intersubjectivity with the mother, centered on the game of disappearing and appearing. Play, representational activity, identification, self-regulation of anxiety: all these elements form an identification model of passage from the intersubjective to the intrapsychic. In *Inhibitions, Symptoms and Anxiety* (Freud, 1926), Freud considered that these processes developing in the preverbal stage give birth to longing and tenderness. In these terms, he presents the evolution from drives and disorganizing anxiety in response to the mother's absence into representational activity and its accompanying affects, essential indicators of the ego's autonomy and development.

In its counterpart, the failures of this link also reveal "the other mother", the mother of identification, whose shadow falls upon the ego. Roussillon calls this trauma of preverbal times the "lost trauma" (Roussillon, 1991), whose consequences affect the ego and involve the ego ideal.

In our contemporary clinical work, the superego-ego ideal undergoes regressions and withdrawal of cathexes, enabling regressive and destructive destinies of the drive. The affects of longing and tenderness, which explain, respectively, the capacity for autonomy and consideration for others in links, are not sufficiently present. We tend to find them dissociated or replaced by ego frontiers constructed on the basis of narcissistic defenses, which often participate in destructive forms of drive satisfaction.

In consequence, isolation accompanied by addictions and other types of drive gratification unable to modify the lack of love tend to be mistaken for exogamy and autonomy. Depressions configure another aspect of this symptomatology.

In this clinical work, we encounter patients diametrically opposed to Freud's ability to direct his attention to the internal world, patients whose narcissistic alterations lead them to a lack of subjective commitment. The ego attributes the cause of all evil to external reality, configuring what I have called "reality illness" (Tebaldi, 2020; Marucco, 2021). I originally described it after observing its rise in patients analyzed during social crises, such as the recent pandemic, who gradually became entrapped in narcissistic problems with a consequent alteration of the reality principle.

I observed how the ego's loss of self-perception of conflicts involving the internal world led inexorably to a process of de-subjectivation that left the subject clinging passively to external reality. At times, analysis lost all meaning for them since the characteristic anxieties accompanying certain clinical pictures would illusorily be soothed "if only the problems of reality were solved".

In analyses able to progress, we observed that the process of withdrawal of cathexes from the internal world responded not only to the circumstantially traumatic but also to activation of the frontier of preverbal trauma. Sometimes, hallucinations, confusion, and depersonalization more openly connoted the loss of reality.

Regression of the ideal is also induced culturally when idealization of drive satisfaction and group identification are proposed, as we see in the mighty sway of the networks on the web.

As we mentioned when discussing Freud's self-analysis, whereas he was able to utilize his childhood history with its significant links to restore his self-esteem, those who suffer from reality illness may totally ignore it.

In current pathology, unlike in Freud's crisis, in this way and other similar manners, with de-objectalization of the internal world and of better developed aspects of the ideal, depersonalizations are intensified and tend to be repeated.

Whereas Freud presents the influence of the pre-oedipal maternal link on oedipal links, in contemporary clinical work, pre-oedipal functioning split in the ego tends to predominate. Its more direct (id) drive expressions, fashioned from an object of satisfaction, accompany and enlarge representational vacuums, leaving room for specific anxieties, such as intrusion, abandonment, and helplessness. Consequently, a narcissistic ideal with excessive disavowal and ego splitting increases the harmful effects of this conflict on the ego. In brief, from this frontier complex of the primary link, the memory traces of preverbal links, far outside of the symbolic-representational mesh, exert their role in the loss of "oedipal efficacy". As an example, we recall that when Green discusses "the dead mother", he describes the corresponding alteration of the Oedipus as "oedipal bi-triangulation" in which the good and bad object is attributed to each parent in a dissociated form (Green, 1986).

In contrast, when Freud describes primary identification as "paternal", he is referring to its function that limits identification activity. In relation to the captive ideal in pre-oedipal conflicts, the balance between self-esteem and identification may become unbalanced in favor of identification with and idealization of the object, heir of the primary object, thereby damaging self-esteem.

In oedipal failure affecting the ego ideal–superego, the idealized object illusorily heals the ego of narcissistic wounds sustained in the "lost trauma". If this object provides drive gratification, as in addictions, the short-circuit of drive satisfaction to the detriment of representational psychic activity is completed.

We have only to observe the influence of the web on self-aggression in adolescence, which may even induce adolescents to commit suicide; it reveals the clinical importance of this disposition to identification since it involves psychic agencies responsible for some stability of the self-esteem and, logically, the reality principle.

The consequent importance of the field of oedipal identification is also a product of retroaction with respect to oedipal times and what was experienced in relation to the real father. In any case, the uncanny power of the idealized object in the present should be attributed to the primary object since, given the baby's early helplessness, the child depends on it absolutely during a period of weakness when the ego is forming.

However, it is obvious that the ego of 1923 is not totally captured by the alienating power of the object of primary identification. What is uncannily alienated that inhabits us is a product of passive primary identification

(Marucco, 1998–2021). This identification is a product of intrusive interference by an object that prevents the ego from appropriating and recognizing its own drive satisfactions and experiences of satisfaction.

This ego, rendered passive by the idealized object, tends to deny its passivity by rationalizing its dependencies in pathologies, such as addictions, transforming them into personal choices. This logic of the uncanny constructs a reality upon disavowal and splitting that threaten destructivity whenever "only drive satisfaction is authentic".

We inevitably face the paradox in which the desirable de-identification is disrupted not only by idealization but also by exiguous representation of vicissitudes in the link with the object of primary representation.

Consequently, contemporary psychoanalysis introduces variants of its settings and analyses centered on countertransference, aiming to promote transference binding of drive and the path of symbolization.

However, excessive attention to what is earliest developmentally and to the "deep" is a path that has dismantled Freudian complexity. Therefore, a technique for clinical work with the limits should contemplate the junctions of frontiers, thereby avoiding the focalization inherent to simplification. These boundaries lie between the oedipal and the pre-oedipal and also between the servitudes of the ego, including present reality itself.

As the history of psychoanalysis has shown well enough, it is problematic to annul the oedipal dimension since it propitiates an analysis assigning priority to a certain psychic zone, such as narcissism, the psychotic nucleus, or preverbal trauma. It could lead to restrictive techniques that also tend to become dogmatic. Metaphorically, it would be "a return to Rank".

The risk of accentuating the model of Freud's self-analysis is sufficiently well-known. It would reside in creating a previous countertransference disposition excluding phenomena not explained within neurotic conflict, where they would be captured in verbal language as a path of remembering.

In other words, Freud's epistemological foundations explain contemporary clinical work in terms of a broad psychic organization that may derive into conflicts between different psychic zones.

The theory of complexity proposes:

> We are going to bring together the one and the multiple, but the one will not dissolve into the multiple, and the multiple will also be part of the one. The principle of complexity, in some way, will be based on the predominance of the complex conjunction.
>
> (Morin, 2015, p. 110)

This proposition responds to the etymology of the word "complex", "complexus": that which is intertwined, an allusion to this intricacy, which burdens Freud's efforts to clarify his own discussion.

Synchronizing with complexity, Freud opens the last chapter of *The Ego and the Id* by excusing himself to the reader for "the complexity of our subject-matter", since "in turning to new aspects of the topic we are constantly harking back to matters that have already been dealt with" (Freud, 1923, p. 48).

In 1933, he warns us against linear thought and explains the methodology of his thinking in terms of complexity:

> In thinking of this division of the personality into an ego, a super-ego and an id, you will not, of course, have pictured sharp frontiers like the artificial ones drawn in political geography. We cannot do justice to the characteristics of the mind by linear outlines. . . . After making the separation we must allow what we have separated to merge together once more. . . . It is highly probable that the development of these divisions is subject to great variations in different individuals; it is possible that in the course of actual functioning they may change and go through a temporary phase of involution. Particularly in the case of what is phylogenetically the last and most delicate of these divisions – the differentiation between the ego and the super-ego – something of the sort seems to be true.
>
> (Freud, 1933, p. 74)

Freud's integrative humanism, his insistence that psychosis and neurosis are not such distant categories, that no patient's suffering is totally foreign to us, illuminate his premises concerning complexity. At the same time, if we take this integrative premise as the starting point of our clinical work, as part of a previous countertransference, we may advance towards the clarification of the analysand's suffering.

Clinical respect for complexity is visible in proposals such as Marucco's (2005–2021). Taking up Freud's models, he identifies different psychic zones, each with its own structure and conflictive character. He discusses the zones of dreams (first "topic"), idealization (narcissism), identifications, repetition compulsion, and splitting of the ego. These descriptive distinctions are integrated in the psyche, characterized by implications between and presence of all the psychic zones while perceiving the predominance of some.

Analyses should start with the assumption that the primacy of a zone must not cancel analysts' broader perspectives as they search for the activity of the whole psyche, although they may need to adjust their technique and setting to the dominant zone for long periods of time. Analysts utilizing their countertransference in the intersubjective context of the therapeutic encounter promote diffraction of the drive. By basing transference on the original link and reactivated oedipal drives, analysts are able to promote binding and patients to construct other destinies of the drives. The psychic zones are not absent but, instead, weakened since they are captured in the link with an object that failed to awaken or nourish them libidinally since it was unable to adequately diffract the drives.

Other epistemological approaches may doubtless be applied to Freud's developments, but complexity emerges as being unavoidable not only because Freud pioneered this type of thinking but also because it is indispensable for understanding the reality of human suffering. We must also bear in mind that the luxuriant arborescence of the theoretical-clinical contributions of post-Freudian authors has need of a common trunk to enable us to integrate different theories. For this purpose, Freud's methodological articulation in *The Ego and the Id* provides us with a fundamental model.

***

References

Bachelard, G. (1948). *The Formation of the Scientific Mind*. M. M. Jones (trans.). Geneva: Clinamen Press. *La formación del espíritu científico*. Madrid: Siglo XXI de España.

Freud, S. (1914). *Introducción del narcisismo*. Buenos Aires: Amorrortu ed., Vol. XIV, 2003.

———. (1920). *Mas allá del Principio del placer*. Buenos Aires: Amorrortu ed., Vol. XVIII, 2003.

———. (1921). *Psicología de las masas y análisis del yo*. Buenos Aires: Amorrortu ed., Vol. XVIII, 2003.

———. (1923). *El yo y el ello*. Buenos Aires: Amorrortu ed., Vol. XIX, 2003.

———. (1926). *Inhibición, síntoma y anagustia*. Buenos Aires: Amorrortu ed., Vol. XX, 2003.

———. (1927). *Fetichismo*. Buenos Aires: Amorrortu ed., Vol. XXI, 2003.

———. (1931). *Sobre la sexualidad femenina*. Buenos Aires: Amorrortu ed., Vol. XXI, 2003.

———. (1933). *Nuevas conferencias de introducción al psicoanálisis*. Buenos Aires: Amorrortu ed., Vol. XXII, 2003.

———. (1936). *Carta a Romain Rolland*. Buenos Aires: Amorrortu ed., Vol. XXII, 2003.

———. (1937). *Análisis interminable y terminable*. Buenos Aires: Amorrortu ed., Vol. XXIII, 2003.

———. (1939). *Moisés y el monoteísmo: tres ensayos*. Buenos Aires: Amorrortu ed., Vol. XXIII.

———. (1940 [1938]). *La escisión del yo en el proceso defensivo*. Buenos Aires: Amorrortu ed., Vol. XXIII, 2003.

———. (1950 [1895]). *Proyecto de psicología*. Buenos Aires: Amorrortu ed., Vol. 1, 2003.

Green, A. (1983). Uno, otro, neutro: valores narcisistas de lo mismo. In: *Narcisismo*. Buenos Aires: Ediciones del 80.

———. (1986). *Life Narcissism, Death Narcissism*. London: Free Association Books. *Narcisismo de vida, narcisismo de muerte*. Amorrortu: Buenos Aires.

———. (1993). *The Work of the Negative*. Andrew Weller (trans.). London: Free Association Books. *El Trabajo de lo Negativo*. Buenos Aires: Amorrortu.

———. (1994). *Urribarri F Del Pensamiento Clínico al Paradigma Contemporáneo*. Buenos Aires: Amorrortu.

———. (2017). *La Clínica Psicoanalítica Contemporánea*. Buenos Aires: Amorrortu.

Jones, E. (1953). *The Life and Work of Sigmund Freud*. London: Hogarth Press. *Vida y Obra de Sigmund Freud*. Buenos Aires: Horme. 1981.

Marucco, N. (1998). *Cura Analítica y Transferencia*. Buenos Aires: Amorrortu.

———. (2005). Current psychoanalytic practice: Psychic zones and the processes of inconscientization. In S. Lewcowics & S. Flechner (eds.), *Truth, Reality and the Psychoanalyst: Latin American Contributions to Psychoanalysis*. London: Routledge.

———. (2021a). Desafíos para el psicoanálisis del siglo XXI: En la clínica, la metapsicología y la técnica. In F. M. Gómez (comp.), *Psicoanálisis Latinoamericano Contemporáneo*. Buenos Aires: APA Editorial, 98–117.

———. (2021b). Introducción de lo siniestro en el yo. *Rev. Psicoanál.*, 37(2): 233–246.

Morin, E. (1999). *Seven Complex Lessons in Education for the Future*. N. Poller (trans.). Paris: UNESCO Publishing. *Los siete saberes necesarios para la educación del futuro*. Buenos Aires: Nueva Visión.

———. (2015). *On Complexity*. R. Postel & S. Kelly (trans.). New York: Hampton Press. *Introducción al pensamiento complejo*. Barcelona: Gedisa.

Roussillon, R. (1991). Le traumatisme perdu. In *Paradoxes et Situations Limites de la Psychanalyse*. Paris: PUF. El trauma perdido. In *Paradojas y Situaciones Fronterizas del Psicoanálisis*. Buenos Aires: Amorrortu.

Tebaldi, R. (2014). Límites en la clínica y la teoría. In Alejandra Vertzner Marucco (comp.), *Metapsicología. Una Clínica con Fundamento*. Buenos Aires: Lugar, 217–230.

———. (2019). Los límites del sueño. In F. M. Gómez (comp.), *Percepción y Sueño. Perspectivas Actuales*. Buenos Aires: APA Editorial, 317–326.

———. (2020). Enfermar de realidad. Aportes al psicoanálisis durante la pandemia. *Rev. Psicoanál.*, 77(3): 117–134.

———. (2021). Comentario. *Rev. Psicoanál.*, 37(2): 247–254.

Vertzner Marucco, A. (2014). Introducción. In Alejandra Verzner Marucco (comp.), *Metapsicología. Una Clínica con Fundamentos*. Buenos Aires: Lugar, p. 15.

Index

For Product Safety Concerns and Information please contact our EU
representative GPSR@taylorandfrancis.com
Taylor & Francis Verlag GmbH, Kaufingerstraße 24, 80331 München, Germany

9 781032 373850